REDISCOVERING MAR █████ ▒▒NS

REDISCOVERING MARGIAD EVANS

Marginality, Gender and Illness

Edited by

Kirsti Bohata and Katie Gramich

UNIVERSITY OF WALES PRESS
CARDIFF
2013

www.uwp.co.uk

British Library Cataloguing-in-Publication Data
A catalogue record for this book is available from the British Library.

ISBN   978-0-7083-2560-5
e-ISBN 978-0-7083-2561-2

The publisher acknowledges the financial support of the Welsh Books Council.

Typeset by Mark Heslington Ltd, Scarborough, North Yorkshire
Printed by CPI Antony Rowe, Chippenham, Wiltshire

Contents

Acknowledgements

The editors are immensely grateful to Cassandra Davis for permission to quote from the unpublished works and private writing of Margiad Evans. We are indebted to Ceridwen Lloyd-Morgan for her involvement in setting up the Margiad Evans Centenary Conference, which formed the impetus for this book and, most importantly, for her willingness to act as unofficial adviser and consultant on countless matters of fact related to Margiad Evans's life, work and archives. Our task as editors has been considerably lightened by her invaluable support. Warm thanks also to Jim Pratt, the nephew of Margiad Evans, whose energy and infectious enthusiasm was an important driving force during Kirsti Bohata's organisation of the conference in 2009. Thanks also to the staff of the National Library of Wales for their support for this event, in practical terms and in kind, including the creation of a small exhibition of some of the Margiad Evans manuscripts from their collections. The editors would like to thank the editorial and production staff at the University of Wales Press and gratefully acknowledge publishing subventions from the University of Cardiff and the Welsh Books Council.

Contributors

SUE ASBEE is a Senior Lecturer at the Open University. She has written a number of articles on Margiad Evans's work, including the introduction to the Honno edition of *The Wooden Doctor* (2005). 'Margiad Evans's *The Wooden Doctor*: Illness and Sexuality' appeared in *Welsh Writing in English* (UWP, 2004), and her conference paper '"To Write a Great Story": Margiad Evans's illness narratives' was published in 2009.

KIRSTI BOHATA is Senior Lecturer in English Literature and Director of the Centre for Research into the English Literature and Language of Wales (CREW) at Swansea University. She is the author of *Postcolonialism Revisited: Writing Wales in English* (UWP, 2004) and editor of Bertha Thomas, *Stranger Within the Gates* (Honno Classics, 2008). She has published widely on Welsh women's writing, most recently '"Unhomely moments": reading and writing nation in Welsh female Gothic', in *The Female Gothic*, Andrew Smith and Diana Wallace (eds) (Palgrave, 2009).

TONY BROWN is Professor of English at Bangor University, where he is also Co-director of the R. S. Thomas Study Centre. He was the founding editor of *Welsh Writing in English: A Yearbook of Critical Essays* (1995–2007) and has published widely on Welsh writing in English, especially on Glyn Jones (including editions of Glyn Jones's *Collected Stories* and *The Dragon has Two Tongues*) and on R. S. Thomas; his *R. S. Thomas* in UWP's Writers of Wales series appeared in 2006 (repr. 2009). He is currently working on a monograph on the English-language short story in Wales.

KAREN CAESAR is completing a PhD on 'Margiad Evans: body and book'. Her conference paper 'Patient, doctor and disease in Margiad Evans's *The Wooden Doctor*' was published in 2009.

MOIRA DEARNLEY was born and educated in Swansea. After completing her PhD and holding a University of Wales fellowship, she worked in educational research before becoming a teacher. She has published *The Poetry of Christopher Smart* (Routledge, 1968), *Margiad Evans* (UWP, 1982) and *Distant Fields: Eighteenth-Century Fictions of Wales* (UWP, 2001). Now retired, she is completing a literary biography of Mary Robinson.

KATIE GRAMICH is Professor of English Literature at Cardiff University. She is the author of *Twentieth-Century Women's Writing in Wales: Land, Gender, Belonging* (UWP, 2007) and *Kate Roberts* (Writers of Wales series, UWP, 2011) and the editor of *Mapping the Territory: Critical Approaches to Welsh Fiction in English* (Parthian, 2010).

A. J. LARNER is a consultant neurologist at the Walton Centre for Neurology and Neurosurgery, Liverpool and Society of Apothecaries' Honorary Lecturer in the History of Medicine, University of Liverpool. He has an interest in neurological disorders in famous artists, and in literary portrayals of neurological illness. He currently edits *Medical Historian: The Bulletin of the Liverpool Medical History Society*.

CERIDWEN LLOYD-MORGAN was formerly Head of Manuscripts and Visual Images at the National Library of Wales, where she catalogued the Margiad Evans manuscripts and archives. She is the author of a critical biography of Margiad Evans (Seren, 1998), as well as books and articles on the art and literatures of Wales.

CLARE MORGAN is Director of the graduate creative writing programme at the University of Oxford. Her novel *A Book for All and None* was published by Weidenfeld & Nicolson in June 2011, and her book *What Poetry Brings to Business* was published by the University of Michigan Press in May 2010. She has published a short story collection, *An Affair of the Heart* (Seren, 1996), and her stories have been commissioned by BBC Radio 4 and widely anthologised. She reviews regularly for the *Times Literary Supplement* and is a Fellow of Kellogg College, Oxford University, and a Fellow of the Royal Society of Arts.

LUCY THOMAS completed a PhD at Cardiff University in 2009, entitled 'The novels of Hilda Vaughan 1892–1985: negotiating the boundaries of Welsh identity'. She has published and given papers on Welsh women's writing in English and continues to work on the Vaughan archive. She is currently working at the Welsh Books Council.

M. WYNN THOMAS is Professor of English and Emyr Humphreys Professor of Welsh Writing in English at CREW (Centre for Research into the English Literature and Language of Wales), Swansea University. A Fellow of the British Academy and Vice-President of the Learned Society of Wales, he has published over twenty volumes in Welsh and in English on American Poetry and the two literatures of Wales. His latest work is *In the Shadow of the Pulpit: Literature and Nonconformist Wales* (UWP, 2010).

DIANA WALLACE is Professor of English Literature at the University of Glamorgan. She is the author of *Sisters and Rivals in British Women's Fiction, 1914–39* (Macmillan, 2000) and *The Woman's Historical Novel: British Women Writers, 1900–2000* (Palgrave, 2005) and co-editor (with Andrew Smith) of *The Female Gothic: New Directions* (Palgrave, 2009).

1

Introduction

KIRSTI BOHATA AND KATIE GRAMICH

In her first published novella, *Country Dance* (1932), Peggy Whistler, born in Middlesex in 1909, and writing under the Welsh pen name 'Margiad Evans', offered her reader the chance to rediscover a lost and forgotten story: that of the life of a mid-nineteenth-century farm girl from the Welsh borders, Ann Goodman. Using the inspired device of the 'found manuscript', Evans allows Ann to tell her own story – the story of countless generations of silenced labouring women, who have been left, as Evans puts it, 'curiously nebulous and unreal'.[1] Taking our inspiration from the author herself, then, in this volume we offer the reader a chance to rediscover the life and work of 'Margiad Evans', a writer whose novels, stories and autobiographical works were much admired during her lifetime but who has subsequently lapsed into the realm of the 'nebulous and unreal'.

Evans published a substantial body of fiction and memoir in the period between 1932 and her untimely death from a brain tumour in 1958. She was a contemporary of women writers such as Rosamund Lehmann, Sylvia Townsend Warner, Storm Jameson, Naomi Mitchison, and Kate O'Brien, all of whom have suffered from critical neglect until quite recent feminist challenges to, and reconstructions of, the accepted literary canon. The disappearance of women from such canons is hardly a new phenomenon, but in the case of these writers, whose major work was published between the 1930s and 1950s, the critical neglect has been exacerbated by the hegemonic status of Modernism. Owing to the generally accepted narrative that the truly important literary work of the first half of the twentieth century was the experimental High Modernist fiction and poetry of writers such as James Joyce, Virginia Woolf and T. S. Eliot (whose work, it should be remembered, continued to be published until the late 1930s, 1940s and 1950s), the literary production of writers who

1

did not conform to the High Modernist template has tended to be denigrated or ignored. Many of these writers were women whose writing may be informed by but does not conform to the dominant modernist tradition.[2] Some attempt has been made in recent years to effect a revival of interest in what has come to be labelled 'middle-brow fiction' by women from the period.[3] Laudable as such attempts are, we do not believe that Margiad Evans should be rediscovered as a 'middlebrow' writer, though a superficial acquaintance with her work might invite such a designation. On the contrary, we and the contributors to this volume believe that Evans is a haunting and innovative writer, whose Gothic reimaginings, questioning of gender, class, and national borders, and disconcertingly frank exploration of the mind and body, illness, and impending death, mark her out as a distinctive and unfairly neglected literary artist.

This collection of essays grew from a one-day conference to mark the centenary of Margiad Evans's birth in 2009. It was an event that also marked a renewed interest in Margiad Evans, not only in literature but also in the clinical field specializing in the study of epilepsy, where Evans's accounts of her illness in published and unpublished works have been the focus of several papers.[4] The present volume comprises essays developed from some of the papers given at the conference, including an important contribution on Evans and epilepsy by the consultant neurologist, A. J. Larner.[5] The remaining essays were commissioned for this collection, with the aim of publishing studies of the broad range of Evans's published oeuvre – novels, short stories and poetry – as well as discussions of important unpublished works such as the pathography, 'The Nightingale Silenced' (*c*.1954–5). Many of the essays that follow draw on the rich collection of manuscript materials by Margiad Evans held by the National Library of Wales at Aberystwyth. It is hoped that future generations of scholars will be inspired by this book to continue such research.

The essays begin with an introduction to the life of Margiad Evans by her biographer, Ceridwen Lloyd-Morgan, who also surveys the autobiographical materials and manuscript resources available to researchers at the National Library of Wales. Lloyd-Morgan examines Evans's constructed identities and literary connections, as well as the traces they have left in the archives. Finally, she offers a short account of the biographical research of Arnold Thorpe, whose work did not lead to the planned biography but did add to the archives in an important way, and appends an invaluable summary of selected

manuscripts and papers held at the National Library of Wales, where Lloyd-Morgan was formerly Head of Manuscripts and Visual Images.

That opening, authoritative account of Evans is followed by a collection of diverse essays which reveal the different dimensions as well as the recurring concerns in the life and work of Margiad Evans. Many common motifs are identifiable, and perhaps one of the most significant in terms of its versatile multivalence is that of hauntings, spectres and ghosts. In a journal entry which figures Wales as a ghostly presence, reaching out to repossess lost territories, Evans writes of the 'sad and oncoming . . . hills today which put out clouds from Wales, as if she would shadow England's stolen marches, and stake her rights with rain and mist.'[6] Diana Wallace's analysis of *Country Dance* (1932) shows how this sense of a haunted landscape is represented in Evans's feminist reappropriation of the historical marriage plot. Wallace explores the subversive narrative of *Country Dance*, to reveal how Evans as author is both a feminist and a 'native' guide, sensitive to the lost histories of women and a ghostly, 'faint murmur which only native ears attuned may hear'. Like Katie Gramich, Wallace sees Evans representing the unresolved trauma of history as a haunting, an unsettling projection of the past into the present. Gramich's 'hauntology of place' highlights the Gothic dimension of Evans's sense of place and of the embodied nature of the self, focusing on that compelling yet daemonic figure of Easter Probert in Evans's recently republished 1934 novel, *Turf or Stone*. She notes how Evans's sense of herself as a *border* writer informs her Gothic visions, seeing the very territory of the borders as haunted by the 'unresolved trauma' of violence and dispossession. While Gramich emphasises Evans's obsessive attraction to the landscape which found suitable expression in the excesses of the Gothic mode, Moira Dearnley discusses the mystical or religious impetus Evans felt in her affinity to the land, particularly in her later work. A year before her marriage to Michael Williams, Evans sees her connection with the land in terms of her spirit (or her 'ghost') reaching out to the hills and to Williams, with whom she shared this connection to the landscape:

> as the earth turns its daily sun and the hills rise to overwhelm that which is now the sky – my strength, my ghost, cries to be with him hand in hand – wearing out the wind against our breasts on a high hill . . . As a child gathers in the body the future spirit assembles in me.[7]

Dearnley traces Evans's Brontëan sense of mortality, eternity and her love for 'mine own country' in the later work, suggesting that Evans's

'ghost' is 'potentially brought into being by her love of place'. For Evans the 'soul' was sometimes interchangeable with or figured as a 'ghost' and yet the troubling difference between an eternal soul that might merge and become one with her beloved country and the disembodied ghost that yet retains something of the individuality of the embodied self is apparent in her poetry and autobiographical prose. In *Autobiography* (1943), Dearnley identifies Evans's conviction that 'the soul pours outward from us . . . to merge with the universal atmosphere' while insisting in a later poem on the survival of individual identity: 'But I would die whole'.

Karen Caesar's study of Evans's recreation of self in *Autobiography* and *A Ray of Darkness* (1952) pursues the theme of Evans's sense of 'herself and others as embodied beings'. Evans's response to the disembodiment of epilepsy may be, Caesar suggests, linked to mysticism and a sense of being *haunted*, of occupying through her epilepsy the liminal space between presence and absence, like a ghost. 'In Evans's case', Caesar argues, 'ghosts represent her sense that she is no longer in possession of herself.' In his essay on memory, time and identity in the short stories, Tony Brown comments too on the proliferation of ghosts in Evans's writing. Brown suggests the representation of memory itself is figured by Evans as a kind of haunting. The ghostly imagery in Evans's fiction is interpreted in the context of lesbian literary history by Kirsti Bohata. Arguing that Evans's writing is an important early twentieth century example of apparitional imagery (a staple of writing by and about lesbians), she traces the language, imagery and metaphors Evans uses in her journals and fiction to represent same-sex love and desire. The centrality of music and sickness in Evans's lesbian fiction reflect two poles between which Evans's own passionate yet ambivalent feelings about same-sex love fluctuated.

Another recurring metaphor revealed by these essays is a 'return to the mother'. Imagined in different ways by Margiad Evans, so too it is interpreted using a variety of conceptual and critical models in this collection. Lucy Thomas, in her comparative study of mixed-blood women characters in *Country Dance* and novels by Hilda Vaughan and Mary Webb, reveals that these three border writers create symbolic female characters who are of mixed descent, with an English father and a Welsh mother. These troublesome hybrid women all inherit their mothers' (often wayward) Welsh characteristics and represent within their very bodies the border that separates the two

national cultures. Ann Goodman, in *Country Dance*, eventually chooses a Welsh rather than an English suitor, and thus 'returns' to her mother's country, endorsing and acting out Myfanwy Goodman's longing to return to the hills: 'lately I have been seeing your mother's blood in you Ann – all that is good in it'. Evans herself often declared a spiritual and emotional affinity with Wales:

> The land beyond the hills means so much more to me than the ground I stand on. For what I stand on only supports my flesh, but the distances uphold my heart and the hills sweep my thoughts across the sky.[8]

Through her nature mysticism she developed a more universal sense of the individual's connection with the land, imagining the Herefordshire landscape, and by extension the whole earth, as a body – the body of *mother* nature. As Karen Caesar argues, in a Lacanian reading of Evans's autobiographical works, nature was a mirror which reflected Evans whole, and thus her sense of unity or existence *in and through* nature is an imaginary 'possession of the mother's body'. In contemplating death, Evans found solace in the idea of her soul merging with the universe and particularly the soil of 'her beloved border country', as Moira Dearnley suggests. Quoting from an unpublished poem in which the speaker, from her grave, is 'loyal to the Death who mothered me in earth . . .', Dearnley identifies an ambivalence about the loss of identity associated with a return to the (mother) earth, while Caesar, using a different conceptual model, sees in Evans a fear of language that 'severs the individual from the mother's body'. In a further permutation, Bohata notes that the sexual desire of one woman for another has been conceived of in terms of a worrying and pathological desire for the mother, where female homosexuality is configured as sterile and morbid (rather than properly reproductive) and as a merging sameness rather than a 'proper' desire for difference. In this negative formulation, a lesbian return to the mother is associated with death, and Bohata explores some of the conflicted and complex imagery of lesbian desire and illness in Evans's fiction and journals. Here, then, several essays work together to identify an important metaphor in diverse areas of Evans's writing which begs further comparative investigation.

As one would expect, there are many other important themes which run through this collection which are not fully explored in our introduction, including place (Katie Gramich and M. Wynn Thomas) and gender (Lucy Thomas, Diana Wallace and Clare Morgan). The

autobiographical turn of Evans's writing is the focus of many of the articles in the latter half of the book, but the function and role of memory is a theme in the essays focused on her earlier fictional works too. M. Wynn Thomas, exploring the confluence and affinities between Evans and the southern American writer Eudora Welty, quotes a line written by Welty that is remarkably apposite to processes of memory and the construction of identity in Evans: 'remembering, we discover'. The role of memory is also the subject of essays by Tony Brown and Sue Asbee although they look at different areas of Evans's work – Brown focusing on the complex slippages between time and memory in her short stories, and Asbee concentrating on the tentative construction of self in Evans's late, unpublished work. Both essays, however, discuss Evans's construction of identity through memory, an undertaking which could be described as a lifetime project.

From the 1950s onwards, Evans's life was dominated by the onset of epilepsy and later the brain tumour that would lead to her death on 9 March 1958, her forty-ninth birthday. In the interests of interdisciplinarity and as an intervention in the field of health humanities, A. J. Larner has contributed a study of the creative impact of epilepsy on Evans from the point of view of a consultant neurologist. And Karen Caesar pursues Evans's illness narratives, both published and unpublished. But life-changing though her condition was, Evans was not wholly fixated by her experience of epilepsy during this period. Clare Morgan's discussion of the frustrations of Evans's life and work in the 1950s is an important counterbalance to the view of Evans as entirely dominated by fits and declining health. Here we see a creatively faltering yet typically combative Evans, wrestling with the infuriating tedium of being a wife (read 'nonentity', as she once put it) and the difficulties of motherhood, but still capable of occasional bursts of successful writing.

The essays are placed in roughly chronological order and reward reading in sequence, although each stands alone. After the biographical and archival introduction by Lloyd-Morgan, the essays move from her first published novel, *Country Dance* (1932), considered as a revisionist historical novel by Wallace and within a postcolonial and comparative framework by Lucy Thomas, through to her last unpublished writings of the 1950s, considered from very distinct perspectives by Clare Morgan and Sue Asbee. Katie Gramich considers her early Gothic fiction, while Tony Brown and M. Wynn Thomas focus on the somewhat later short fiction, which has been seen as a form in which

she excelled. Kirsti Bohata considers both published and unpublished writings from different periods in Evans's writing life in her pursuit of the recurrent lesbian themes in her work. Two contributors, Andrew Larner and Karen Caesar, then focus on Evans's unflinching expression of illness, probing the fascinating interface between epilepsy and creativity, while Clare Morgan explores the autobiographical and creative tensions of the 'frustrating fifties'. The final essay in the collection, by Moira Dearnley, offers a sensitive response to the later poems of Evans up to her untimely death in March 1958. It is a sad yet fitting close to the collection.

Notes

[1] Margiad Evans, *Country Dance* ([1932] Cardigan: Parthian, 2006), p. 4.

[2] Daniel G. Williams considers Margiad Evans as a modernist writer and compares her to Kate Roberts in his chapter on 'Welsh modernism', in *The Oxford Handbook of Modernisms*, Peter Brooker, Andrzej Gasiorek, Deborah Longworth and Andrew Thacker (eds) (Oxford: Oxford University Press, 2010), pp. 797–816, and in comparison with Zora Neale Hurston in his book *Black Skin, Blue Books: African Americans and Wales 1845–1945* (Cardiff: University of Wales Press, 2012).

[3] See Nicola Humble, *The Feminine Middlebrow Novel 1920s to 1950s: Class, Domesticity, and Bohemianism* (Oxford: Oxford University Press, 2001) and Faye Hammill, *Women, Celebrity, and Literary Culture between the Wars* (Austin: University of Texas Press, 2007).

[4] Jim Pratt, 'Margiad Evans: centenary of an artist with epilepsy', paper delivered to the 28th International Epilepsy Congress, Budapest, 28 June – 2 July 2009; A. J. Larner, '"A ray of darkness": Margiad Evans's account of her epilepsy (1952)', *Clinical Medicine*, 9 (2009); A. J. Larner, 'Margiad Evans (1909–1958): a history of epilepsy in a creative writer', *Epilepsy & Behavior*, 16 (2009); Sue Asbee, '"To Write a Great Story": Margiad Evans' illness narratives', in *The Patient: Probing Interdisciplinary Boundaries*, Aleksandra Bartoszko and Maria Vaccarella (eds) (Witney: Inter-Disciplinary Press, 2011). E-book, available at *www.inter-disciplinary.net/publishing/id-press/ebooks/the-patient/*; I. Iniesta, 'Epilepsy and literature', *Medical Historian*, 20 (2008–9), 31–53 (available online at *www.lmi.org.uk/Data/10/iniestaa.pdf*) discusses 'The Nightingale Silenced', but is otherwise poorly informed about Margiad Evans's work, claiming erroneously that *The Old and The Young* (1948) is 'a book almost entirely devoted to her experiences with epilepsy'! Earlier interest in Margiad Evans's epilepsy was primarily medical; see for instance W. G. Lennox and

M. A. Lennox, *Epilepsy and Related Disorders* (London: J. A. Churchill, 1960) and Walter C. Alvarez M.D., *Minds That Came Back* (Philadelphia & New York: J. B. Lippincott, 1961), full text available at *www.archive.org/ stream/mindthatcameback007026mbp#page/n7/mode/2upw*.

5   Two papers given at the conference do not appear in this volume. Daniel Williams's comparison of Margiad Evans and Zora Neale Hurston as 'ethnographic modernists' forms part of his chapter 'In the wide margin: modernism and ethnic renaissance in Harlem and Wales', in *Black Skin, Blue Books* (see note 2), while Jim Pratt's moving personal discussion of his aunt's life and work forms the basis of an article published to coincide with this volume, 'The Nightingale Silenced: Margiad Evans's manuscript on the "self-disaster" of her epilepsy', *New Welsh Review*, 99 (forthcoming 2013).

6   NLW MS 23577C, 2 October 1935.

7   NLW MS 23577C, August 1939, f. 125.

8   NLW MS 23577C, 2 October 1935.

2

The Archivist's Tale: Primary Sources for the Study of Margiad Evans

CERIDWEN LLOYD-MORGAN

Personal archives can be exciting, frustrating, disappointing, illuminating and misleading. Some are deliberately weeded, by writers or
their heirs who rigorously destroy anything they think too personal,
too incriminating, or of insufficient interest or relevance. Some
creators or owners of personal archives may cherry-pick so that, as in
the case of the artist Ceri Richards, for example, only the correspondence with a handful of famous names and with a few close relatives
and friends remain.[1] Others may deliberately retain letters to incrim-
inate their enemies, sometimes gleefully informing the archivist that
they have done so; others, like the novelist Glyn Jones, preserve most
if not all their letters, however trivial, overwhelming the archivist
attempting to catalogue them or the researcher striving to sift the
wheat from a mountain of chaff.[2] The archive of manuscripts and
papers which Peggy Whistler and her literary alter ego Margiad
Evans have left is fortunately substantial. Not only is it quite extensive in time and scope, it is remarkably informative, with very little
dross. The papers comprise drafts of literary works in both prose and
verse, published and unpublished, which are contextualised and often
illuminated by a wealth of more personal documents. The latter
include journals and autobiographical writings, correspondence,
photographs and sketches.

Although the main body of Margiad Evans's papers in public
hands, which will be discussed below, is preserved at the National
Library of Wales, no discussion of the primary sources for the study
of the life and work of Margiad Evans would be complete without
reference to the significant groups elsewhere, in both private and
public collections. Much material remains in the hands of relatives

and friends, though small collections or individual items continue to surface and find their way into public collections. A notable example is the series of utterly characteristic letters which she wrote to her brother, Roger, between 1940 and 1944, while he was a prisoner of war in Germany. These letters have been studied and generously made available to researchers by their nephew Jim Pratt, son of their sister Betty, who has also unearthed a number of photographs, hitherto unknown outside the family, showing Peggy in her younger years. Letters from writers can end up scattered very widely for they will normally, of course, remain in the hands of the recipients. These might be friends, publishers or editors as well as relatives; at their death letters to them would normally pass to the recipient's heirs. Of course, many letters will not have survived, as some people destroy letters once they have been dealt with, or when moving house or after a death in the family, while heirs do not always recognise the value of inherited bundles of old letters and destroy them or throw them away. Fortunately there are exceptions, where heirs realise the significance of personal papers and take steps to ensure their preservation.[3]

Turning to papers in collections with public access, the most important single group outside Wales is held in the Beinecke Rare Books Library, at the University of Yale. This archive consists of papers donated to the Beinecke by Margiad Evans's fellow author and generous patron Winifred Ellerman (1894–1983), better known as the writer 'Bryher'. It comprises Margiad's letters to her, together with the journal of her holiday trip to Ireland in 1949, paid for by the award which Bryher funded via the Society of Authors, a manuscript of *A Ray of Darkness* and a series of sketches and drawings, all of which the author sent to Bryher as gifts. Again in the USA, the State University of New York at Buffalo holds a notebook, 1948–50, and a few letters and poem drafts, some donated by Margiad Evans herself. But smaller groups and single items can also be found in British collections. Reading University Library, for example, holds letters relating to the author's work, from publishers' records.[4] A file of letters to Rosamund Lehmann in the archive of modern literary manuscripts held at King's College, Cambridge, includes only two letters from Margiad Evans, written in March and April 1945, but both are of interest. One is accompanied by a poem and the other by a very characteristic self-portrait sketch, in which she portrays herself in trousers and wellingtons holding in one hand the manuscript of a poem, marked 'masterpiece'.[5] Even so small a find as this can be

useful to the researcher, for it may flesh out references elsewhere, in diaries or in other correspondence, for instance. Further examples can be found in the invaluable online Location Register of 20th Century English Literary Manuscripts (*www.locationregister.com*) developed by the University of Reading's Library Services. This database is a useful starting point for researchers on many modern writers in English and it is updated periodically, though it may not include the newest acquisitions by repositories.

For the study of the life and work of Margiad Evans, the extensive papers at the National Library of Wales, Aberystwyth, remain indispensable. The core of the collection is her *Nachlass*, comprising papers generated by the writer and still in her hands at her death, most generously donated to the library by her husband, Michael Williams. Given the descriptive title Margiad Evans MSS when they were acquired, they are supplemented by material subsequently acquired through donation and purchase; details of the holdings are given in the appendix below. This main archive covers the life of Margiad Evans from about 1932, when she was twenty-three years old and working on her second novel, *The Wooden Doctor*, until her death. It includes drafts of works in prose and verse, both published and unpublished, journals and notebooks, autobiographical writings, photographs, sketches, and letters addressed to her. To these, Michael Williams kindly added the long and illuminating series of letters which she wrote to him, including those she wrote almost daily during his wartime absences in the navy.[6] As I have suggested elsewhere, the letters of Margiad Evans to her husband not only provide a valuable record of her daily life in Llangarron, and help to establish when she was working on a particular text and how she felt about that work's progress, but they also show how important letter-writing was to her as a literary exercise.[7] Like her journals they allowed her to fix impressions, images and turns of phrase, and because her own life experience was the starting point for so much of her writing they may reveal the precise source of a key incident or image in a story or a poem. Similarly some of the journals, especially those from the war years are to all intents and purposes literary drafts, to be quarried later. Thus one journal (NLW, Margiad Evans MSS 32, dated 1942) constitutes an early draft of the 'Beet Hoeing' section of *Autobiography*.

The second major group at the National Library is a secondary archive, the so-called Margiad Evans Papers, compiled in the years immediately following her death by W. Arnold Thorpe, a man who knew intimately the Ross-on-Wye area which was so central to her

work. He had intended to write her biography but in the end was only able to assemble the raw material and write an outline and a few brief notes. In 1982, however, his widow, Mrs Josephine Thorpe, recognised the potential value of these papers to future researchers and generously donated them to the library. These papers proved to be an essential source for the biographer. Armed with his detailed knowledge of what he calls 'Margiad Evans country', Arnold Thorpe had been assiduous in collecting relevant material. His research was timely, for at that date – in the early 1960s – he was able to have photographs taken of places connected with Margiad Evans, while they were still little changed from how she would have known them. Now that so many of the places, such as the old mill that features in *Creed*, have altered beyond recognition, these photos have become particularly valuable. Thorpe was also able to collect information from the writer's friends, acquaintances and relatives, many if not most of whom have since died. Thus he extracted from her cousin Kitty Meredith (née Lane), for instance, a description of their visit to a ruined cottage which was to prove the starting point for *Country Dance*.[8] He also persuaded people who had letters from her to let him borrow them; his partial transcriptions of her letters to David Garnett from the early years of her career as a writer, and her letters to Thomas Butcher when she was at Springherne, are two typical examples.[9] Thorpe tended not to transcribe documents in their entirety, which initially raised some concern about their reliability, and the accuracy of his transcriptions. But where the original letters have by now become available, it has been possible to establish that he was in fact a very careful transcriber and possessed an unerring eye for the meat of a letter. In general, little of what he left out was of any real significance, as I was able to establish when the original letters to Thomas Butcher surfaced in 2003 after the death of the recipient. Fortunately his son recognised the significance of this series, which covers the important years 1938–43, and donated them to the National Library of Wales, where they are now NLW MS 23893E. These letters provide an amusing and extraordinarily vivid impression of the chaotic, hand-to-mouth life at Springherne guest house as well as being a superb example of the writer's liveliest, most entertainingly extravagant style.

As well as borrowing and transcribing letters, Arnold Thorpe also asked people who knew Margiad Evans for their personal recollections of her, as well as putting specific questions to them. For this

reason his papers provide a valuable source of independent information about her earlier years, which are under-documented in her own archive. Thorpe's archive can therefore help to tease out how far the raw autobiographical material was fictionalised and transformed – 'translated' to use her term[10] – as part of the process of literary creation. In addition to collecting material from friends of Margiad Evans, such as Marjorie Byolin of Bridstow, and from relatives such as her cousin Kitty Lane, Thorpe extracted information from a host of the author's literary contacts, including Sir Basil Blackwell, Bryher, whose generosity had so helped Margiad Evans in her later years, Arthur Calder-Marshall, David Garnett, Robert Herring, Glyn Jones, Professor Gwyn Jones, Keidrych Rhys and Derek Savage.[11] This is precisely the kind of information which all too often is lost or never recorded. Judging by the surviving, fragmentary drafts of Thorpe's proposed biography, it is perhaps a mercy that he did not live to complete his task, but the archive of material he assembled is of great and lasting value.

Apart from these two main groups of archives – the papers compiled by Thorpe and the writer's own *Nachlass* acquired from the family – further Margiad Evans papers are scattered through various other collections at the National Library. These, as one would expect, consist mainly of correspondence, of which the small but highly illuminating short sequence of letters in the Kate Roberts archive is a good example.[12] Letters to editors of periodicals to which Margiad Evans submitted work form an important category, within which those to Professor Gwyn Jones are particularly informative.[13] Jones first came into contact with Margiad Evans in the autumn of 1938, when he was launching his new periodical, *The Welsh Review*, and asked her permission to include her name in a list of well-wishers; at the same time he invited her to submit work for publication in its pages. She offered a piece based on her Iceland journal, but asked anxiously, 'Would it pay and *on the nail?*'[14] As well as publishing and, indeed, paying her promptly, Gwyn Jones encouraged her to write to the BBC offering to do a reading from *Country Dance* or perhaps 'The Widower's Tale', the never-completed novel on which she had embarked after *Creed*, and which was already proving intractable.[15] When the BBC did invite her to Cardiff to broadcast a reading on the Welsh Home Service, she stayed with Gwyn Jones and his first wife, Alice, and they remained in friendly contact for the rest of Margiad's life. The fact that Gwyn Jones was himself a writer as well as

magazine editor and academic was probably a factor. That the two of them found themselves very much on the same wavelength is evident from her letters to him, which are very open and honest about her difficulties, ready to accept criticism about the value of the poetry and prose she submits, yet with no sign of false modesty. The affinity and sympathy she felt was not one-sided. This is shown in the only two surviving letters to her from Gwyn Jones and in Gwyn Jones's letters to Arnold Thorpe,[16] but it was confirmed by Gwyn Jones himself when I talked to him as I was embarking on the biography.[17]

Perhaps because of the sympathy between them, the letters from Margiad Evans which Gwyn Jones preserved so carefully offer valuable insights into her literary aims and even her analysis of herself as a writer. It is in these letters that she most clearly defines her role as a writer – not Welsh, not English, but of the Border:

> I'm *not* Welsh. I never posed as Welsh and it rather annoys me when R[obert] H[erring] advertises me among the Welsh short stories because *I am the border* – a very different thing. The English side of the border too. I don't speak fretfully: you know how I honour the Welsh writers and how hospitable they have been to me. But people who judge my 'characters' as Welsh can't understand much, with the exception of *Country Dance* of course. Most of them are stolid English, flavoured with Celtic ancestry and named from a very far past.[18]

She also discusses the contrast, if not conflict, between her private self as Mrs Peggy Williams, and the author 'Margiad Evans', whom she often externalises as a kind of alter ego. The only other place where she explores this dichotomy to quite the same extent is in her own private journals. Sending in her poem 'The Passionate Refusal' for *The Welsh Review* in December 1943 she explains to Gwyn Jones:

> There are at least two distinct writers in me – that I do know. The 'poem' was written by the thump-thump one who wrote most of *Turf or Stone* ... Just as there are two sides to the country – the loveliness and peace, and the brutal, human side which cannot ever be exaggerated.[19]

Although the precise characterisation of Peggy Williams and Margiad Evans varied, the opposition between the two remained. 'Margiad Evans', she declared to Gwyn Jones in January 1946, 'is an insufferable highbrow but Mrs Peggy Williams likes horrors', gobbling up fiction by Le Fanu, Surtees and 'the people who write for the *Woman's Weekly*.'[20] In his capacity as editor of *The Welsh Review* Gwyn Jones retained, as editors often do, original MSS submitted by authors,

including ones by Margiad Evans. In this way a number of final drafts of both her poetry and prose have been preserved with her letters in the Gwyn Jones Papers, such as the fair copy of the short story 'A Party for the Nightingale'.

Taken together, the author's own papers, the Thorpe archive and the various scattered letters and related documents provide a remarkably rich resource for both biographer and critic, and incidentally to the historian as well, for Margiad Evans in her letters often provides a telling detail to bring contemporary circumstances into sharp relief. From the archivist's standpoint it is curious and indeed disappointing to observe how often critics of literature, visual arts or music neglect to study the essential primary sources which such archives provide and thus make statements easily refuted by documentary evidence. A writer's archive and the letters and other documents which he or she has sent to others provide far more than biographical information or the bald fact that X corresponded with Y at such and such a time and on a particular topic, though that information alone can sometimes save a critic from many a glaring error. Literary drafts may be dated, and above all can throw light on the evolution of a particular work. The surviving manuscript of Margiad Evans's *The Wooden Doctor*, for example (NLW MS 23357B), reveals the extensive rewriting that took place before publication in 1933, including the complete excision of a long section based on the author's stay at Pouldu in Brittany in 1926. Yet the manuscript also confirms how closely autobiographical the novel was, for the first person narrator is sometimes named as Peggy – the author herself – rather than the fictional Arabella; it seems likely that the author was working directly from her journals.

Letters to others in the literary world, be they other writers or journal editors, publishers or literary agents, can shed considerable light on a writer's aims and purposes, or simply how they felt at a particular time about their own work or that of others, or where they locate themselves in respect to a tradition, a fashion or a movement; in retrospect, of course, the critic may not agree with that judgement. Margiad Evans rarely minces her words when expressing her opinion and her letters often contain very trenchant remarks, such as her comment in 1946 to Kate Roberts on H. E. Bates, who had reviewed Roberts's *A Summer Day* so unsympathetically in *The Welsh Review*:

> Bates? My dear he is no good. I never believed in him – in his integrity, genuine[ne]ss or inspiration. He is no writer. Such epithets as 'primitive' and so on are just stuck on – Such reviewers say anything just to be

clever. They are like bad accompanists who merely wish to draw attention to themselves. Reviewers should be humble and TRY – at least I think so.[21]

Another typical example is found in a letter, dated 30 April 1937, to Keidrych Rhys, editor of *Wales*, where she characterises surrealism as 'false cheating rubbish made to hide an utter lack of originality, thought or ability'.[22]

Journals as well as letters can yield important information not only on the chronology or progress of the author's work but also on, for example, the author's own taste in reading, establishing which books she was reading at a given time, or which writers from past or present she admired or disliked and why she held particular opinions. In a letter to her husband in November 1944, for example, she remarks:

Sometimes K[atherine] M[ansfield] is so profoundly good – at others she doesn't seem to *know* and puts down bathos – an awful sort of tripping drivel like a young green girl – she has nothing like the power and fury of our Eudora [Welty] and could never have written *The Worn Path*.[23]

Archives can be as valuable to the critic as to the biographer, as a corrective as well as an informative resource.

Nonetheless, there are many pitfalls to avoid. Anyone who has worked on original documents will be all too aware that these can be incomplete or misleading. Chance plays such a major role in the survival of personal archives that it is essential to guard against jumping to conclusions from negative evidence. Letters and other personal papers, not least those of artists and writers, are almost always skewed to the later years, in some cases because the individual creating the archive becomes increasingly aware of those papers' interest, especially if they have an eye to posterity, as many do. More commonly, perhaps, especially where the lifetime is longer or death or infirmity comes suddenly, papers are not so much preserved as survive passively, when, as a result of inertia, lack of time or less energy, with the passing years the individual has never got round to sorting or disposing of them. Poverty or constant changes of address or both tend to typify the early life of professional writers and artists and both are inimical to the preservation of personal papers, with the unfortunate consequence that the individual's youngest, most formative years, are often the most poorly documented. In the case of Margiad Evans this process can also be observed in the later period of her life, for there is evidence that many of her papers were destroyed or lost in the process

of repeatedly moving house between 1947 and 1953.[24] This is indicated not only by the evident gaps but also by her own comments in letters. Unfortunately, among the casualties were all but one of the letters she received from Kate Roberts. Drafts of poetry and prose probably suffered the same fate as these and letters from other correspondents, for she sometimes mentions conducting a purge on her old manuscripts and papers; the preponderance of literary manuscripts dating from the later years may well reflect a lack of selection as much as conscious preservation. Sometimes, however, there is clear evidence that literary drafts were deliberately kept, notably *The Wooden Doctor*, or the unfinished drafts of 'The Widower's Tale', which date from about 1938 to as late as 1955.[25] Another example would be the unpublished short stories which she began to assemble in the late 1940s with a view to publishing another collection like *The Old and the Young*, once again to be decorated with her own pen and ink drawings. This she describes in a letter to Lindsay Drummond, publisher of *The Old and the Young*, as 'a collection of uneasy stories which I call The Blessing of the Trumpets . . . I want to draw for them all.'[26] Some of the provisional drawings survive too, notably five intended to accompany a story called 'The Master Died'.[27]

Archives are inevitably incomplete, uneven and can be downright misleading if not used with care. It is always horribly tempting to assume that because someone *wrote* this or that, it must be true. But narratives of events and feelings always depend on context: the same writer may give widely conflicting opinions or versions of the same event, even on the same day, depending on the intended reader and the impression the writer seeks to give. Two letters on the same topic may be contradicted by another while a contemporary journal entry may provide yet another narrative. Similarly, it is also essential to bear in mind the date of a document, since ideas and feelings may change rapidly over time. A statement made one year may not hold true at another time, even if a change of view is undocumented elsewhere in surviving documents. Journals can be a minefield, for people in general seem to write more when their work is going badly, for instance, or when they are feeling unhappy, creating what may be an entirely false impression of a writer suffering in unbroken gloom.[28] Lively, extravagant letters to friends and informal family photographs often present a very different picture of Margiad Evans from what is contained in contemporary entries in her journals, which seem often to have been used as a cathartic outlet as well as a literary exercise.

This is especially true of the earliest surviving journals, from the 1930s. Both letters and journals, however, consistently reflect and document the pressures of conflicting roles and duties on the professional writer, especially the woman writer, for whom domestic and family duties as daughter, sister, wife, mother, even neighbour, together with the necessity sometimes of taking paid work, too often competed with the urge to write. Sometimes Margiad Evans describes the two sides of her life with cheerful good humour: 'I feel terribly eccentric sometimes – mostly in the mornings. At midday I'm a good housewife & in the evenings, a genius.'[29]

Sometimes, too, she seems to use the act of writing to lighten her own mood after what she describes as 'A day spent in Hell (K. Mansfield)' as she struggled to wash sheets by hand in the back kitchen with the fire smoking:

> In a great heat I was (Mr Pepys) . . . Couldn't see the windows. Couldn't make up my mind to die. 'Another thing going wrong and I'll cut my throat'. Wring squeeze. 'I will' slop, wring, toss and heave the bucket 'I'll cut my throat'. All the time wanting to saw and tie up the raspberries . . . rushed in terrific passion down garden path and tore mangled washing off line. Terrible oaths. Pushing of Pussy, scolding of Gladys [her dog], malevolent spirits. 4 o'clock threw rice pudding on floor. Kitchen wet hair. Hopped over wall & sawed. A bit calmer in mind . . . Why can't I ever get out and dig and have nice long quiet hours. My minutes are like stones in my shoe . . . [evening] Decided as it grew dark not to run away today.
> No book from Blackwell.
> What should I do if I had a little Williams too?[30]

The further strain, anxiety and frustration which wartime brought Margiad Evans are amply documented in letters to her husband:

> Why are we treated so abominably by our horrible foul fat Bevins & ministerial louts? Why don't we kill 'em and salt 'em? *We* feed Malta – we're *still* having bombs. That Bevin has just said food control's got to go on after the war. I'm blasted sick of it – sick of crumb & salt sausages & inconvenience & [. . .] *bossiness*.[31]

> I'm told that people say I should be working – they who have time to stand about any hour & talk – *me* sitting up till one two & three to write when they aren't about to interrupt. I know who says it – the Sherrifs who turned a man out of his farm to get their son in & keep him from the War. P'raps that's not fair for Betty says people in Ross say it too. 'Writing', says Ellen, 'I'd rather go out & peel a potato & help the War.' That's the mind I have to live in . . . One of the things I hate most in war

18

is people's complacency about their own 'effort'. Well, I look at my poems & I think they're worth it . . . I think I'll circumvent 'em all & go to work 2 days a week in Ross – get something to *eat* there . . . I feel bitter and sad – I don't know that I want to live here after the War even.[32]

But here again letter-writing emerges as a crucial activity, as a way of keeping her literary muscles toned, of working towards literary texts, as well as keeping in touch with friends, relatives, other writers, editors, and so on.

Both critics and biographers, then, ignore archives at their peril. Provided the user is aware of the many traps for the unwary, archives are an invaluable source against which to test one's ideas and theories and to throw light on the creative process and the writer's own purposes. Without the Margiad Evans papers preserved here and elsewhere our knowledge of both her life and her work would be scanty indeed. Without these written sources we could not set her work in its proper context nor understand the relationship between her life as she lived it and the body of extraordinary work she produced.

Appendix: Archives of Margiad Evans
at the National Library of Wales

Margiad Evans MSS

1–31	Drafts of published and unpublished prose and poetry, 1930s–1958.
32–42	Notebooks and journals, 1942–1950s.
43–939	Correspondence, 1934–58.
940	Cuttings of book reviews, 1943–52.
941–59	Drawings for the *Panchatantra* (1930).
960–2	Christmas cards drawn by Peggy Whistler, 1956 and undated.
963–87	Miscellaneous family papers, snapshots and ephemera, 1939–1950s.

Margiad Evans Papers

1–13	Transcripts by W. A. Thorpe, including poetry and prose by Margiad Evans; letters, 1936–55, from Margiad Evans to friends and relatives; extracts of Margiad Evans's published prose works.
14–23	Copies of letters from W. A. Thorpe to relatives, friends and publishers of Margiad Evans, with their replies, 1936–55.

24–34	Miscellaneous biographical and other material relating to Margiad Evans, compiled by W. A. Thorpe.
35	Photographs of Margiad Evans and the Whistler family and of places associated with her and her work, 1920–65, together with copies of drawings by Margiad Evans, 1930–*c*.1951.
36–38	Miscellaneous notes and cuttings compiled by W. A. Thorpe.

Other Manuscripts at the National Library of Wales

NLW MS 22432D	Letters, 1954–6, from Margiad Evans to Alan and Dorothy Hancox.
NLW MS 23357B	Early MS draft, *c.*1932, of *The Wooden Doctor*, here entitled 'A Divine Image'.
NLW MS 23358A	Incomplete MS draft, *c*.1938, of 'The Widower's Tale'.
NLW MS 23359D	Incomplete MS draft, ?1940s–50s, of 'The Widower's Tale'.
NLW MS 22360C	Incomplete manuscript draft, ?early 1950s, of 'The Widower's Tale.'
NLW MSS 23361–2B, 23363C	Manuscript drafts, *c*.1953–*c*.1955, of the unpublished short novel 'The Churstons'.
NLW MSS 23364E, 23365D	Manuscript drafts of short stories.
NLW MS 23366D	Journal, February 1933–July 1934.
NLW MSS 23367–8B	Manuscript drafts, 1954–5, of the unpublished autobiographical work 'The Nightingale Silenced', with a draft poem.
NLW MS 23369C	Typescript draft, 1957, of the unpublished autobiographical essay 'The Immortal Hospital'.
NLW MS 23370C	Autobiographical notes and fragments, *c*.1934–*c*.1955, together with three letters, 1943–50, to Margiad Evans.
NLW MS 23371B–72C	Essays, 1950–3, including one on Emily Brontë and on John Clare, together with an apparently unpublished short story and drafts of four poems.
NLW MS 23373E	Four typescript radio scripts by Margiad Evans or based on her work: 'The Silver Lining' (1953), 'December Day' (1956), 'Dear Desdemona' (1950s), 'Country Dance' (1960).

NLW MS 23374E	Manuscript and typescript drafts, *c*.1946–56, of published and unpublished poems by Margiad Evans, some of those included in *Poems from Obscurity* (1947) and *A Candle Ahead* (1956).
NLW MS 23577C	Margiad Evans's journal, 1935–9.
NLW MS 23893E	Letters, 1938–43, to Thomas Kennedy Butcher.
NLW MS 23994F	Manuscript drafts, *c*.1953–6, of poetry and prose, including a fragment of 'The Widower's Tale'.
NLW MS 23997D	Manuscript drafts, 1941–2, of eight sections of *Autobiography* (1943), together with two letters, ?1950s, to Alan and Dorothy Hancox.
NLW MS 23999E	Two holograph poems and an autobiographical sketch, 1952, written for *Promenade: The Weekly Review for Cheltenham*, together with a copy of the publication.
NLW Facs 870	Photocopy of Margiad Evans's diary, 1947.

Notes

[1] National Library of Wales (hereafter NLW) MSS 23005–14.

[2] The most substantial holdings, including extensive correspondence, are held at the National Library of Wales (Glyn Jones Papers), though there are significant groups elsewhere, notably at the University of Wales Trinity Saint David, Carmarthen. I am grateful to Sally Wilkinson and Sandra Stedman for information about the Carmarthen holdings.

[3] A good example is the series of lively and informative letters from Margiad Evans to her friend Thomas Kennedy Butcher, now NLW MS 23893E (see p. 12 and appendix to this essay).

[4] A file of correspondence relating to her works is included in the archives of Chatto & Windus and the Hogarth Press, Reading University Library.

[5] Cambridge, King's College Library, Rosamund Lehmann Papers, MISC 42A/17.

[6] These constitute the bulk of the correspondence files in Margiad Evans MSS 51–875.

[7] The same can be said of her letters to Roger Whistler, or those to Bryher. On the literary importance of her letters see Ceridwen Lloyd-Morgan, *Margiad Evans* (Bridgend: Seren, 1998), p. 81.

[8] NLW, Margiad Evans Papers, file 13.

[9] I have not been able to establish with certainty whether any letters from Margiad Evans to David Garnett still survive; none are listed in the Location Register of 20th Century English Literary Manuscripts (*www. locationregister.com*). For those to Thomas Butcher see Margiad Evans Papers, file 4, and NLW MS 23893E, cf. p. 12.

[10] 'The reality of my manuscript is myself *translating what I have learned* into scribbled words on thin paper' [my italics], *Creed* (Oxford: Basil Blackwell, 1936), foreword (unpaginated).

[11] NLW, Margiad Evans Papers, files 6–7, 10, 12, 17, 22–3.

[12] Since these have been published and discussed in detail, no further discussion is necessary here. See Ceridwen Lloyd-Morgan, 'Diwrnod o haf: llythyrau Kate Roberts a Margiad Evans', *Cylchgrawn Llyfrgell Genedlaethol Cymru/National Library of Wales Journal*, 33 (2003), 201–16, and Tony Brown, '"Stories from foreign countries": the short stories of Kate Roberts and Margiad Evans', in Alyce von Rothkirch and Daniel Williams (eds), *Beyond the Difference: Welsh Literature in Comparative Contexts* (Cardiff: University of Wales Press, 2004), pp. 21–37.

[13] NLW, Gwyn Jones Papers 74/115–73, 5 November 1938–January 1958. Gwyn Jones continued to write to her in her last weeks and received replies from Michael Williams and from her mother, Mrs Katherine Whistler (NLW, Gwyn Jones Papers 74/207, 218–221, 5 February–26 March 1958). Gwyn Jones was also instrumental in the reprinting of *A Ray of Darkness*, with the support of the Academi Gymreig in 1978, acquiring a small group of W. A. Thorpe's papers at the same time. See Gwyn Jones Papers 74/18–74.

[14] NLW, Gwyn Jones Papers 74/116, November 1938.

[15] See National Library of Wales, Gwyn Jones Papers 74/117–18. It was Gwyn Jones who urged her to publish part of 'The Widower's Tale', and a section entitled 'The Black House' appeared in *The Welsh Review*, 1 (1939), 242–6. No further material from the unfinished novel has hitherto been published. For details of manuscript drafts and fragments of this work see the appendix at the end of this chapter.

[16] NLW, Margiad Evans MSS 677, 717, dated 1945; NLW, Margiad Evans Papers, files 7, 23.

[17] In a further example of the importance of preserving oral testimony, I offer the following curious anecdote which Gwyn Jones recounted to me shortly before his death in 1999 and which further illustrates the sympathy between him and Margiad Evans. He telephoned me at home and in a voice of what sounded like great intensity, related how on one occasion, quite out of the blue, he had suddenly had a strong conviction that she was experiencing some kind of crisis or disaster and nothing could prevent him from going over to see her. All was well by the time he got there, but he remained convinced that something had been wrong – some *Weltschmerz* perhaps, he suggested – which had passed by the time he arrived. But he had no doubt whatsoever that he had done the right thing and that some telepathic sympathy had forced him to such precipitate action.

[18] NLW, Gwyn Jones Papers 74/144, 6 March 1946.

[19] NLW, Gwyn Jones Papers 74/126.

[20] NLW, Gwyn Jones Papers 74/143.

[21] NLW MS 20062B, item 1. For full transcript and discussion see Lloyd-Morgan, 'Diwrnod o haf', 204, 212. Bates's review appeared in *The Welsh Review*, 5 (1946), 217–20.

[22] NLW MS 22744D, ff. 145–6. The letter also includes a sketch of herself holding out her letter to dry in the sun. See also John Harris, 'Not a Trysorfa fach', *New Welsh Review*, 3/3 (1990–91), 28–33.

[23] November 1944, NLW, Margiad Evans MSS 495.

[24] The first move was within Llangarron from Potacre to Tower Hill in the summer of 1947 and then, forced to leave Llangarron in January 1949, she lodged for over a year with relatives in Chalfont St Peter, Buckinghamshire, and in Gloucester, before moving to the Black House in Elkstone, Gloucestershire, in March 1950 and later to Cheltenham, and finally to Hartfield in Sussex in 1953.

[25] For the draft of *The Wooden Doctor* see NLW MS 23357B; fragmentary drafts of 'The Widower's Tale' are preserved in NLW MSS 22358A, 23359D, 22360C, 23361–2B, 23363C, 23994F. The only published part of 'The Widower's Tale' is 'The Black House' (see note 15).

[26] NLW MS 23364E, f. 65ᵛ.

[27] NLW, Margiad Evans MSS 12 and NLW MS 23364E.

[28] This is undoubtedly true in the case of the artist Gwen John (1876–1939); see Ceridwen Lloyd-Morgan (ed.), *Gwen John: Letters and Notebooks* (London: Tate Publishing, 2004), p. 11.

[29] Letter to Michael Williams, 23 January 1943, NLW, Margiad Evans MSS 152.

[30] Letter to Michael Williams, 9 February 1943, NLW, Margiad Evans MSS, no. 161.

[31] Letter to Michael Williams, 12–13 March 1945, NLW, Margiad Evans MSS, no. 559.

[32] Letter to Michael Williams, 14 March 1945, NLW, Margiad Evans MSS, no. 560.

3

'Two Nations at War Within it': Marriage as Metaphor in Margiad Evans's Country Dance *(1932)*

DIANA WALLACE

The marriage plot as a metaphor for the 'union' of two nations is a key device in many of the early historical novels and national tales of the late eighteenth and early nineteenth centuries. Marriage between an English man and a Scottish girl in Sir Walter Scott's *Waverley, or 'Tis Sixty Years Since* (1814) or an English man and an Irish girl in Sydney Owenson's *The Wild Irish Girl: A National Tale* (1806), for instance, functions as an allegory of reconciliation and national unity between warring nations which have recently been brought together as one. As a historical novel, Margiad Evans's *Country Dance*, published in 1932 but set in 1850, revisits that metaphor, disrupts it, and revises it in a Welsh context in important ways. Evans's protagonist, Ann Goodman, herself of mixed English and Welsh blood, is caught between two suitors, one Welsh, the other English, and dies as a result. Reading *Country Dance* against those earlier novels by Scott and Owenson, as I want to do in this essay, enables a comparative analysis which works both across time (from the 1930s back to the late eighteenth and early nineteenth centuries) and across nationality/geography (Wales/ Scotland/Ireland). Evans's novel lays bare the inequality and coercion at the heart of the marriage metaphor, exposing the gendered and national violence which is buried in the earlier texts.

Questions of nationality have been central to the historical novel from its earliest inception. Regarded as the founder of the historical novel until very recently, Walter Scott has been hugely influential, both in terms of his influence on subsequent writers and in his central place in accounts of the development of the genre. His first novel, *Waverley*, about the 1745 Jacobite rebellion, was hailed as the

exemplary 'classical historical novel' by Georg Lukács in his seminal *The Historical Novel* (1962). Working with a Marxist model, Lukács argues that Scott depicts history as a series of dialectical conflicts between opposing forces, which produce a synthesis, or middle way, which represents progress. The marriage ending crucially figures that synthesis in *Waverley*. Written over a century after the 1707 Act of Union between England and Scotland, *Waverley* looks back to the '45 as the last major conflict between the two countries. The English Edward Waverley 'wavers' across various borders – Hanoverian/ Jacobite, England/Scotland, Highland/Lowland – and between two women (both Scottish) Flora MacIvor and Rose Bradwardine, before wedding Rose in a marriage which symbolises (in the words of the toast offered by her father) 'the united houses of Waverley-Honour and Bradwardine'[1]– or of England and Scotland. While Scott may be nostalgic about elements of the Scottish past, he clearly positions union with England as the way forward.

In *Ivanhoe* (1819) Scott looked even further back to depict conflict between the conquering Normans and conquered Saxons. Again, this is symbolically resolved through the marriage of Wilfred of Ivanhoe, a Normanised Saxon to the Saxon Rowena, a descendant of Alfred. The narrator comments:

> these distinguished nuptials were celebrated by the attendance of the high-born Normans, as well as Saxons, joined with the universal jubilee of the lower orders, that marked the marriage of two individuals as a type of the future peace and harmony betwixt two races, which, since that period, have been so completely mingled, that the distinction has become utterly invisible.[2]

Scott presents the mixture of 'races' through intermarriage as an image of national peace and harmony which leads to the erosion of the distinction between them, as well as the development of what Scott (mistakenly) characterises as 'that mixed language, now termed English' (*I*, p. 398). In this plot of historical progress, then, dialectical conflict leads to synthesis, figured by a cross-nation marriage. Scott's work is, however, in many ways more complex than Lukács's account allows. Tensions in this neatly dialectical plot are suggested, for instance, by the fact that in both of these novels, there is an excess which has to be excluded in the shape of the woman not married by the protagonist: the Jewish Rebecca in *Ivanhoe*, and, in *Waverley*, Flora MacIvor, sister of the executed Jacobite leader.

Lukács's positioning of *Waverley* as *the* 'classical historical novel' exerted a stranglehold over accounts of the genre which led to novels which did not fit this paradigm being ignored. However, more recent work by critics such as Katie Trumpener has shown Scott's indebtedness to a host of earlier historical novels and 'national tales', many of them by women. *The Wild Irish Girl* by Sydney Owenson, known after her marriage in 1812 as Lady Morgan, is one of the most important of these, and obvious parallels with Scott's novel suggest its influence on him. Both *The Wild Irish Girl* and *Waverley* use a male English protagonist who travels into Ireland or Scotland respectively and there falls in love with and marries an Irish/Scottish girl. Furthermore, Scott's Flora MacIvor, the girl Waverley does not choose to marry, closely resembles Owenson's harp-playing, auburn-haired Irish princess, Glorvina.

Owenson's earlier depiction of the marriage union plot is much more ambivalent than Scott's. The historical setting of *The Wild Irish Girl* is intentionally blurred. The opening letter is dated 17____ but Claire Connolly points to internal evidence which sets it around and after the United Irish rising of 1798,[3] just eight years before its publication date. It is not, therefore, a historical novel in the sense (borrowed from Scott's 'sixty years since' formula) in which we now usually understand the term. But it is a novel which is saturated in history. Owenson's English protagonist, Horatio 'Mortimer', has been banished to his father's Irish estates as a punishment for dissipation. Travelling incognito through what he regards as this 'semi-barbarous, semi-civilised' country, to the west coast of Connaught, he writes letters home to a friend in England describing what he encounters.[4] As Horatio falls in love with both the country and Glorvina, the 'wild Irish girl' he encounters there, he comes to see himself as turning '*historiographer*' (*WIG*, p. 92, original emphasis) to her father, the Prince of Inismore. It is, however, Glorvina herself who is the real historian and she educates Horatio about the history, culture and language of Ireland, much of it lost through colonisation by England. Owenson uses this epistolary format to mediate the English reader's introduction to this unfamiliar country but she supports Horatio's depiction of Ireland with extensive and scholarly footnotes documenting a range of historical, cultural, social and linguistic information.

The determining power of history is forcibly demonstrated when it emerges that Glorvina is the descendent of an Irish king deposed by

Horatio's own ancestors. In a dramatic denouement Horatio discovers his father, the Earl of M., also in disguise, about to marry Glorvina in recompense. The revelation kills her father the Prince, and the Earl steps aside to allow Horatio and Glorvina to be married. Tellingly, it is the Earl who interprets their union in politically symbolic terms:

> [. . .] let the names of Inismore and M____ be inseparably blended, and the distinctions of English and Irish, of protestant and catholic, for ever buried. And, while you look forward with hope to this family alliance being prophetically typical of a national unity of interests and affections between those who may be factiously severe, but who are naturally allied, lend your *own individual efforts* towards the consummation of an event so devoutly to be wished by every liberal mind, by every benevolent heart. (*WIG*, p. 250, original emphasis)

The marriage of Glorvina and Horatio can be read in several ways. Kevin Whelan suggests that it signals Owenson's 'collapse back into the weary Whig teleology which she had spent the more successful part of her book resisting'.[5] Julia Anne Miller, in a more feminist reading, argues that it exposes the 'coercion evident in the "marriage" of English and Ireland': 'The Act of Union,' she points out, 'like most marriages of the early nineteenth century, was an annexing, rather than a union of equals.'[6] Claire Connolly's reading of the novel's 'politics of love' suggests that neither the romantic relationship nor the Act of Union can be assimilated to a 'single reading', but that *The Wild Irish Girl* 'reinvent[s] "the resources of sensitivity" [. . .] putting them to the service of the language of "nationness"'.[7]

As examples of what becomes known as the 'national tale', *The Wild Irish Girl* and *Waverley* are both typical in their use of an allegorical marriage plot to explore what Katie Trumpener in *Bardic Nationalism* (1997) calls 'the contrast, attraction, and union between disparate cultural worlds'.[8] Such a plot typically ends, Trumpener argues, with 'the traveller's marriage to his or her native guide, in a wedding that allegorically unites Britain's "national characters"'.[9] However, the many examples of this plot which Trumpener discusses in *Bardic Nationalism* are almost all about England's relationship with Scotland and Ireland. As Jane Aaron has pointed out, Trumpener makes very little reference to Wales or Welsh writers in *Bardic Nationalism*, suggesting that she failed to find fictions which fit the particular patterns she identifies in Scottish and Irish fiction. Although there is no shortage of novels located in Wales, Aaron

argues, 'it is certainly more difficult to find ones focusing on the type of aspiring nationhood that [Trumpener] ascribes to the Scottish and Irish fictions of the period.'[10]

Written over a century later, *Country Dance* is particularly interesting because it rewrites the marriage union plot in a Welsh context and through the viewpoint of 1930s debates around gender and nationality. Moreover, *Country Dance* is part of a wider post-First World War reclamation and refashioning of the historical novel by women writers. This was inspired partly by the opening of university education to women and partly by women's new-found sense of citizenship once they were enfranchised. Writers like Naomi Mitchison, Rose Macaulay, Hilda Vaughan, Sylvia Townsend Warner, Margaret Irwin, Virginia Woolf and Bryher used historical fiction to re-imagine women's history. In this context, *Country Dance* is both typical of its period, and unusual in its focus on Wales and Welshness.

As the title metaphor indicates, questions of nationality and marriage are central to *Country Dance*. Playing on the double meaning of 'country' as both 'territory of a nation' and 'rural district' (*OED*), it suggests a dance between countries, or across country borders, as well as an old-fashioned, traditional rural pastime. Dancing is a common metaphor for courtship and marriage, as Jane Austen reminds us in *Northanger Abbey* where Henry Tilney tells Catherine:

> I consider a country-dance as an emblem of marriage. [. . .] You will allow that in both, man has the advantage of choice, woman only the power of refusal; that in both, it is an engagement between man and woman formed for the advantage of each; and that when once entered into, they belong exclusively to each other till the moment of its dissolution.[11]

Austen's analysis makes very clear the gendered inequalities of a marriage system where the woman has only the 'power of refusal'. Evans's novel makes the violence inherent in the marriage system even clearer, but she also uses the historical novel form to allow us to read the marriage metaphor back to explore the violence of colonialism.

The narrative structure of *Country Dance* uses several of the conventions of the historical novel established by Scott and, earlier, Owenson. These have interesting implications in terms of the relationship between the implied reader and nationality. *Country Dance* is presented as the diary of Ann Goodman, written in 1850, but framed by an introduction and postscript written in the present day by

'Margiad Evans' who has 'discover[ed]' the diary and offers a commentary on it.[12] The book is illustrated by 'Peggy Whistler'. 'Margiad Evans', of course, was the pen name chosen by Peggy Eileen Whistler, who was English but whose paternal grandmother (Ann Evans) was possibly of Welsh extraction.[13] The 'found' manuscript (diary, letters, historical document) presented by a fictionalised present-day narrator (which is one way of seeing the narrative voice of 'Margiad Evans' here), is a typical convention of historical novels. *Ivanhoe*, for instance, has a dedicatory epistle by 'Laurence Templeton' introducing the main text, while *The Wild Irish Girl* is an epistolary novel, with a third person conclusion. These conventions create an illusion of historical authenticity, but also mediate access to and offer ways of reading the text. Like Scott and Owenson, Evans also includes epigraphs and quotations – mainly from Welsh songs – and scraps of the Welsh language, usually given with translations. The epigraph to the novel – from an 'Old Song' – is given first in Welsh and then an English translation is included below in brackets. Such inclusions serve several complex functions: they attest to the scholarly credentials of the author but (as with *The Wild Irish Girl*) they also educate an implied English reader about the history and language of this 'other' country.

In both *The Wild Irish Girl* and *Waverley* the male English protagonist travelling into Scotland or Ireland acts as a mediator for such an implied English reader, introducing them to an unfamiliar, even exotic landscape and history, symbolised by the girl they fall in love with. In contrast, Evans centralises the first person voice of her female protagonist, who is of *mixed* nationality. However, her framing narrative serves a similar mediating function for the present-day (English) reader. The first lines of the text direct the reader towards a particular reading of the 'theme' of Ann's diary in terms of warring nationalities, contained within a single body, and duplicated in what is a version of the classic nineteenth-century dual suitor plot.

> The struggle for supremacy in her mixed blood is the unconscious theme of Ann Goodman's book.
> She writes of Gabriel, her sweetheart, English, jealous and sullen, of Evan ap Evans, her father's master, Welsh, violent and successful. (*CD*, p. vii)

Moreover, this claims (using a semi-Freudian language) to be able to decode the subtext of the diary, to be able to interpret an underlying meaning which is hidden even from Ann herself.

Ann Goodman is the daughter of a Welsh mother (Myfanwy) and an English father (John Goodman), and has lived for the last fifteen years in Wales on a farm with an English name (Twelve Poplars) and an English owner. Her parents live on the English side of the border where she was born, but her father works there as shepherd for a Welshman, Evan ap Evans. These complex border crossings (figured in the 'country dance' of the title) complicate any straightforward alignment of nationality with place of birth or habitation. Ann is courted by two men, the English shepherd Gabriel Ford to whom she is initially betrothed, and the Welsh farmer, Evan ap Evans. It is Gabriel who gives her the diary and asks her to keep a record of her life for him 'until we shall be married' (*CD*, p. 3). The first sections are, therefore, written for his eyes. Increasingly alienated from Gabriel by his jealousy when Evan ap Evans repeatedly speaks to her in Welsh, Ann breaks off the engagement, and finally becomes engaged to Evans. The diary ends there with a hope of 'some peace at last' (*CD*, p. 93). However, the final framing narrative in the voice of 'Margiad Evans' tells us that Ann's body was found in a pool in the river, with a 'great wound' on her temple (*CD*, p. 94).

Both Gabriel and Evan are suspected by the community, although the narrator tells us that 'Gabriel was undoubtedly the murderer' (*CD*, p. 94). The narrator then offers another interpretation of the 'subtler underlying narrative' of Ann's diary which again draws on a Freudian language of repression. It is, she tells us,

> the record of a mind rather than of actions, a mind which though clear in itself was never conscious of the two nations at war within it. Here is represented the entire history of the Border, just as the living Ann must have represented it herself – that history which belongs to all border lands and tells of incessant warfare.
>
> Wales against England – and the victory goes to Wales; like Evan ap Evans, the awakened Celt cries: 'Cymru am byth!' with every word she writes. (*CD*, p. 95)

There's an unresolved tension in the text between the attempt in the framing narrative here to present Ann as emblematic – representing the 'entire history of the Border' – and the individual 'living' voice of her diary. This seems to be partly the result of the tradition within the historical novel of positioning the woman as a symbol of her country. Evans partly reverses this to make Ann's choice of prospective husband a choice between the nationalities they represent. In choosing Evan ap Evans she is aligning herself with her mother's country,

as well as with the colonised/defeated nation. However, the 'victory' assigned here to Wales seems bizarre in the face of Ann's death. In fact, there's a slippage in the pronouns in this passage so that the 'awakened Celt' who is aligned with Evan ap Evans seems to be not Ann but 'Margiad Evans', the writer who shares his surname. The 'victory' here seems to be Peggy Whistler's choice of an elective Welsh identity as the writer 'Margiad Evans'.

The notion of the 'border' is also problematic. In the quotation above it represents conflict ('incessant warfare'). Ann's body is the ground of that conflict both as her two suitors literally fight over her, and as the 'two nations [are] at war within her mind'. The suggestion of the framing narrative is that she dies because of the internal conflict within her 'mixed blood': that is, because she herself is the result of a mixed marriage. However, in Ann's diary the border also represents a kind of middle way or reconciliation, when Gwen Powys (Gabriel's employer) to defuse drunken nationalistic conflict offers as toast, 'I give the Border' (*CD*, p. 61). This hints at the kind of reconciliatory middle way that Scott offers, but which Evans problematises in important ways.

Evans's use of the marriage union plot is closer to Owenson's than Scott's, but she makes three radical changes. First, she centralises and gives a strong voice to a female protagonist. Her privileging of the female point of view allows her to re-imagine a lost or erased Welsh/ Borders female history. The introduction offers an interpretation of the gender of history which echoes the more famous analysis in Virginia Woolf's *A Room of One's Own* (1928) where Woolf comments that women have been 'all but absent from history'.[14] But a further absence from Woolf's own very English-centred text is that of women from Wales. Evans is similarly interested in the ways in which women have been erased from oral history but she places this in a specifically Welsh context:

> Circumstances have dimmed the memory of this woman and ironically accentuated that of the rivals, Gabriel Ford and Evan ap Evans, shepherd and farmer, Englishman and Welshman. The glare which at her death picked them out with horrible distinctness, has left her curiously nebulous and unreal, a mere motive of tragedy. (*CD*, p. vii)

Men, defined by their trade and their nationalities, leave their marks on history in a way that women do not. Like Woolf's imaginary Judith Shakespeare, Evans's Ann Goodman is a lost possibility – indeed, a lost woman writer. Her diary recreates the possible life of a rural

woman in the mid-nineteenth century and restores that imagined life to a central place in history and the historical novel.

The second major difference from the novels of Scott and Owenson, is that in Evans's reworked marriage union plot it is her fully-realised central female protagonist who chooses between two male suitors who represent different nationalities. In fact, Evans is using here a version of the dual suitor plot which is typical of many nineteenth-century novels by women. The most important example here is Emily Brontë's *Wuthering Heights* published in 1847, just three years before the time *Country Dance* is set. Emily Brontë's work was an important influence on Evans's writing.[15] In 1948 Evans published an essay on 'Byron and Emily Brontë' in which she explored the affinities between the two writers.[16] *Wuthering Heights*, which she characterises in the essay as being, like *Manfred*, a 'hate poem',[17] is clearly an important influence on *Country Dance*. In both novels the heroine chooses between two suitors (Heathcliff and Linton, Evan ap Evans and Gabriel Ford) who represent different potential identities. Both are so-called 'regional' novels organised around the spatial representation of difference where characters move between two places: Ann Goodman moves across the Welsh–English border as Brontë's characters move between Thrushcross Grange and Wuthering Heights. Finally, both feature a Byronic hero, or anti-hero (both Gabriel and Evan ap Evans resemble Heathcliff).

Equally importantly, *Wuthering Heights* is itself a historical novel although it is rarely read as such (it opens in 1801, and the key action takes place a generation before).[18] Emily Brontë was, as Juliet Barker has shown, strongly influenced by Scott's work and Barker notes strong echoes of Scott's *Rob Roy* in *Wuthering Heights*.[19] Ian Jack links *Wuthering Heights* firmly to *Waverley*, arguing that Brontë got the idea for Lockwood from Scott's eponymous protagonist and that her narrative structure is what he calls 'the Scott technique modified [. . .] by the use of a first person narrator'.[20] Margiad Evans's reworking of Scott's marriage union plot, then, comes through her reading of Brontë's reworking of Scott. In *Wuthering Heights* Brontë plays out the dual suitor plot in terms of class: despite her famous assertion that 'I *am* Heathcliff',[21] Catherine marries Linton because he is a gentleman while Heathcliff is a poor orphan. Evans takes this plot and reworks it in terms of nationality, offering Ann Goodman a choice of suitors who represent different national identities.

However, and this is the third difference between her novel and those of Scott and Owenson, Evans swerves away from the marriage

union they use to give her marriage plot a tragic rather than a happy ending. *Wuthering Heights* has, in a sense, two endings: the tragic story of Heathcliff and Cathy in the first half, and the final ending with the marriage of Hareton and the second Catherine which can be read as reconciliatory. In contrast, the ending of *Country Dance* with Ann dead, Gabriel fled and Evan ap Evans eventually emigrating, might be more accurately called a missed or failed marriage plot. This refusal to provide a marriage ending is particularly striking in biographical terms given that Evans gives her heroine the name of her own Welsh grandmother – Ann – and gives her grandmother's surname (the name she herself adopted) to the chosen suitor.

There are at least three potential reasons why Evans doesn't give us a marriage ending. The first reason is perhaps personal to Evans. As Ceridwen Lloyd-Morgan has shown, Evans became increasingly fascinated by a sense of her own split personality.[22] In *Country Dance* the title page itself indicates an authorial split between 'Margiad Evans' and 'Peggy Whistler', and Evans explores the theme of duality in Ann's 'mixed blood' and her choice of nationality in the plot. Later, in *A Ray of Darkness* (1952) Evans suggests the strain caused by such a split and connects it to her epilepsy: 'I was an ordinary domestic woman by day, a poet or novelist or essayist by night. It was too much for me.'[23] Evans was clearly drawn to Wales, especially the notion of the border, as a place where she could explore her duality. But she also seems to have been using the issue of nationality to explore ambivalences about marriage. At the end of Evans's second and recognisably autobiographical novel, *The Wooden Doctor* (1933), Arabella breaks off her engagement to Oliver Austen, ostensibly because of her attachment to the much older doctor. However, Arabella is also finishing a book which seems from internal evidence to be a version of *Country Dance* and her refusal to marry Oliver can be seen as freeing her to be a writer. In 1850 Ann has only a choice between two suitors, but in 1933 Arabella can choose to be a writer instead of marrying.

The second reason I want to explore is more broadly historical and counters what might seem the reductiveness of any merely biographical reading. This is a crucial difference between the histories of Scotland, Ireland and Wales (which explains why Trumpener did not find Welsh novels which fit her patterns). Both Owenson and Scott were writing in the context of relatively recent Acts of Unions – the 1800 Act of Union between England and Ireland, and the 1707 Act of Union which united England and Scotland. However, as John

Davies has pointed out, whatever 'deception and trickery' was necessary to get them passed, both those Acts of Union were 'pieces of legislation passed by the parliaments of *both* countries concerned'.[24] In contrast the so-called Act of 'Union' of 1536 was passed solely by the parliament of England, and it simply assumed that the union of Wales and England already existed.[25] Davies quotes the preamble as follows: 'Wales . . . is and ever hath bene incorporated, annexed, united and subjecte to and under the imperialle Crown of this Realm as a verrye member . . . of the same.'[26] Not only is the 'union' of Wales and England further back in the past, it is also far more difficult to represent as a 'marriage' of equal partners. Given the formation of Plaid Cymru in 1925, which foregrounded the reassessment of Wales's status, past and present, Evans would have found it far more difficult (whatever her personal feelings) to offer a marriage ending as a symbol of the progressive union of the two countries.

The third important context here is the lively public debate around the meaning of marriage in relation to women's changed status in the 1930s. There was, for instance, a six-part series in *The Listener* in 1931 on what was called 'The Present Crisis in Marriage'. Novelists like Vera Brittain, Margaret Kennedy, Rebecca West, Naomi Mitchison and Hilda Vaughan all produced novels in the 1930s which interrogated and rewrote the marriage plot. Brittain's *Honourable Estate* (1936), for instance, offers a historically informed account of the shifts in marriage from what Brittain called the 'master-servant relationship of most nineteenth-century marriages' to the twentieth-century model of 'companionship between equals'.[27]

A particularly hot topic was the inequity of the law around nationality and marriage. Up until 1933 a British woman who married a foreigner could lose her British citizenship without acquiring her husband's nationality and thus find herself stateless. Brittain quotes a letter from the London *Evening News* of 1928 which described the predicament of a woman who married a Canadian soldier during the First World War and, after he was killed, found she had lost her British nationality. She was therefore 'compelled to report herself regularly to the police in her native village, where she has lived for over thirty years, and where her mother, brothers and sisters live.'[28] Although the British Nationality and Status of Aliens Act of 1933 made it possible for a woman who did not acquire her husband's nationality to retain her own, it was not until 1948 that the Nationality Act enabled a woman marrying an alien to retain her British

nationality. Virginia Woolf wrote acerbically of the effect of this on women's sense of national belonging in *Three Guineas* (1938):

> That [women] are stepdaughters, not full daughters, of England is shown by the fact that they change nationality on marriage. A woman, whether or not she helped to beat the Germans, becomes a German if she marries a German. Her political views must then be entirely reversed, and her filial piety transferred.[29]

The situation Ann Goodman faces – that a choice of husband is also a choice of national identity – was one that had continued relevance in the early 1930s. While Peggy Whistler elected a 'Welsh' identity as 'Margiad Evans' her novel makes it clear that women have not traditionally been able to chose their nationality with such freedom.

In the 1930s it was no longer possible, for a woman novelist at least, to use marriage straightforwardly as a metaphor or allegory of 'union' between equal partners because the historical inequalities of the institution were under debate. Frances E. Dolan's exploration of the ongoing connections between marriage and violence is perhaps particularly helpful here. Dolan discusses the various models of marriage which have persisted since the early modern period into the twentieth century, as well as their importance as metaphors for political relations. One of the most important of these models is what she calls the 'legal fiction of coverture' which had a far-reaching resonance.[30] The concept of coverture is most famously expressed in the much-quoted passage from William Blackstone's *Commentaries on the Laws of England* (1765–9):

> By marriage, the husband and wife are one person in law; that is, the very being or legal existence of the woman is suspended during the marriage, or at least is incorporated and consolidated into that of the husband; under whose wing, protection, and *cover*, she performs everything [. . .].[31]

Dolan draws attention to the violence which is involved in this unequal union as one 'spouse absorbs, subordinates, or eliminates the other'.[32] The similarity between this model of marriage and the wording of the 1536 Act of 'Union' I quoted above between England and Wales is striking. Both describe a merging of two entities into one in which the weaker member is 'incorporated' into the other. And both gloss over the violence which is implicit in this incorporation.

As a particularly sophisticated exploration of the ways in which the marriage metaphor maps onto the colonial 'union' of countries,

Evans's *Country Dance* also exposes this violence. Both Gabriel *and* Evan ap Evans are depicted as violent men and their violence is directed against Ann as well as each other. One of Evan's first acts towards Ann is to 'compel [. . .]' (*CD*, p. 15) her to dance with him, and Gabriel nearly brains her with a faulty mallet before, probably, murdering her. It is particularly telling that *both* men are suspected of Ann's murder. Evans explores the marriage metaphor for national 'union' precisely to suggest that there can never be a proper reconciliation or 'union', either in marriage or colonisation, where the two parties are so unequal. In *The Wild Irish Girl* the Earl of Mortimer hopes that with the marriage of Horatio and Glorvina, 'the distinctions of English and Irish, of protestant and catholic, [will be] for ever buried' (*WIG*, p. 250). The ironic and haunting ending of *Country Dance*, like that of *Wuthering Heights*, suggests that those things which have been buried are not necessarily forgotten:

> But new furrows are ploughed in old fields, harvests are sown and gathered, and names that sprang from the red earth itself have died away to a faint murmur which only native ears attuned may hear.
>
> It is well that men's doings, like the leaves after their season, fall to the earth, and beneath the boughs, crowded with fresh green growth, lie buried and forgotten. (*CD*, p. 96)

The 'incorporation' of the defeated/conquered party, whether a woman or a nation, will always be a violent erasure of identity which leaves traces of historical trauma in the memory for those whose ears are 'attuned' to hear them.

Notes

1   Walter, Scott, *Waverley: Or, 'Tis Sixty Years Since*, ed. Claire Lamont ([1814] Oxford: Oxford World's Classics, 1986), p. 339. Further references are given in the body of the text.

2   Walter Scott, *Ivanhoe*, ed. Graham Tulloch ([1819] London: Penguin, 1998), p. 398. Hereafter *I*.

3   Claire Connolly, 'Introduction', Sydney Owenson, Lady Morgan, *The Wild Irish Girl: A National Tale*, ed. Claire Connolly and Stephen Copley, foreword by Kevin Whelan ([1806] London: Pickering and Chatto, 2000), p. lii.

4   Sydney Owenson, Lady Morgan, *The Wild Irish Girl: A National Tale*, ed. Kathryn Kirkpatrick (Oxford: Oxford World's Classics, 1999), p. 10. Further references are to this edition, hereafter *WIG*.

5   Kevin Whelan, 'Foreword', Sydney Owenson, Lady Morgan, *The Wild Irish Girl: A National Tale*, ed. Claire Connolly and Stephen Copley ([1806] London: Pickering and Chatto, 2000), p. xxix.

6   Julia Anne Miller, 'Acts of union: family violence and national courtship in Maria Edgworth's *The Absentee* and Sydney Owenson's *The Wild Irish Girl*', in Kathryn Kirkpatrick (ed.), *Border Crossings: Irish Women Writers and National Identities* (Tuscaloosa and London: University of Alabama Press, 2000), p. 28.

7   Connolly, 'Introduction', pp. xxvi, xlvii.

8   Katie Trumpener, *Bardic Nationalism: The Romantic Novel and the British Empire* (Princeton, NJ: Princeton University Press, 1997), p. 141.

9   Ibid.

10 Jane Aaron, *Nineteenth-Century Women's Writing in Wales: Nation, Gender and Identity* (Cardiff: University of Wales Press, 2007), p. 11.

11 Jane Austen, *Northanger Abbey*, ed. Anne Ehrenpreis ([1818] London: Penguin, 1985), p. 95.

12 Margiad Evans, *Country Dance* ([1932] London: John Calder, 1978), p. vii. Further references are to this edition, hearafter *CD*.

13 Ceridwen Lloyd-Morgan, *Margiad Evans* (Bridgend: Seren, 1998), p. 7.

14 Virginia Woolf, *A Room of One's Own* ([1929] London: Granada, 1977), p. 43

15 See Lloyd-Morgan, *Margiad Evans*, p. 33.

16 Margiad Evans, 'Byron and Emily Brontë', *Life and Letters Today*, 57/130 (June 1948), 193–216, 208.

17 Evans, 'Byron and Emily Brontë', 198.

18 Emily Brontë, *Wuthering Heights*, ed. and introduction by Ian Jack (Oxford: Oxford World's Classics, 1981).

19 Juliet Barker, *The Brontës* (London: Weidenfeld and Nicolson, 1994), pp. 274, 501.

20 Jack, 'Introduction' to Brontë, *Wuthering Heights*, pp. ix, x.

21 Brontë, *Wuthering Heights*, p. 82.

22 Lloyd-Morgan, *Margiad Evans*, p. 127.

23 Margiad Evans, *A Ray of Darkness* ([1952] London: John Calder; Dallas: Riverrun Press, 1978), p. 27.

24 John Davies, *A History of Wales* ([*Hanes Cymru* (1990)] London: Penguin, 1994), p. 232.

25 Ibid.

26 Ibid.

27 Vera Brittain, *Lady into Woman: A History of Women from Victoria to Elizabeth II* (London: Andrew Daker, 1953), p. 170.

28 Brittain, *Lady into Woman*, p. 63.

29 Virginia Woolf, *Three Guineas* ([1938] London: Hogarth, 1986), p. 168.

[30] Frances E. Dolan, *Marriage and Violence: The Early Modern Legacy* (Philadelphia: University of Philadelphia Press, 2008), p. 77.

[31] Quoted in Mary R. Beard, *Woman as Force in History* (New York: Macmillan, 1946), pp. 78–9, original emphasis.

[32] Dolan, *Marriage and Violence*, p. 4.

4

'Born to a Million Dismemberments': Female Hybridity in the Border Writing of Margiad Evans, Hilda Vaughan and Mary Webb

LUCY THOMAS

There is a stone on the river bank with a rail around it to keep off the cattle. It was placed there by the master opposite the deep pool where Ann was found, her body wrapped in water weeds, her head no more than an inch or two from the surface.

On her temple was a great wound that cried aloud for justice. The cry was taken up all along the border . . .[1]

This, the most arresting image in Margiad Evans's novella, *Country Dance* (1932), is the final glimpse of its heroine, Ann Goodman. The haunting, painterly description, strikingly reminiscent of John Everett Millais's painting *Ophelia*, builds layers of myth and allusion that make it difficult not to read her lifeless body as symbolic.[2] This is something the very narrative struggles with as it performs a dance of its own, back and forth between its purported endeavour to uncover a female identity that death has rendered 'curiously nebulous and unreal' (*CD*, p. 4) and a portrayal of Ann that is weighted down with symbolic meaning. Her murder is marked upon the landscape not with a grave but with a stone behind a rail that more closely resembles the markers used to commemorate a battleground. Indeed, the wounded body is the casualty of a battle between Welsh and English nationality experienced both within and outside Ann Goodman. A hybrid character, she struggles with her own sense of identity while two male suitors from opposing sides of the border fight to win her. The implications of this death are not immediately clear. While the cry for justice reverberates 'all along the border', does it more

39

forcefully trace the divide between two nations as they suspect either the Englishman or the Welshman of murder, or does it unite the border country in collective outrage and anguish? In either scenario, Ann's hybrid body *becomes* the border, scarred, inscribed and dissected by seemingly opposing ideologies.

This is no isolated incident. Ann's death is one of a series of brutal endings for hybrid women in border fiction, the striking parallels among which would intrigue any armchair detective. Writing in the previous decade, Hilda Vaughan also presents a scene near the end of her novel *Here Are Lovers* (1926) where the characters frantically search for the body of the heroine, Laetitia Wingfield, in a turbulent river late at night.[3] Almost a decade before this, Mary Webb ends her novel *Gone to Earth* (1917) with the particularly gruesome death of its protagonist, Hazel Woodus, who is torn to pieces by a pack of hunting dogs.[4] A cruel fate is not the only thing these three female characters have in common: all are the offspring of mixed marriages between Welsh and English parents, all have a crisis prompted by their hybrid identity, and all must make a choice which ultimately leads to violent death. Thus, the call for justice and investigation made by Margiad Evans's narrator in *Country Dance* must surely be extended. The narrator's consciously articulated attempt to tell Ann's story, to uncover the identity of a woman whose face has been forgotten, forms part of a wider examination that is demanded of female identity in border writing.

Set in the region where the border divides Herefordshire and Monmouthshire, *Country Dance* depicts the life of Ann Goodman as she makes several border crossings between her cousin's farm in Wales, where she has been working, to the place of her birth on the English side of the borderlands. In England, Ann's English father and Welsh mother live on land owned by the Welsh farmer Evan ap Evans. She is aggressively courted by two suitors: the English shepherd Gabriel Ford, and the Welsh farmer ap Evans. Written in the form of Ann's diary, the text records her thoughts as she chooses between the two men and ultimately between the two nationalities that comprise her mixed identity. A hybrid work in numerous senses, Ann's story is placed within a framing narrative in which Margiad Evans introduces Ann's journal as a rediscovered text and concludes with the author's explanation that Ann's own account has ended because she was murdered by the English lover that she rejected in favour of his Welsh rival. The writing is interspersed with illustrations ascribed to Peggy

Whistler and so both Evans's real name and her nom de plume dually contribute to the text. Its focus on the border and the thematic concerns specific to that area have led Ceridwen Lloyd-Morgan to describe the novella as Evans's 'manifesto' as a border writer.[5] The precisely-constructed, sparse text incorporates tropes and tensions that have previously appeared in border writing by women such as Webb and Vaughan in each of the preceding decades of the twentieth century. Her assured and highly focused novella strips these previous works down to their bare constituent components in order to consolidate a specifically feminine narrative of the border and the hybrid heroine who dwells in this liminal zone.

The hybridised nature of this region is made abundantly clear in *Country Dance*. Though the narrative hinges on the opposition between Ann's Welsh and English identities, the border territory and its inhabitants challenge these binaries in the complex relationships encountered in both nations. The Welsh-speaking Evan ap Evans and his sister live in England, while the Welsh-hating Englishman, Gabriel Ford, lives in Wales; characters with Welsh names such as Olwen Davies are English while Ann's Welsh cousin, Mary, voices a general dislike of the Welsh. A telling scene from the book sees a charlatan going from door to door, selling to one household the wares that he has stolen from another; he disguises his national identity, playing the cultural part that will be seen most favourably by each inhabitant, thus displaying the fluidity of identity while exploiting the xenophobic prejudices of each nation in turn (*CD*, p. 54).

The cultural complexity of the border region can also be seen in the Shropshire setting of *Gone to Earth* by Mary Webb. Webb was one of the most prominent of the female regional writers of the early twentieth century; while her novels were parodied by Stella Gibbons in *Cold Comfort Farm* (1932), elements of her border writing were in the same year, consciously or otherwise, being reworked very differently by Margiad Evans. Though the setting of Webb's novel is Shropshire, the proximity with Wales is marked in the text as Welsh culture is seen to encroach into the English countryside. Hazel Woodus's father is a gifted harp player and we hear snatches of the Welsh airs he plays, such as the 'Ash Tree' and 'Ap Jenkyn' (*GE*, p. 14). Father and daughter continually traverse the border country, playing at a culturally mixed range of events such as eisteddfods, 'flower shows, country dances, revivals and weddings' (*GE*, p. 19).

Here Are Lovers by Hilda Vaughan is set on the Welsh side of the border, in Radnorshire. The action here is primarily restricted to one small valley, creating a sense of confinement which is symbolic of the unhappiness and frustration felt by the novel's heroine, Laetitia Wingfield, who, like many other characters in this text, is unable to escape the strict social boundaries that limit the expression of her identity. At the bottom of the valley is the Squire's Manor, while the homes of his tenants are scattered over the surrounding slopes, with the very poorest living high on the mountainside. There is a palpable sense of social hierarchy, though its spatial manifestation upon the landscape is in a curiously reversed form. While the boundaries here are ones of social class, national identity also has a role to play within these distinctions. The novel was intended to be the first of a trilogy that would trace social change in rural Wales; a project that, unfortunately, was never realised.[6] The valley is divided into the tenants, the servants and the squire and his family. Even within these classes, however, there are subdivisions firmly linked to national identity: the 'Anglicised upper servants' keep company 'in the housekeeper's room, sipping cordial and vying with one another in gentility [while those] in the kitchen were the Welsh . . .' (*HL*, p. 238). The English house-keeper, Mrs Smith, sacks her Welsh servants who engage in the courting practice of bundling (*HL*, p. 43), so ardently condemned by the infamous Blue Books report.[7] The housekeeper's misunderstand-ing of the practice is described by Laetitia as a 'little tragedy . . . of two races and two traditions' (*HL*, p. 44). In a novel in which the female hybrid character is violently dispatched, it is significant that one of the most notable differences between the nations is so closely associated with anxieties surrounding gender and sexuality and particularly the need to govern female behaviour.

There are many mixed marriages to be seen in all three texts. The national identities of Ann's parents in *Country Dance* are repeated in the parentage of the heroines of both Webb and Vaughan. In all three cases, the parental union between an English father and a Welsh mother adheres to the gendered depiction of these nations and the way in which colonial and imperial discourse implicitly draws upon sexual paradigms to present itself.[8] The trope may be seen as a devel-opment from the eighteenth- and nineteenth-century texts termed 'first-contact romances' by Stephen Knight, in which an English suitor travels to Wales, woos and wins a native Welsh woman in an allegory of the colonial relationship.[9] The three texts can be read as

the next step in this process as they examine the consequences for identity in the hybrid progeny of such romances. Hazel Woodus, the protagonist in *Gone to Earth*, is the daughter of Abel, an Englishman who met his Welsh gypsy wife at an eisteddfod, where he won a prize for his harp playing (*GE*, p. 12). Bringing her back to his home, though, he finds that his Welsh wife is unhappy, 'hating marriage and settled life and Abel Woodus as a wild cat hates a cage' (*GE*, p. 12). Though Ann Goodman's parents enjoy a happier partnership in *Country Dance*, Myfanwy Goodman on numerous occasions informs her daughter of her desire to return to Wales, a wish that is not granted until after her death, when she is buried in the Welsh soil.[10] Laetitia Wingfield, the heroine of Vaughan's second novel, *Here Are Lovers*, is the daughter of the widowed English squire of a Radnorshire estate who had loved his deceased wife possessively but without understanding her character or her Welsh culture (*HL*, p. 195).

It is significant that the Welsh mothers of all three heroines in the texts examined here have died or die during the course of novels.[11] It might be expected that the severed link with the maternal culture would lessen its influence over the heroines but this is not the case. In *Country Dance*, though Ann's strengthened identification with her Welshness is a cumulative process and is also intertwined with her feelings for Evan ap Evans, there is a marked difference after her mother's death. It causes her cousin Mary to inform her that 'Lately I have been seeing your mother's blood in you, Ann – all that is good in it' (*CD*, p. 66). It is this increased identification with her mother's nationality that, in part, leads Ann to make the choice between her suitors that results in tragedy. In Webb's novel, Maray Woodus has died long before the narrative begins but her fierce independence has been passed on to her daughter:

> All the things she felt and could not say, all the stored honey, the black hatred, the wistful homesickness for the unfenced wild – all that other women would have put in their prayers, she gave to Hazel. The whole force of her wayward heart flowed into the soft beating heart of her baby. (*GE*, p. 12)

Hazel inherits her Welsh mother's close identification with an untamed landscape, a trait characteristic of Welsh women's writing, as Jane Aaron has observed:[12] indeed, 'the blood in her veins was not slow-moving human blood but the volatile sap' (*GE*, p. 163). Her mother's wild ways are transferred to the young Hazel, who is

unconscious of the fact that her behaviour falls outside the expectations of society. She is 'unlike the women of civilization, who are pursued by looking-glasses, [and] was apt to forget herself and her appearance' (*GE*, p. 166). Waking early to pick mushrooms, Hazel lets her hair fall free, removes her stockings and pulls up her skirts, a shocking and provocative sight to the man who stumbles across her. It is a scene reminiscent of that found in *Country Dance* as the lascivious parson calls Ann a 'gypsy' when he encounters her in the garden with her 'skirts tucked up' and her hair loose on her shoulders. When she also responds brusquely to him, he declares, 'I don't think you are very civil, Ann; one can see as you have lived in the mountains.' (*CD*, p. 17) Like the wild behaviour that Hazel has inherited from her mother, Ann's 'Welsh' ways are viewed as transgressive on the English side of the border.

The relationship between mothers and daughters is poignant in Vaughan's book, which is dedicated to her own daughter, Shirley. Laetitia Wingfield in *Here Are Lovers* has, like Hazel, lost her Welsh mother as a young child. The heroine's resemblance to her mother creates a painful divide between father and daughter that the squire repeatedly attempts to broach, but he reasons that the two women are 'Welsh both of them; and nobody could understand these moody Celts' (*HL*, p. 39). This lack of understanding replicates the difficult relationship between Ann Goodman and her father, and the indifference between Hazel and Abel Woodus. Laetitia wilfully challenges the boundaries of propriety in behaviour that the squire ascribes to her mother's side of the family. She delights in shocking her servants by riding alone at night, (*HL*, p. 176) and rebels against the etiquette and decorum that govern the behaviour of ladies of her class (*HL*, pp. 229–30). This is linked by the squire with another trait that he blames on his daughter's Welsh relatives: her interest in Welsh folklore (*HL*, p. 71). Laetitia is drawn to the Wishing Chair, which her working-class lover, Gronwy, explains is 'a slab of stone down by the river. Old folks believe it has supernatural powers' (*HL*, p. 67). It is from this reputedly magical place that the secret couple commit suicide near the end of the novel. Similarly, when her mother dies, Hazel is left 'an old, dirty, practically illegible manuscript-book of spells and charms and other gipsy lore' (*GE*, p. 12). She uses these spells to determine her actions, thus setting her on a path that leads to her death at the close of the narrative. Hazel feels intermittent terror when passing an old quarry and when overcome by her thoughts of the 'Black Huntsman' and the

'death pack' (not unlike the ancient Welsh myth of the Cŵn Annwn),[13] prefiguring her macabre death at the end of the novel. In Evans's text, though she laughs at the superstitious Gwen Powys, 'who is very fanciful, like most of the Welsh folk' (*CD*, p. 81), Ann is forewarned of her death by the Welsh woman's reading of her future in her tea cup (*CD*, p. 80). Ann, like the other Welsh characters, is afraid of the whirlpool called Llyn Tro, though the English Gabriel is not (*CD*, p. 64). A sense of impending doom is thus built into all three novels in the myth and folklore of the maternal traditional culture and its implicit links with the landscape.

The dual influences of the maternal and paternal cultures on the three heroines provoke an internal struggle over their identity. For Ann Goodman this takes the form of a crisis of national identity, described by Margiad Evans as the 'struggle for supremacy in her mixed blood' (*CD*, p. 3) and is represented by a choice of either the English suitor, Gabriel Ford, or his Welsh rival, Evan ap Evans (often referred to as the Master, since the Goodmans are his tenants). Initially, Ann is vociferous in her hatred of ap Evans (*CD*, p. 18) and is unsettled by his use of his native tongue: 'He speaks to me always in Welsh; and often I make believe not to hear him . . . Why does he always speak to me in Welsh?' (*CD*, p. 20). Her hostility gradually diminishes, however, and soon Ann is rendered the embodiment of the border region as she is physically fought over by the Englishman and the Welshman:

> [Gabriel] says nothing and neither does the Master: like two bulls they come together and I cannot stay them. There is blood on their mouths and running down their chins; their breath comes panting, their eyes are red. (*CD*, p. 73)

The fight is followed by ap Evans's cry of 'Cymru am byth!' and he is symbolically given buttermilk by Ann from a trophy previously won by Gabriel. Gradually Ann succumbs to what is an unconscious, involuntary Welshness, as is implied in a passage where she converses with Olwen about ap Evans:

> I don't know what comes over me that I cry out.
> 'Ni fedrwch gael ei debyg yn Lloegr!'
> Olwen stares at me.
> 'Why, what does that mean?'
> 'I hardly know myself.' (*CD*, p. 96)[14]

Days later, Ann is engaged to ap Evans but is murdered by the jealous Gabriel before the wedding can take place.

Hazel is also fought over by two men, who again represent binary values: the spiritual vicar, Edward Marston, and the virile squire, Jack Reddin. Both men characterise different aspects of Hazel's identity and, in her agonised attempt to choose between them, 'her soul became the passive battleground of strange emotions' (*GE*, p. 183). Reddin awakens the young Hazel's carnal desire. The text presents his extreme masculinity as equally compelling and threatening. His approach is often forewarned by the sound of hoofs, linking him with the 'death pack' that Hazel fears, and for much of the first part of the novel he is indeed travelling the countryside, hunting her down. He likens his rough courtship of Hazel to the breaking of horses, which is reminiscent of the country dance in Margiad Evans's text, where ap Evans traps Ann in his grip and 'gallops' her to the tune of the 'Black Nag' and 'A-hunting we will go' until she is too breathless to voice her fury (*CD*, pp. 20–1). Ann writes of this experience, 'I am compelled, though I am not at all content' (*CD*, p. 20), and this also accurately describes Hazel's feelings for Reddin. Here, too, the men violently tussle over the heroine but in this text it is suggested that neither man will be able to make Hazel truly happy:

> It was as if evil and good, angels and devils, fought for her. And which-ever won, she was equally forlorn. She did not want heaven [or hell]; she wanted earth and the green ways of earth. (*GE*, pp. 228–9)

Similarly, Jane Aaron has commented that Ann Goodman's choice between Gabriel Ford and Evan ap Evans cannot be entirely satisfactory because 'neither of the two males is going to allow her to express the side of herself which they do not share'.[15] Following Ann's death, suspicion is 'divided' (*GE*, p. 101) between her two suitors. Though it is heavily implied that it was Gabriel who struck the blow that killed her, it is indeed the battle between the two men and the choices they represent that lead to Ann's death. The unsatisfactory choice between suitors is made even more explicit in *Gone to Earth* as the narrator admits that '[b]oth men saw her as they wanted her to be, not as she was' (*GE*, p. 125). Though she marries Edward early in the text, Hazel makes several border crossings between the two homes and the two men, since she is unable to fully stand by either decision. The unsuitable nature of the choice she feels obliged to make provokes the text to question the relevance of binaries to a hybrid female character such as Hazel.

A variation on this choice between binaries can be found in *Here Are Lovers*. In this text Laetitia Wingfield is torn between her wish to conform to the expectations of her family and friends of her own class, and the realm of romanticism and rusticity into which she escapes. As she prepares for a Christmas ball to be held in her honour, Laetitia realises that she will never find contentment either among her social peers or outside in the wild landscape. She declares, '[i]f only I could be utterly indifferent to their opinion or else conform to it in all things!' (*HL*, p. 218) A lover of literature, Laetita's hybrid identity is reflected in her reading tastes: she enjoys the work of Byron and Shelley (*HL*, p. 54) as well as ancient Welsh tales of mystery and romance. The crisis in her identity is linked with literature and mythology, allusions to which are used to connote her unstable and fragmented identity. She is described as a 'bewitched princess in the fairy tale' (*HL*, p. 185) and as Helen of Troy (*HL*, p. 59), imagining herself to be the heroine of romantic adventures (*HL*, p. 68), which is mildly ironised by the text. Though she has a choice of two rivals, the working-class Welshman, Gronwy Griffiths, and the anglicised son of a neighbouring squire, the latter is dismissed almost immediately. The real choice in this novel is between Gronwy, a poor scholar, who appeals to Laetitia's romantic ideas and urge to break social conventions, and her over-possessive father, in whom the observance of social decorum is deeply entrenched. In this novel the romantic hero, Gronwy, is himself a hybrid character as a Welshman who has been sent briefly to a school in Cambridge. He has scholarly leanings, but further intellectual advancement is thwarted by his family's poverty; the little learning he has experienced has resulted in a division between Gronwy and his family. His sense of detachment is depicted as he attempts to read *Romeo and Juliet* to them:

> Gronwy, with his fingers among the pages of the book, looked at the little group as a lonely man might look at the upturned faces of his dogs, grateful for their company but saddened by its incompleteness, wishing they might understand the language he spoke. (*HL*, p. 9)

There is a hint of disapproval in the text, since the preceding passages recount in detail the many ways in which his family have toiled in the hope of saving enough money to advance Gronwy's education. Having finished his reading he is 'recalled . . . to his own world' (p. 10). Both Gronwy and Laetitia cross repeatedly between reality and fantasy worlds, unable to find a middle ground that can accommodate the multiple facets of their identities. Running away together to

live out the reality of their love never appears to be a viable consideration. In this novel both hybrid hero and heroine see no option but to commit suicide.

Notwithstanding Gronwy's hybridity, most male characters in all three texts appear to have a fixed and static identity. Several critics have noted the significant scene in *Country Dance* where at a social gathering of both Welsh and English, the men are 'hot as coals' and aggressively toast their own nations to rouse the fury of those considered their enemies. It is left to the female hostess, Gwen, to negotiate a compromise as she embraces hybridity, raises her glass and declares, 'I give the Border' (*CD*, p. 67).[16] In *Here Are Lovers* the squire's refusal to submit to Laetitia's repeated entreaties to help Gronwy's advancement show him imposing the demarcations of social class as an act of patriarchal oppression over his daughter and the community as a whole, with a hint of casual imperialism thrown in for good measure. He asserts that

> [w]e have each of us our duty to perform in our appointed station in life. I have never aped those who are in a higher position than myself . . . I do not, therefore, expect my tenants to envy or attempt to copy our class. The nobility, gentry and common people of this realm have each their proper sphere. In my opinion, it would be the ruin of England to change this. (*HL*, p. 178)

Laetitia's hybridity positions her within a class whose foibles she can simultaneously criticise as an outsider figure. Preparing for a Christmas ball she ridicules the structure of society seen in microcosm in the seating arrangements:

> Papa calls the lord lieutenant's wife 'a skinny old harridan' and the high sheriff's wife bores him . . .; but it is proper that they should sit on either side of their host. And their husbands will sit on either side of me. I must not be seen to talk more to the one that can hear what I say than to the one that is deaf. Charles, as son of the house, will have to take in the high sheriff's wife and sit between her and Aunt Emily, who will not relish a chit of a child like myself taking the head of the table. But she can't openly resent it because my being there is quite the correct thing – of course! (*HL*, pp. 229–30)

Her scepticism goes unappreciated both by the gentry and her servants alike but seems to be endorsed by the narrative. The hybrid identity is feared by those who embrace the dominant ideology as dangerous, subversive and iconoclastic but is cautiously presented by Vaughan as a potential path to freedom and enlightenment.

Throughout the texts, the hybrid heroines of the border country attempt to inhabit the 'in-between spaces' that Homi K. Bhabha explains 'provide the terrain for elaborating strategies of selfhood – singular or communal that initiate new signs of identity, and innovative sites of collaboration, and contestation, in the act of defining the idea of society itself'.[17] Evans, Vaughan and Webb identify, to varying extents, the redemptive hope offered by hybridity and the hybrid character's ability to inhabit the border, offering what Bhabha has described as the borderline engagements of cultural difference which

> may as often be consensual as conflictual; they may confound our definitions of tradition and modernity; realign the customary boundaries between the private and the public, high and low; and challenge normative expectations of development and progress.[18]

None of the three authors appears able to fully realise this challenge, however. Instead, all three writers kill off their heroine rather than allow her to make a choice that would be limiting and reductive, a choice that would inevitably constitute the death of a significant aspect of their identity. The death becomes a symbolic comment upon the tyranny of binary values which has brought about this end. Thus, the border cuts painfully through the hybrid female character, violently wrenching her apart.

For Laetitia, Ann and Hazel alike it is only the horror provoked by their deaths that can bring about a true questioning of binary values and the boundaries they create. In choosing one part of her identity, Ann is killed by the embodiment of the other part of herself. Laetitia embraces the romantic aspect of her nature and leaps from the Wishing Chair with her lover to her death. The struggle between her contesting identities comes to an end for Hazel as she is literally torn apart by the hounds. As all three texts come to a close, boundaries are questioned and once closely demarcated divisions are no longer clear. Seeing the similarities that grief has wrought in the characters of all social classes, the final word in *Here Are Lovers* is given to Gronwy's confidante and his brother's sweetheart, Elizabeth Evans. She remarks that it is 'the small little differences atween folk as do make them able to harden their hearts one against another. But if you were onst to see the great big likenesses o' all human folk, you wouldn't be able to hate your enemies no more' (*HL*, p. 321). In *Gone to Earth* all who hear her screams and witness Hazel's violent death are united in universal horror:

Once again it rang out, and at its awful reiteration the righteous men and the hunt ceased to be people of any class or time or creed, and became creatures swayed by one primeval passion – fear. (*GE*, p. 288)

Though the narrator of *Country Dance* declares that in this tale of warring nations, the Welsh have been victorious (*CD*, p. 102), this is immediately undermined by the fact that Ann is dead and ap Evans exiled in Canada. Instead, the last lines of the text suggest that, in fact, the landscape is gradually ridding itself of the divisive ways in which it has been demarcated by human beings: 'It is well that men's doings, like the leaves after their season, fall to the earth, and beneath the boughs, crowded with fresh green growth, lie buried and forgotten' (*CD*, p. 104). In all three texts the sacrifice of the hybrid female characters leads to the levelling of the boundaries that have cloven their identities. As Margiad Evans reminds us, however, 'new furrows are ploughed in old fields' (*CD*, p. 103). This is not the end of the story of the border. Old values will be replaced by new ones and long into the future the border itself will be negotiated and renegotiated by succeeding generations. All three female writers can be read as part of an ongoing process of questioning and examining the border and border identities.

The border is, of course, still a focus for discussion in contemporary culture and Welsh writing in English. A recent issue of *Planet* has focused on borders, and within its pages the Welsh writer Horatio Clare has celebrated the ease of crossing the Welsh/English border, in contrast with this experience in other nations, where walls both literal and bureaucratic hamper the freedom for many to cross national boundaries.[19] Writing recently in *New Welsh Review*, Gwyneth Lewis has explored the decision she made in her twenties to return to Wales from America, in order to safeguard her identity as a Welsh writer.[20] Though there are still choices to be made, Welsh women of our own generation, such as Gwyneth Lewis and Fflur Dafydd are writing confidently in both English and Welsh. For these writers, as Margiad Evans, Hilda Vaughan and Mary Webb tentatively envisioned, there are exhilarating possibilities presented by the ability to embrace multiple facets of identity.

Notes

1. Margiad Evans, *Country Dance* ([1932] Cardigan: Parthian, Library of Wales, 2006), p. 101. All further references are to this edition, hereafter *CD*.
2. John Everett Millais, *Ophelia* (1852) (London: Tate Gallery).
3. Hilda Vaughan, *Here Are Lovers* (New York and London: Harper & Brothers, 1926), p. 329. All further references are to this edition, hereafter *HL*.
4. Mary Webb, *Gone to Earth* ([1917] London: Jonathan Cape, 1974), p. 288. All further references are to this edition, hereafter *GE*.
5. Ceridwen Lloyd-Morgan, *Margiad Evans* (Bridgend: Seren, 1998), p. 31.
6. In a review in *The Observer* it is stated that 'In the love of her plough-boy hero for the squire's daughter, Miss Vaughan begins a trilogy which intends to trace through the fortunes of two families, the decline of the landed gentry and the rise to wealth and influence of the farming classes, from the time of Disraeli's Reform Bill down to the period following the late war.' See *The Observer*, 25 May 1926, 9.
7. The custom was condemned by the commissioners, who particularly objected to the 'want of chastity' allegedly found in Welsh women in particular. Reverend William Jones of Nefyn in the *Report of the Commissioners of Inquiry into the State of Education in Wales*, 1847, iii, pp. 67–8.
8. See, for example, Deirdre Beddoe, 'Images of Welsh women', in Tony Curtis (ed.), *Wales: The Imagined Nation* (Bridgend: Poetry Wales Press, 1986), pp. 225–38, and Jane Aaron, 'A national seduction: Wales in nineteenth-century women's writing', *New Welsh Review*, 7/3, 27 (1994), 31–8.
9. Stephen Knight, *A Hundred Years of Fiction* (Cardiff: University of Wales Press, 2004), pp. 10–14.
10. Much of Vaughan's personal correspondence reveals that she was longing for a permanent residence back in Wales. In a letter from her husband Charles Morgan, undated but most likely to have been written in 1922, he writes, 'I wonder about that Welsh cottage . . . You know we shouldn't be in that Welsh cottage very much – at any rate not in our early years, at least I shouldn't I'm afraid.' Twenty years later, Vaughan's dream remained unrealised as we can see in a letter from Morgan to Vaughan dated 19 June 1941, in which he writes that after the war they might try 'to find the real country house you would like' in Wales. Reproduced by kind permission of Mr Roger Morgan.
11. This must be seen in the context of the strong emphasis placed on the influence of the mother in English imperialist discourses and Welsh nation-building discourses of the early twentieth-century, such as: Marie Stopes, *Mother England: A Contemporary History* (1929), reproduced in

ed. Lesley A. Hall, *Marie Stopes: Birth Control and Other Writings*, vol. I (Bristol: Thoemmes Press, 2000); O. M. Edwards, introduction to *Cymru'r Plant*, vol. XVI (1907); and Mallt Williams, *A Maid of Cymru: A Patriotic Romance* (1901), cited in Marion Löffler, 'A romantic nationalist', *Planet: The Welsh Internationalist*, 121 (1997), 58–66 (60).

12 See Jane Aaron, 'Introduction', *A View Across the Valley: Short Stories by Women from Wales* c.*1850–1950* (Dinas Powys: Honno, 1999), pp. ix–xx.

13 Cŵn Annwn were the supernatural hounds of Annwn, the ancient Welsh underworld, which took part in the Wild Hunt presided over by Gwyn ap Nudd, king of the Tylwyth Teg.

14 The Welsh sentence, which remains untranslated in Margiad Evans's text, means 'You will not find his like in England!'

15 Jane Aaron, 'Taking sides: power-play on the Welsh border in early twentieth-century women's writing', in ed. Jane Aaron, Henrice Altnik and Chris Weedon, *Gendering Border Studies* (Cardiff: University of Wales Press, 2010), pp. 127–41 (p. 140).

16 See Aaron, 'Taking Sides', p. 140; Lloyd-Morgan, *Margiad Evans*, p. 31; and Katie Gramich, *Twentieth-Century Women's Writing in Wales: Land, Gender, Belonging* (Cardiff: University of Wales Press, 2007), p. 86.

17 Homi K. Bhabha, *The Location of Culture* (London: Routledge, 1994), pp. 1–2.

18 Ibid., p. 3.

19 Horatio Clare, 'The borders of reason: a reflection on boundaries', *Planet: The Welsh Internationalist*, 201 (February 2011), 50–61.

20 Gwyneth Lewis, 'The poet I might have been', *New Welsh Review*, 91 (Spring 2011), 9–13.

5

Gothic Borderlands: The Hauntology of Place in the Fiction of Margiad Evans

KATIE GRAMICH

Margiad Evans invariably roots her writing in a particular place. As a child, Evans was labelled as 'dreamy' because, as she herself records, she 'liked ... to make up stories about places.'[1] Ceridwen Lloyd-Morgan observes that Evans 'had to be able to visualise clearly the place where her characters lived, and feel the atmosphere of that place ...'[2] Indeed, according to Lloyd-Morgan, 'without a location ... there could be no narrative, and the setting could be as important a protagonist as the characters themselves.'[3] There is no doubt that it is the Welsh border country that first awoke Evans's passionate creativity. In her journal in 1934 she records:

> the mountains of Wales, indigo beyond low transparent clouds, were gathered in one splendid vision spinning backwards as we fled over the Hereford road. The ocean which crashed about Herman Melville's brain, and the thrashing of enormous waves in his ears, could never have meant more to him than those hills to me, an unsealable ponderous mystery which could drive me to frenzy and beyond if I looked at them too long.[4]

The terms of Evans's description of the Welsh hills here indicate that her attraction to this landscape was by no means fond and gentle; on the contrary, her words gesture towards obsession and madness. It is no surprise, then, to find that her earliest attempts to render the 'ponderous mystery' of the Welsh border country in the settings of her novels are in a decidedly Gothic mode.

In the Gothic novel of the 1790s, as James Henderson has observed, Wales was represented as a remote, wild setting full of what R. S. Thomas has mordantly described as '[w]ind-bitten towers and castles/ [w]ith sham ghosts'.[5] Jane Aaron has shown how nineteenth-century

novels by women frequently represent the taming of a female wild Wales with transgressive Gothic propensities by a civilising masculine England in an allegorical marriage plot which she terms 'a national seduction'.[6] By the later nineteenth century, Matthew Arnold considered the 'Celtic Temperament' to be 'admirably suited to figure in . . . the works of the Gothic novelists', suggesting that the characteristic melancholy, excessive emotion, and attachment to the past, which he designated as 'Celtic' were particularly suited to the un-Saxon excess of the Gothic mode.[7] By the turn of the twentieth century, Wales's borderland with England had become one of the sites of the resurgence of Gothic fiction in the hands of the Caerleon-born writer of supernatural tales, Arthur Machen.[8] From the eighteenth century onwards, then, Wales and its borders have frequently featured as a Gothic location for writers of fiction, so it is within an already well-established tradition that the Border writer, Margiad Evans, in her fiction of the 1930s and 1940s creates a literary landscape of Gothic excess and anxiety.

The Gothic is a complex and multifaceted literary mode; it tends to focus on terror, the transgressive, and the taboo. It has also long been associated with women writers and female protagonists; Ellen Moers in her influential coining of the term 'Female Gothic' states that it is easily defined as the work produced by women writers in this literary mode, which is primarily 'to do with fear'.[9] Moers also argues, convincingly, that Female Gothic is peculiarly associated with 'the body itself, its glands, muscles, epidermis, and circulatory system, quickly arousing and quickly allaying the physiological reactions to fear'.[10] In this regard, the Gothic mode lends itself perfectly to Margiad Evans's challenging early experiments in fiction, in which she dwells on the human body, its vulnerability and sensitivity to pain, and goes on to explore areas of psychology and sexuality which are often unsettling or unmentionable. Moers takes Emily Brontë's *Wuthering Heights* as one of her primary examples of the Female Gothic and it is no accident that Brontë was one of Margiad Evans's most admired authors. Nevertheless, Evans's deployment of the Female Gothic is not an exercise in neo-Victorianism; on the contrary, her Gothic mode is strikingly modern, using supernatural tropes and haunted landscapes to figure states of psychic imbalance, obsession, and trauma.

Evans is a self-conscious inheritor of the Gothic mode in fiction, both from her admired heroine, Emily Brontë, and from the more

recent Gothicised Celtic landscapes of Gwent as found in the works of Arthur Machen. Clare Morgan has argued convincingly that Evans is a neo-Romantic writer longing for, yet never quite recuperating, the lost kingdoms of Celticity and childhood.[11] She has also suggested that Evans was not essentially either a Welsh or even a Border writer but rather an English writer searching for somewhere to belong. I will be arguing that Evans is, as she herself asserted, very much a Border writer, who constructs in her fiction a specific liminal territory where people are haunted by ghosts of their past. This spectral border is the other face of Margiad Evans's neo-Romanticism, for Romanticism was always Janus-faced, one face radiating glimpses of the transcendental sublime and the other glowering with doom-laden Gothic violence. Clare Morgan has ably documented and analysed Evans's attempts to attain the Romantic sublime, but this essay will examine her persistent and pathological haunting by the Gothic. In doing so, it will draw on some of the critical vocabulary of Jacques Derrida, as used in his seminal work *Specters of Marx* (1994), which provides the subtitle, 'the hauntology of place'.[12] 'Hauntology' is a characteristically witty coinage on Derrida's part, suggestive of the 'science' of ghosts and haunting and at the same time echoing 'ontology', the philosophical study of the nature of being. Since ontology is partly concerned with what entities can be said to exist, ghosts are test cases: do they/can they exist, and if so, how might they be defined? Margiad Evans is a writer fundamentally interested in such metaphysical concerns, so it seems appropriate to explore her writing through a 'hauntology of place'.

Evans herself recognised the spectral duality of her own vision, which might be identified as her split Romantic/Gothic nature; as she said in a letter to Gwyn Jones: 'There are at least two distinct writers in me . . . ,' one who wrote the contemplative and often beatific *Autobiography* (1943) and the other whom she characterises as 'the thump-thump one who wrote most of *Turf or Stone*'.[13] In the same letter she expresses her duality as the difference between 'Miss Margiad Evans', who 'is an insufferable high brow', and 'Mrs Peggy Williams' [her married name], who 'likes horrors'.[14] Interestingly, she also identifies this dichotomy as a reflection of 'the two sides of the country – the loveliness and peace, and the brutal, human side which cannot be exaggerated'.[15] D. S. Savage remarks in his 1950 study of Evans that her novels 'glow with a dark, sombre, passionate light',[16] a description which certainly hints at the Gothic ghostly atmosphere

which they persistently conjure. Nevertheless, Evans goes far beyond the use of Wales as an exotic place of Otherness as found in the work of some early Gothic novelists; she is influenced by the Celtic twilight rediscovery of the Welsh borders as the site of Gothic haunting but she transcends neo-Romantic Celticity to re-imagine her borderland 'country' as an emblem of what might be described as unhealed psychic wounds. In this way, Margiad Evans's fiction of the 1930s and 1940s may be viewed as a Gothic literature of psychological trauma.

The Gothic as a recurring literary mode is frequently concerned with the unwelcome and pathological return of the past in the present; it is fiction haunted by ghosts and characterised by violence and by repetition, which, in Freudian terms, links both with trauma and with the uncanny. Thus, as David Punter suggests, 'the Gothic . . . provides us with a language in which to address our ghosts.'[17] Evans characteristically depicts the Welsh border landscape as being haunted, riven, and often tormented by its past while the dead – eerily – appear to be at least as energetic and vibrant as the living. Ghosts trouble us, arguably, because of their ambivalence and liminality; they have no bodies and yet they are body-shaped; they are not human and yet they are troublingly twinned with human lives. Karen Caesar suggests elsewhere in this volume that Evans's feeling of being haunted 'may have had a neurological base' and have been connected with the ghostly 'absences' she felt even before the onset of her epilepsy in 1950. The fascinating neurological evidence is examined by others far more qualified to judge but what is certain is that there is a self-conscious awareness of *literary* precedent and possibility in Evans's use of Gothic, ghostly forms.

Evans published four novels in rapid succession in the 1930s: *Country Dance* (1932), *The Wooden Doctor* (1933), *Turf or Stone* (1934) and *Creed* (1936), and it is these texts which will be explored in this essay. As many readers have noticed, there is a marked change in her later work when she shifts from fiction, however autobiographically-based, to the memoir form of *Autobiography* (1943) and *A Ray of Darkness* (1952). Put simply, if the novels of the 1930s are Gothic and haunted by the past, the memoirs of the 1940s and 1950s are Romantic and obsessively focused on the present. The mode of her writing changes dramatically from one of overblown violence and excess to one of quiet, often mystical contemplation. As Moira Dearnley puts it in her monograph, by the time she came to write *Autobiography*, Evans 'would have approved Llewellyn Powys's

dictum in *Earth Memories* (1934): 'The past is nothing, the future is nothing, the eternal *now* alone is of moment', for as Dearnley observes, 'She too aimed to express in *Autobiography*, "The Now of It"'.[18] *Autobiography* focuses on precise sensory experience; as Evans puts it: 'The body has no past. The limbs and the skin feel minute by minute – the physical is always the now.'[19] There could hardly be a starker contrast with her earlier fiction, where the body is very much marked, even scarred by its history, and where there is no place to hide from the past's intrusion into the present.

In the determined phenomenological abandonment to the present that one witnesses in *Autobiography*, we can see that Evans is, perhaps despite herself, influenced by her immediate Modernist predecessors, notably Virginia Woolf, who were wedded to the impossible notion of fixing the fleeting moment of being, as much as by the Romantic, Wordsworthian notion of capturing the 'spot of time'. But, as Jacques Derrida reminds us, such devotion to the present is doomed to failure. 'Learning to live', he asserts, 'is learning to live with ghosts [which] . . . secretly unhinge the living present.'[20] However much the past seems to be dead, it will reassert itself, rising up like the ghost of Hamlet's father, clamouring for attention, and asserting its spectral presence. One might even suggest that the tragic diagnosis of Evans's epilepsy, which the doctors believed was linked with a childhood riding accident, is a demonstration of the unavoidable spectrality of existence.

Country Dance (1932) was Margiad Evans's first published work of fiction. It is a novella which is overtly concerned with the resurrection of a ghost from the past, the conjuring of the protagonist, Ann Goodman, herself. On one level, *Country Dance* is clearly a work of feminist recuperation, the recovery of a lost women's history, as I have argued elsewhere;[21] it is also, as Diana Wallace has argued, an example of what she calls 'histories of the defeated', typical of British women's historical novels of the 1930s in which women authors 'took the sides of the defeated and conquered peoples . . . as a way of exploring the gendering of power inequalities'.[22] But in this essay it is the text's Gothic hauntology which engages our attention: the way in which it conjures Ann's ghost, exorcises it and finally lays it to rest.

Country Dance is deeply concerned with the interpenetration of landscape and memory – right from the opening pages, the landscape of the border country is read – together with the found manuscript which tells Ann's story in her own voice – as a palimpsestic narrative

of unexpiated crime and unresolved trauma. Ann's ghost – like that of Hamlet's father – continues to haunt the landscape, continues to return, in the characteristic repetition of traumatic experience. Repetition is the key element of traumatic neurosis, according to Freud. In *Beyond the Pleasure Principle* he worries about the repetitive dreams experienced by traumatised individuals, partly because they so markedly diverge from his main theory that dreams are basically wish-fulfilments. As Freud scrupulously admits, 'Dreams occurring in traumatic neuroses have the characteristic of repeatedly bringing the patient back into the situation of his accident, a situation from which he wakes up in another fright.' As Freud puts it, the subject is 'obliged to repeat the repressed material as a contemporary experience, instead of, as the physician would prefer to see, remembering it as something belonging to the past'.[23] In creating the haunted landscape of *Country Dance*, Evans represents Border history as trauma, in the sense adumbrated by Freud, in which the past is spectrally replayed in the present. Locations function as triggers of these haunting memories of the past, and yet that past remains stubbornly inaccessible and therefore irredeemable. The past is a place of terrors which can resurface at any time; the present is therefore where we live, paradoxically, in the nightmare of history.

Evans's Gothic fiction can be seen as a missed encounter with history. She repeatedly narrates dreams, visions and quests in a landscape permeated with memories of the past, yet those narrations never succeed in telling a story which is restorative. Her characters seem doomed to repeat but seldom to redeem the past of her Gothic borderlands. In fact, *Country Dance*, her first published work, comes closest to a successful exorcism. *Country Dance* performs the work of mourning in identifying the dead Ann Goodman and allowing her to speak and bear witness in her own voice; it also locates her dead body, where it lies in the landscape, and explains why it lies there. At the same time, the final paragraphs, so strongly reminiscent of the ambivalent ending of Emily Brontë's *Wuthering Heights*, exude a palpable sense of restfulness, and yet there is also an address to the reader which sounds like 'beware!' for we are told:

> live awhile in these remote places [and. . .] you will come to know how the dead may hold tenure of lands that were once theirs, and how echoes of their lives that are lost at a distance linger about their doorways. Here among the hills and valleys, the tall trees and swift rivers, the bland pastures and sullen woods, lie long shadows of things that have been.[24]

It is suggested that the traumatic past is related both to nation and to gender divisions for, in the same closing paragraphs, Evans, masquerading as the editor of the text, concludes: 'Here is represented the entire history of the Border, just as the living Ann must have represented it herself – that history which belongs to all border lands and tells of incessant warfare' (*CD*, p. 95). The fact that the 'shadows' of that history still 'linger' in the present are indicative of a continuing and recurrent hauntology: the warfare that has been remorselessly narrated in the text is still with us; our doorways are still haunted by the spectre of domestic violence.

The novella is death-haunted to an extreme, a Gothic degree. It begins with the suicide of the sexton who, despairing, drowns himself in the flooded river: 'Three days later they find him, when the floods have gone down, fast in the hedge where the waters have carried him' (*CD*, p. 8). The insertion of the dead man into the landscape is important here: repeatedly, Evans's Gothic corpses become part of the body of the landscape itself, so that the Border territory becomes one vast necropolis. Ann herself, when alive, sees spectres in the landscape; as she enquires of Gabriel: 'Have you seen the Roman soldiers marching through Craig Dinas and the White Lady that drowned herself in Llyn-Tro?' (*CD*, p. 55). These ghosts are suggestive of the 'incessant warfare' of this border territory, as well as foreshadowing Ann's own death in a deep pool of water. Death by drowning and the trope of the whirlpool (Llyn-Tro) recurs in Evans's next novel, *The Wooden Doctor*, and is echoed several times in the short stories of the 1940s. Significantly, Gabriel, the man who will one day murder Ann, is untroubled by ghosts – he simply does not see them. Gwen Powys's father, though, has seen the same spectres as Ann at Llyn-Tro, suggesting perhaps that this Gothic spectrality is associated particularly with the Welsh, as opposed to the more stolid and, as it turns out, brutal, Saxon.

Evans's next novel, *The Wooden Doctor*, is, if anything, more extreme in its Gothic imagery. Arabella's domestic life is shadowed by violence, largely on account of her father's alcoholism. She remarks with jarringly cool matter-of-factness: 'our home among the quiet fields became a cage of savagery' and 'we sharpened our claws in one another's flesh.'[25] Arabella, like Ann in *Country Dance*, is a seer of ghosts. While she is in France, she visits a house which is believed to be haunted, described in the following terms:

The Marechals lived at the very top of the hill: the front door opened straight on the road, and across the powder-blue paint was scrawled in huge white chalk letters:
MAISON HANTÉE. (*WD*, p. 38)

Arabella asks the Englishman:

> 'Why do people think this house is haunted?'
> 'Oh, it's just nonsense.' [he replies] . . .
> 'Do you believe it?'
> 'Why no, of course not. I don't think there are such things as ghosts. Do you?'
> 'Yes, I'm sure there are.'
> 'Why, have you ever seen one?'
> 'Yes, I have.' (*WD*, p. 40)

Interestingly, this ghost she has seen is associated with her father, who has terrifying visions when he is drunk. In this novel, the monstrous spectre may well be that of sexual abuse (just as that in *Country Dance* might be seen as domestic violence). As both Sue Asbee and Karen Caesar have argued, there are a number of indirect hints in the novel that Arabella is the victim of such abuse at the hands of her father, and that the terrible physical pain she suffers in the course of the novel is a kind of ghostly residue or symptom of that traumatic experience.[26] Certainly the repetitions of her visitations by the terrible pain unforgettably figured as being 'like a fox in a bag scratching and rending to get out . . . with flaming feet and famished jaws, rending, biting, tearing' (*WD*, p. 71) are reminiscent of the repetitive dreams of trauma victims. Karen Caesar has argued that Arabella's love for 'the wooden doctor' represents 'the transference of the compromised love she felt for her father'.[27] Moreover, her illness can be seen as a way of repeatedly gaining his attention. Evans expresses the extremity of the pain which ensues from trauma in vividly memorable ways; Arabella states, for example, 'My body [w]as the axle of that red wheel of pain, and to the axle like the deep heart in a whirlpool, there was an unutterable centre' (*WD*, p. 98). This language again picks up the image of the whirlpool, ineluctably associated with female death, its cone-like shape acting as a kind of bore into the inner self. But the use of the adjective 'unutterable' suggests the failure of language to name the ultimate cause of the suffering. The fox here is the ghostly presence, a kind of monster or succubus, feeding off Arabella's body. The fox is exorcised, albeit temporarily, by writing: once Arabella escapes

to north Wales and succeeds in writing her book, the fox vanishes and the wooden doctor too is summarily dispatched from the text. Writing conjures ghosts and dispels them, makes them walk in all their monstrosity and has the power to lay them to rest. Evans's Gothic tropes demonstrate again and again the therapeutic nature of her writing practice.

Evans's next novel, recently republished in the Library of Wales series after having been out of print for many years, was *Turf or Stone*. This is probably the most overtly Gothic of all of her published novels. Its main locale is a house called the 'Gallustree' on account of its position 'standing near a cross roads, where there had been a gibbet; . . . it was said that a portion of the cross beam had been worked into the porch.'[28] Seen from afar, it is a handsome Georgian building, set on high ground 'five miles out of Salus in Brelshope parish' but 'a nearer view exposed its painful demission' (*TS*, p. 26). It is dilapidated and ineptly patched up, its interior 'decorated through-out in vile standard taste [which] testified to the plebeian strain in the inhabitants' (*TS*, p. 27). Matt's father, a wealthy Herefordshire gent, had married his housekeeper and 'The blood was running thin from its antique source' (*TS*, p. 26). The setting thus appears to be a modern version of the Gothic ruin in the late eighteenth-century works of Ann Radcliffe or Horace Walpole, a location haunted by past violence and simmering with present tensions and resentments. The book enacts a reverse comedic structure, beginning with a grim wedding, and ending with a brutal murder. The two central characters are Matt Kilminster, owner of the Gallustree, and his groom, the half-gipsy Easter Probert. Both of these characters inhabit internal landscapes which are haunted and tormented; Matt's is described as a 'blind island' which consists of a 'vague state where nothing held any significance' (*TS*, p. 88), a state of terminal ennui, while the sadistic yet mesmeric Easter Probert is seen as living in a 'lonely and abandoned . . . wilderness' (*TS*, p. 104). The Gallustree is a location of mutual torment for all who live there – it is still a place of execution, death and revenge, as it has been in the past.

The novel is full of extreme violence and sadism, which perhaps explains why it did not match the popularity of its autobiographical, female-centred predecessor, *The Wooden Doctor*. Easter is both malevolent and strangely vital, in contrast to the effeteness of his master, Matt. The temporal setting of the novel is the 1920s and there are a number of echoes of the Great War reverberating through the

text. The carter, William Dallett, for example, who befriends Easter Probert's poor abused wife, Mary, is himself maimed and wounded, having lost an arm in the war; he poignantly gives Mary a gunmetal ring instead of the wedding ring which Easter has spitefully taken away from her. Evans's fiction, though containing unmistakable echoes of *Wuthering Heights*, is therefore a distinctively twentieth-century modulation of the Gothic, for the gloomy atmosphere is one of aftermath; there is unresolved and often unspoken trauma here which emerges in Gothic, spectral imagery.

The novel is full of the transgression of social norms, the breaking of taboos. Mary gets pregnant out of wedlock; up to then she has been living in a quasi-lesbian relationship with her employer, Miss Tressan; Mary has transgressed her social role by more or less being the dominant partner in this relationship, despite her lower social status as lady's companion; Mary later has an illicit affair with the married Matt Kilminster; but all these transgressions pale into insignificance compared with Easter's behaviour, which is frequently promiscuous, sadistic and highly unsettling. Margiad Evans seems to go out of her way to mention the unmentionable: stinking dead rats, used by Easter to terrify and torment women; the drowning of kittens and the killing of birds and dogs; stones thrown at his new wife; foul-smelling liniment poured over his wife's underclothes, pillow and hairbrush. The focus is constantly on defilement and humiliation, bodily pain and disgust.

Mary Probert is the main female character, but the story is not the classic Gothic one of a female victim of patriarchy who resists heroically and is eventually saved. Oddly, Mary is not the central consciousness of the text, unlike Ann and Arabella in Evans's previous two novels. *Turf or Stone* actually gives the reader far more insight into the psyche of the loathsome Easter Probert, her husband, than of Mary, bringing the reader uncomfortably close to the source of Gothic horror.[29] For Easter is described as being 'like a goblin' (*TS*, p. 43); he is a lurid, threatening figure, reminiscent of Peter Quint, the predatory male ghost in Henry James's 1898 novella, *The Turn of the Screw*, and prefiguring the 'horrid sideshow of freaks' contained in Djuna Barnes's 1936 novel, *Nightwood*.[30] Yet the glimpses we have of his memories, dreams and nightmares reveal to us a man haunted by his past and forever searching in vain for a lost well-beloved.

The text associates Easter with dead rats, which he produces in order to torment womenfolk. But the rat is tellingly placed alongside

Easter's dream of childhood with his mother 'in a sort of encamp-
ment with other half-bred gipsies . . . "Mammy" he cried in his sleep
. . . He awoke terrified . . . The dead rat smelled like a dirty drain' (*TS*,
p. 73). Julia Kristeva's concept of abjection is helpful in reading the
meaning of Easter's association of the dead rat and the lost mother.[31]
The abject, according to Kristeva, is something outside ourselves
which prompts disgust and revulsion, such as a dead rat or a corpse.
She suggests, moreover, that the abject inhabits a liminal space
between inside and outside, and as such is something which exists
outside the 'symbolic order', namely the patriarchal system of
language. Connecting it to the infant's development, she suggests that
the mother is precisely that which we must abject or cast out in order
to establish our own identity. Easter Probert is a character still fixated
on the lost mother, who has died while incarcerated in the poorhouse,
suffering from a 'bleeding cancer' in Chepsford Poor Law Infirmary;
though she wants to escape and cure herself with herbs, the rules and
regulations close in on her. His relationships with other women are, as
a result, pathological and often sadistic – he subjects them to appalling encounters with the abject as if forcing them into some kind of
defilement, an encounter with abjection. Easter repeatedly attempts
to rid himself of the ghost of the lost mother but repeatedly fails,
leading to his increasingly extreme sadism. It is as if Easter infects the
atmosphere around him, so that the novel as a whole is suffused with
deliberately repulsive, disgusting detail: there are references to cat
faeces, dog fleas, worms wriggling out of human noses, and the
callous killing of animals and birds. The use of such deliberately
repulsive detail may indicate Evans's literary debt to the
Naturalist-inflected work of Caradoc Evans, of which she was
certainly aware, but the frighteningly amoral world of *Turf or Stone*
sets it apart from the other Evans's moral parables.

At the end of the novel, Easter Probert is swiftly and brutally
murdered by having a pike impaled through his eye; as readers we
cannot feel empathy with a character who has functioned as such an
extremely oppressive and destructive force, like an unglamorous
Heathcliff, and yet it is difficult not to be left with a sense of pity for
this 'lonely and abandoned spirit [who] dwelt in a wilderness where as
yet none had ever penetrated. None. Never' (*TS*, p. 104). Ultimately,
Easter is a kind of savage indigene – a barbaric, mad, yet strangely
compelling figure, intimately connected with the landscape, even from
infancy; the link is reminiscent of Evans's description of the Border

territory as 'an unsealable ponderous mystery which could drive me to frenzy'.[32] Easter's earliest memory is described like this:

> He was lying on a shawl on the grass beside a rough stony road which went straight up hill and stopped dead at the top as though it had been shorn off at the horizon. Within a foot of his head a colt was grazing. It moved forward; he lay between its forelegs and then, without troubling him, it walked right over him. He did not stir. Its belly was silky, almost white. This was the first thing he could remember; not very clearly, for he was hardly able to walk. (*TS*, pp. 92–3)

Nothing could indicate more clearly the way in which Easter is associated with the Border landscape, and with a refusal of civilised society which amounts to an indictment of all of its values.

Creed, Evans's fourth work of fiction, offers an interesting variation on the Gothic landscape since it is set largely in an industrial Border town, in an area called Mill End in Chepsford. This is a place of violence and dissipation; as the self-conscious first-person narrator exclaims, 'Ha, what a town!' She goes on to assert that she is 'possessed by' Mill End and its surrounding countryside: 'I see it night and day . . . this secret and defended country, with its red fields flogged by the rain, its floods, storms in the elms, clouds tossed over the hills and dissolving in moonlight, wild moods of unleashed winds and pathetic stillnesses . . .'[33] The imagery of possession and night haunting clearly positions this as a Gothicised realm, passionate and sombre, extreme in all its moods. The tormented characters live in an unappetising setting nicknamed Rats' Ramble: 'The street was narrow, like a cañon cleft in sulphur-coloured brick; it was sickly with the smell of boiling from the brewery. Rows of gloomy incavated windows stared straight into their opposites' (*C*, p. 49). One of the main characters, Florence Dollbright, finds that she is suffering from cancer – she is, as she says, 'feeding the frightful crab' (*C*, p. 73) and as a result she views everything around her in terms of affliction and disease: 'The gutters, running like sores, the black fissures in the pavement, the angles where the buildings met the ground all seemed filled with poison, with secret diseases ready to fall and feed upon the fair and tempting' (*C*, p. 85). Even the glare of the street lamps is seen as 'cadaverous' (*C*, p. 73).

Creed is a novel which, as the title suggests, addresses religious questions, and in so doing might be seen as returning to some of the earliest preoccupations of the Gothic novel. There is a juxtaposition between the clergyman, Ifor Morris, and Francis Dollbright, an iron-monger's clerk from Mill End, Chepsford, who believes in damnation

and that only the good will be saved – this is his fanatical 'creed' (*C*, p. 15). As the narrator remarks, 'Poor wretch, he loved his flinty God, who came at him like a hammer' (*C*, p. 45). Yet there are plenty of characters in the text who are utterly Godless, such as the monstrous alcoholic bully, Mrs Trouncer, who is in some ways similar to Easter Probert – a devilish, grotesque figure full of maniacal energy. That she has a similar function to Easter is suggested by her violent death at the end of the novel. Dollbright's employer, John Bridges, is also an unabashed unbeliever; as he says: 'demons have no dominion in me. I *killed* the gods long ago . . . they died without a kick . . . a row of bogy men, smoky and dabbled in the fire of their makers' tongues' (*C*, p. 101).

The novel, despite its elements of Gothic excess, does gesture towards the meticulous rendition of the real in Evans's later works, especially the memoirs of the 1940s and 1950s, in its frequent recourse to description of domestic detail, such as one might observe in a painting of an interior scene by a Dutch master:

> Near the door an iron spout was dripping into a grated drain. Thick dusty cobwebs were stretched between it and the bulging wall. A scrubbing brush and knotted house flannels like grey fists had been put on top of an upturned bucket. A Tabby cat stalked along the narrow ribbon of dry ground under the wall. (*C*, p. 105)

Nevertheless, we have not yet reached the realm of 'the eternal *now*'. Physical pain and bodily mutilation feature here as in the earlier three novels, particularly in the scene in which Dollbright visits the hospital where his wife has undergone a mastectomy. He meets the matron dressed in an apron 'marked all over the front with . . . blotches of his wife's blood, from fresh pink to deathly scarlet' (*C*, p. 124). Again, as in the earlier novels, women characters suffer from dreadful bodily afflictions, while the male characters, when not downright malevolent, are at best ineffectual, like Dollbright himself, who feels guilty about his wife's suffering because he believes that it is a punishment for his own sin: 'He saw the evil in himself like a humpback's swollen shadow' (*C*, p. 139).

After the publication of *Creed* in 1936, Evans received an advance from her publisher, Basil Blackwell, for another novel, one which she would never actually finish. The projected novel was *The Widower's Tale* and, according to Ceridwen Lloyd-Morgan, its 'mood was dark, Gothic even . . . set in the 1860s or 1870s in a forest parish called Gwias Harold on the English side of the border, [it] is full of macabre

and mysterious events'.[34] She herself referred to it as her 'ghost novel' and it was due to appear in 1939 but it never materialised. Its unfinished state perhaps suggests that Margiad Evans had come to the end of her Gothic imaginings – she was ready to move on to a more Romantic, phenomenological quest for the sublime in the everyday.

Nevertheless, some of the stories in the volume *The Old and the Young* (1948) do draw on the Gothic tropes used in the novels of the 1930s. In the story 'People of his Pasture', for instance, the setting has a spectral bleakness reminiscent of scenes from *Turf or Stone*: here, the 'land was one great pasture, one loneliness so large, so lost as to stir a kind of abstract pity'.[35] There is a stark contrast between the young man, Daniel, a visitor to the place, who is concerned and horrified by the suffering of a ewe with garget, and the attitude of the young mother who lives on the land and has a callous, realistic attitude. Yet underneath that indifference, she is verging on madness: 'There are days when I could scream and scream and scream,' she gasped, 'days when I could go mad' (*OY*, p. 59). Even Margiad Evans herself thought this 'a grim story . . . Almost a horror if one stops to think' (*OY*, p. 197). In another story in the collection, 'The Boy Who Called for a Light', the first-person narrator, Derry Painter, recalls the farmer, Mr Gregory, who sees 'visions . . . Hundreds of 'em. Hundreds. But . . .The-the-they d-don't see you. They-they don't sp-sp-speak, do 'em? Never . . . They look 1-1-like any other m-man you mid m-meet on the road. H-h-how be, be, be you to tell? I guessed he meant *ghosts*. His stammering increased my horror' (*OY*, p. 65). Though Mr Gregory's ghosts are those of 'fellows hedging', another character, Kate Prosser, recalls seeing the ghost of her dead brother, Henry, killed in Mesopotamia during the First World War; on the day he died she saw him back in this familiar landscape and, in a sense, he is still here: 'His name be on the Memorial . . .' (*OY*, p. 69). In the story entitled 'Thomas Griffiths and Parson Cope' the rectory appears haunted:

> There was scarcely space for a trap to turn and branch off to the stable yard, but if a wheel so much as grazed the lawn Parson Cope had an 'attack'. When this happened, resurgent noises, apparently detached from the parson, tumbled about the hollow house. Sobs in the attics – but the parson was in the conservatory. Cries and lights, buckets swilling, rags being wrung – but the parson was sitting lampless in his owly study. (*OY*, p. 27)

'Lampless in his owly study' is a phrase which could have come straight from the pen of Dylan Thomas, who was also writing

exaggerated Gothic tales set in the mysterious never-neverland of the 'Jarvis Valley' during the 1930s. Margiad Evans's Gothic writing, though, is very specifically located and her work in this mode can be seen as deeply unsettling forays into the bruised psyche of the Border region.

Evans's concern with Gothic haunting and the supernatural gradually bleeds out of her published writing in the 1950s. Arguably, even the most lurid figures of Gothic tales must have seemed to her mere painted monsters in comparison with the actual monstrosity of her appalling illness which became her everyday reality from the moment of her first epileptic fit in 1950. From then on, the ghost that haunts her is her own. Evans's use of the Gothic mode in her earlier fiction thus uncannily predicts her own later situation in life. Perhaps Margiad Evans's inventive and exaggerated Gothic fictions did indeed partly originate in an undiagnosed neurological condition.

Notes

[1] Ceridwen Lloyd-Morgan, *Margiad Evans* (Bridgend: Seren, 1998), p. 9.
[2] Ibid., p. 20.
[3] Ibid.
[4] Margiad Evans, National Library of Wales (hereafter NLW) MS 23366D, journal entry, 6 May 1934.
[5] James Henderson, 'The Gothic novel in Wales', *The National Library of Wales Journal*, 11 (1956–60), 244–54; R. S. Thomas, 'Welsh landscape', *Song at the Year's Turning* (London: Rupert Hart-Davies, 1955), p. 63.
[6] Jane Aaron, 'A national seduction: Wales in nineteenth-century women's writing', *New Welsh Review*, 7/3, 27 (1994), 31–8.
[7] Matthew Arnold, quoted by Henderson in 'The Gothic novel in Wales', 244.
[8] For example: *The Great God Pan* (1894), *The Hill of Dreams* (1907), *The White People* (1904).
[9] Ellen Moers, 'Female Gothic', in *Literary Women* (London: The Women's Press, 1986), p. 90.
[10] Ibid.
[11] Clare Morgan, 'Exile and the kingdom: Margiad Evans and the mythic landscape of Wales', vol. 6 (2000), *Welsh Writing in English: A Yearbook of Critical Essays*, 89–118.
[12] Jacques Derrida, *Specters of Marx*, tr. Peggy Kamuf (New York: Routledge, 1994).
[13] Margiad Evans, letter to Gwyn Jones, 28 January 1946, quoted in Lloyd-Morgan, *Margiad Evans*, pp. 126–7.

14 Ibid.
15 Ibid., p. 93.
16 Ibid., p. 108.
17 David Punter, *The Literature of Terror: A History of Gothic Fictions from 1765 to the Present Day* (London : Longman, 1980), p. 2.
18 Moira Dearnley, *Margiad Evans* (Cardiff: University of Wales Press, 1982), p. 32.
19 Ibid., p. 62.
20 Derrida, *Specters of Marx*, p. xix.
21 See Katie Gramich, *Twentieth Century Women's Writing in Wales: Land, Gender, Belonging* (Cardiff: University of Wales Press, 2007), pp. 85–6.
22 Diana Wallace, 'Mixed marriages: three Welsh historical novels in English by women writers', in ed. Christopher Meredith, *Moment of Earth* (Aberystwyth: Celtic Studies Publications, 2007), pp. 171–84, p. 175.
23 Sigmund Freud, 'Beyond the pleasure principle', *Complete Psychological Works*, vol. XVIII (London: Hogarth, 1961), p. 13.
24 Margiad Evans, *Country Dance* (London: John Calder, 1978), p. 96. Further references are to this edition, hereafter *CD*.
25 Margiad Evans, *The Wooden Doctor* (Dinas Powys: Honno, 2005), p. 12. Further references are to this edition, hereafter *WD*.
26 Sue Asbee, 'Introduction', *The Wooden Doctor* (Dinas Powys: Honno, 2005); Karen Caesar, 'Patient, doctor and disease in Margiad Evans's *The Wooden Doctor*', in Aleksandra Bartoszko and Maria Vaccarella (eds), *The Patient: Probing Interdisciplinary Boundaries* (Witney: Inter-Disciplinary Press, 2011). E-book, available at *www.inter-disciplinary.net/ publishing/id-press/ebooks/the-patient/*.
27 Caesar, 'Patient, doctor and disease'.
28 Margiad Evans, *Turf or Stone* (Oxford: Basil Blackwell, 1934), p. 26. Further references are to this edition, hereafter *TS*.
29 Ibid., p. 43. It is telling that Evans refers to the novel in her journals as *Easter*.
30 The phrase is T. S. Eliot's; he admired Barnes's Modernist novel greatly; quoted in Moers, *Literary Women*, p. 108.
31 See Julia Kristeva, *Powers of Horror: An Essay on Abjection*, tr. Leon S. Roudiez (New York: Columbia University Press, 1982).
32 Margiad Evans, NLW MS 23366D, journal entry, 6 May 1934.
33 Margiad Evans, *Creed* (Oxford: Basil Blackwell, 1936), p. 23. Hereafter *C*.
34 Lloyd-Morgan, *Margiad Evans*, p. 72.
35 Margiad Evans, *The Old and the Young*, ed. Ceridwen Lloyd-Morgan (Bridgend: Seren, 1998), p. 52. Hereafter *OY*.

6

Time, Memory and Identity in the Short Stories of Margiad Evans

TONY BROWN

Proust says (or at any rate if he doesn't he ought) that the very worst form any ill that befalls us can take is in the form of its memory. The reverse is true: it is the best.[1]

The operation of personal memory, the sudden unpredictable flow of images, events and, above all, emotions from the past into present consciousness, is so recurrent a feature of Margiad Evans's short stories as on occasion to become a thematic concern in itself: 'So chamber leads into chamber, passage into passage of remembrance, as in a garden the smell of lilac leads us on to the violets and the first pansies.'[2] As with Proust, it is usually a sensory experience in the present which releases the vivid flow of past experience in Evans's characters. In 'Miss Potts and Music', Miss Potts suddenly enters the narrator's mind, years after she had known Miss Potts briefly in childhood, as the talented niece of her piano teacher:

Why I thought of Miss Potts and my music lessons when I looked at the tree was because it is a birch. Birches grew outside the room where B.B.S.H. taught me. [. . .] I can see those grey-green three-cornered leaves now. [. . .]

Perhaps, too, my being in the orchard this morning unconsciously opened my mind to her image. Down there with the smell of the long grass and nettles and the horse mushrooms under old perry and cider trees the sense of an intimate past is always more powerful than anywhere else: under those trees my childhood grows over me.[3]

Ceridwen Lloyd-Morgan points out the similarly Proustian moment in 'The Lost Fisherman' when, hearing in her mother's house the canaries 'cracking their seeds with a tiny insect-like pop', Emily is suddenly back in the heat of the countryside: 'It was so hot that the

stones were tepid in the shade. The pods of broom and gorse burst in the sun with that wee minute crack, with only the linnet to make the stillness alive. Emily remembered, as if she saw the burnt grass and the sky above, the whirring world of heat' (*OY*, p. 88).[4] In the unpublished 'And Every Day of their Lives' (*c*.1951–3), the sight of hydrangeas in a garden reminds Ellen, as she walks through the town one evening with her husband, of the 'half-wild hydrangeas' under the windows of the cottage above the sea shore where she and her husband had lived in the early, happy days of their marriage: 'The smell of it! The sweet grass, the honeysuckle, and the salt, sunny breeze. It was midsummer.'[5] But the happiness which the hydrangeas bring into her mind is long past; she has discovered that her husband has committed adultery with a girl in the town and had a child by her; by now Ellen detests the self-satisfied bully who walks beside her: 'Haberdasher Evans the Freemason, the lay-preacher, the sing-song psalmer'. The sensations and memories aroused by the hydrangeas are soured and the security of the escapist fantasy she has constructed is suddenly destroyed: 'Why, she wondered, had she been forced to pass by hydrangeas at the moment when she was so satisfied with the real, solid little farm she had created for herself? Now it was nowhere and neither was she.'

'The Immortal Hospital', from which the passage about Proust at the head of this essay comes, was written in 1957 when Evans was 48 and seriously unwell with the tumour that would ultimately kill her; it is a deeply-felt recollection of the year which she and her sister spent, when Evans was eleven, living on the farm at Benhall with her Aunt Fran and her husband. It was, as other commentators have suggested, a crucial period in the development of Evans's individual identity. Barbara Prys-Williams, for instance, emphasises the ways in which Benhall, and the devoted attentions of her aunt, provided for the imaginative young girl a refuge from the domestic tensions created not only by the increasingly unpredictable behaviour of her alcoholic father but also her ambiguous relationship with her mother, born one assumes of Evans's sense of dependence on the mother, her sensitivity to her mother's feelings for her, given the father's behaviour.[6] Benhall and the loving attention she received from her aunt clearly provided a sanctuary which allowed the young girl the security to grow as an individual. In her account of that crucial year the landscape around the farm becomes suffused with the feelings of affection, tranquillity and security inculcated by her relationship with her aunt; such

feelings are epitomised in her recollections of the relaxed, content interludes before bedtime when Aunt Fran brushed and curled her niece's hair in her room:

> It was a beautiful old room in the front of the house which bowed gently over the garden. Beyond the lawn and the wych elms and the blue shadow of the Wellingtonia to the right of the expanse, lay a marshy piece of land matted with bullrushes and, in spring, violet with the alder catkins – a bit of near landscape as tender and indescribable in colour as were the goodnight moods between my Aunt Fran and me.[7]

Even when the insertion of the curling rags pulls at her hair, 'between my Aunt and me was such sympathy, such peace, that I didn't mind very much'. Again, writing of the room at the farm which became the playroom of Evans and her sister, she reflects that there are 'enough memories in that one room alone to make up a whole person'. The sense of security, of feeling at home in the world, which she experienced at Benhall emblematised for the rest of Evans's life a state of being, of secure selfhood in harmony with the natural landscape around her, which is in many ways at the core of her stories, albeit often evoked as an aspiration or as a state only to be remembered, usually in recollections of childhood.

The present essay seeks to consider the function and significance of the frequent recourse of the narrators and characters in Margiad Evans's short stories to memory and what this might indicate about her sense of the nature of human consciousness in time and place, in the world she inhabits. Some paradoxes in her attitudes are in themselves revealing and might be seen to take us to the heart of some of the central tensions in her creative concerns.

In her remarkable *Autobiography*, composed primarily of extracts from the journal she kept in the late 1930s and early 1940s, mainly while living at Potacre, the small cottage at Llangarron, near Ross, Evans shows herself to be unafraid of being alone, even to relish it: 'I love the alert freedom of being alone.'[8] One notices that 'alert': it was an aloneness which allowed her to focus with remarkable, almost obsessive, intensity on the natural world around Llangarron through which she walked, and the detailed observations which are recorded in the *Autobiography* are repeatedly suffused with a sense of security which she found to be intimated in the natural world, a unity and wholeness in which the separateness of the self and its anxieties could be transcended. In January 1940 she writes, 'I'm not a naturalist or a scholar in leaves and birds, but something is there which makes me

stand quite still and look. I do feel a rooted certainty then' (*A*, p. 44).
At one point, as she lies on the hillside, she reflects:

> No more grief and pain and betrayal. Only joy. *Thou* Father knowest
> me. [. . .] God be between us all like the lovely air.
>   It was pure delight to lie there with my dear home winds coming over
> the tops of the elms and my own country lapping around its incompar-
> able hills . . . (*A*, p. 10)

The invocation of God is unusual – Evans was no orthodox Christian
– but the link between God as Father and the sense of security and
'at-home-ness' which she feels in the natural world might suggest that
at some level of consciousness such feelings are a substitution for the
anxiety, the lack of stability which she associates with her own father
and her childhood home.

Not infrequently, such moments are intuited in essentially mystical
terms. On one occasion, she comes upon an old countryman collecting wood in the fields, in a scene which echoes Wordsworth's meetings
in his poetry with rural figures, beggars and leechgatherers, who seem
to dwell in another, more visionary realm than the poet; 'almost as
old as the oldest root under him', the old man sits smoking his pipe:

> On his left hand was the sun, the sky, the beautiful thunder pillar, below
> him the trees, the stream, the ant and molehills, the golden sunny turf,
> always above him gray hazel branches.
>   He told me of them all, not as one describes a place but as a time. He
> was away from time, not 'out' with it but in a different variety of it. The
> clock pendulums swing backwards and forwards in time; but in his vari-
> ations of it the sun did not hurry and the cloud remained, and by them
> he existed away from indoor clocks. [. . .]
>   He felt the gladness in the ground, and the still joy in the trees and the
> smoothing out of icy currents in the air under the sun's influence. [. . .]
>   His 'now' lasted all one afternoon long with the thrush's notes,
> thoughtful with the trees. His brain did not tell him what he felt but it
> came to him straight from the touch of the ground from the height of
> the sky and the directness of the birds' descents to grass and bough.
> (*A*, pp. 69–70)

The perception of the old man and that of Evans seem to coalesce as
she reflects on, and enters, what she takes to be his vision of the world:

> The idiot sway of the pendulum is no more time than the baton is
> symphony. What marks on a clock-face are there for that moment when
> the crow, tired of flight, droops his wings in the air and you see the
> lustrous contour of his back, the hanging pinions like blue-black leaves.

It is only a second by artificial time, yet he *dwells* in the air – the eye
registers him as something belonging to eternity. [. . .]
    Life is lived outside this penny round in a vaster and roomier circula-
tion. [. . .] The true time is the spirit in places, the era in your mind, the
pleasure in your soul. [. . .] It is consciousness, but not the consciousness
of time. Rather it is the intermittent feeling of space, air, loveliness and
life. The now is the time of all times. (*A*, pp. 70–1, emphasis in the
original)

Such states of mind, such intuitions of a wholeness and timeless unity
in the natural world around her, and her sense of herself as a joyful
and secure part of it, form a recurring thread in *Autobiography*, fleeting, elusive moments as Evans walks the hills and fields around
Llangarron: 'All is continuous, connected; all is one perpetually
breathing, changeless power; all is of one. [. . .] Ah, how impossible it
is to keep those moments, to hold down for more than a single instant
that joy of being oneself contained in all one sees!' (*A*, pp. 91, 95).
Such moments of security and wholeness, experienced in the late
1930s, still bring to Evans's mind the remembered security and
moments of heightened awareness she had experienced at Benhall; on
the previous page of *Autobiography*, she writes:

NOVEMBER. I am twelve years old, reading on the window sill in the
fruit shed. [. . .] I have read myself out of existence. [. . .] My crowded
head feels suddenly clear, empty and airy as craning out of the window,
I look hungrily around. This is real, I think, the colours, the brick, the
ivy. [. . .] Why have I never seen them like this before? A moment ago
they existed but quietly and without me. (*A*, p. 94)

But now she feels herself to be part of the scene, at one with it, and,
almost inevitably, the moment of wholeness is associated with
memory: the adult Evans not only remembers the scene, but remembers being determined *to* remember it: 'Something is happening which
makes me able to say and know that it is true: "I shall remember this.
I shall remember each vein on each leaf. I shall be able to see this
whenever I want to, wherever I am!"' (*A*, p. 94). Such remembered
moments of awareness, of connection with the world, are immediately associated with continuity of consciousness, the continuity
which is fundamental to personal identity.
    As is evident from her *Autobiography*, Margiad Evans was not
always alone in the countryside; part of the security she felt in her
growing love for Michael Williams, whom she married in 1940,

stemmed from her sense of how profoundly he shared, and gently enhanced, her intimacy with the natural world:

> Presently, I heard his voice speaking out of a trance of peace. [. . .]
>
> I often feel when M—— suddenly speaks like that that he thinks from inside Nature, that he has some thought with it, flowing with it. To go with him into the fields is to see further than my own sight, and to understand without effort, from within. When we worked together out of doors [. . .] he seemed of himself to create a harmony, like a third person whose presence befriended us both. (*A*, p. 92)

It was a harmony, manifestly, in which she could feel secure, at home.[9] However, in 1942 Williams was called up to serve in the Royal Navy, being posted to the Mediterranean for most of the war, while his wife remained alone at Llangarron, undertaking farm work to bring in an income, as well as writing.[10] The stories collected in *The Old and the Young* were, with the exception of the earlier 'The Wicked Woman' (1933), written in this period, between 1943 and 1946, and it is striking that such moments of harmony with the natural world, such intimations of security as we have noted in the *Autobiography* are for the most part absent from these short stories. Rather do we find a recurring sense of uneasiness, of the fragility and elusiveness of individual consciousness in the processes of time. The connectedness of individual memory is present, but seems shadowed by uncertainty and vulnerability. Though one might suggest that such impulses are essentially modernist, exacerbated by the tensions of war, this is not to suggest of course that these are bleak or even unrelievedly anxious stories; the depth and delicacy of feeling, the rich and detailed sense of the natural world like that in *Autobiography* and the recurring childhood perspectives continue, to give a tone of lyrical richness.

And in a couple of the stories there is certainly still present an elusive sense of the possibility of a fuller life, a more unified and secure world. 'Into Kings', narrated in the third person but almost in free indirect style, has the child's elusive, fluid sense of time; we are told firmly at the outset that 'Harry was five', though after an initial visit with his mother to the tiny rural cottage of the Lackitt family (the name is perhaps uncharacteristically laboured) to buy eggs, '[. . .] now for years and years he had been coming by himself. [. . .] Each day the Harry of yesterday seemed somebody else' (*OY*, p. 46); the story has in some ways the sense of being a memory, and contains an intuitive, almost visionary moment akin to those remembered in *Autobiography*. Like other protagonists, the boy is a middle-class

outsider in the country community; his mother is hesitant about his visiting the working–class rural family, with the '[h]alf-gipsy' mother: 'It was rather as if the Lackitts' kindness had fleas in it' (*OY*, p. 47). But for Harry contact with the Lackitts becomes a transformative experience. When he enters the main room in the cottage for the first time by himself, his sense of intrusion and uncertainty means that he can at first 'hardly breathe for terror'; but despite the ambiguous presence of the crippled daughter, slumped at the fireside dozing, Harry's fascination grows. The room he finds 'full of lovely things', little porcelain ornaments, china cups and saucers with gold bands bathed in the reflected light from a large, old, ornamental, gold-framed mirror. It is the mirror which focuses for the boy the central experience of the story as he experiences a new and unexpected sense of calmness, continuity and security:

> With the poetry of all mirrors, whether sixpenny or Sheraton, it seemed to reflect not only light, but *stillness*. The quality of abidingness which poverty, closeness, and use had given to the chairs and tables was compacted in the mirror into a tilted but solid peace. (*OY*, p. 48, emphasis in the original)

He seems to undergo the kind of almost epiphanic shift in awareness, a heightening of the imagination akin to that which Margiad Evans records herself as having experienced in the calm security of Benhall. When Harry sees his reflection in the mirror – 'a little boy in a green sou-wester. [. . .] He felt his shoulders, the top of his head, his breast, and saw himself repeating the touches' (*OY*, p. 48) – he experiences not a disturbing defamilarisation but a sense of himself as part of this rich, tranquil scene. The world outside, through the window, is 'strangely altered' (*OY*, p. 49); the Lackitts themselves are seen for a moment in regal terms, 'crowned and wearing trains' (an idea stimulated in the boy's imagination by his earlier puzzling over why the little cottage has a sign over the door proclaiming it to be 'Peewit Castle': 'Kings, not birds, lived in castles', *OY*, p. 44). The mysterious new mood of security enables him to approach the crippled daughter ('he could feel how calm she was' (*OY*, p. 49)) who wants him to sit on her knee. It is this tableau of calm togetherness which greets the Lackitts when they re-enter the cottage. Harry cannot express the feelings which he has been experiencing – 'It was something he could only have himself, to keep and to question' (*OY*, p. 50) – but there is something in the elusive mood which Mrs Lackitt and her crippled daughter can also sense and share; Mr Lackitt shuffles off to get on

with other tasks, 'the only person of the four to whom nothing could possibly have been otherwise than as it was'. 'Otherwise' not in economic terms – Evans does not engage the actual hardship of the Lackitts' lives – but the three seem to be aware of qualities beyond the material, of emotional stability, calm and 'abidingness'; 'it's something they've got', Harry later tells his mother (*OY*, p. 46).

One of the finest stories in *The Old and the Young*, 'The Lost Fisherman', is also the story which most directly engages the experience of the war, the very real fears and insecurities which haunt those on the home front and which make the 'longing for peace and fulfilment' which Emily, the young woman at the centre of the story, experiences more than merely an individual longing. Emily, living in a small town on the Welsh border – evidently based on Ross – becomes aware of an enigmatic young man whom she regularly sees fishing in the calmness of the nearby river. They converse only casually but she comes to associate him with the tranquillity that is missing not only from the world around her but from her own life, living with her mother and then also with her sister and her children, who have been evacuated from the London Blitz. For Emily, the fisherman is 'part of something that's being lost. And I want it to come back. It's life. At least it is to me' (*OY*, p. 76). The first time the reader encounters the fisherman is when Emily sees him one afternoon asleep in the warmth of the sunshine, in what had been the garden of an old cottage, demolished years before; in the quiet intense scent of the overgrown garden in the sunlight, 'his powerful, innocent face free from eagerness, away from the frightening smell of people, he slept like a lad in a field' (*OY*, p. 75). This place was once somebody's home; Emily always wonders 'where was his home'.

Emily's relationship with the fisherman is drawn with remarkable delicacy of feeling: her attraction to him is not sexual in any conventional way – they never kiss. But he comes to represent to her a sense of authenticity, fulfilment and security remembered from her childhood in the area but lacking in her adult life:

> He recalled to her a beam of the true meaning of freedom and fulfilment: with him or thinking of him she became again the real Emily who used to swim across the river in the early mornings, who was free, whose being absorbed and radiated the harmony of the countryside in which she was growing. (*OY*, p. 83)

Again personal security is associated with 'that kind of order' (*OY*, p. 90), which can be found when you are at one with, at home in, the

natural world. The climax of the story comes when the fisherman rows her, late in the evening, to her aunt's riverside house, where she is staying; the scene is one of remarkable tranquillity as they glide through the darkening trees. But then he tells her that he is likely to leave the area soon:

> 'Called up probably. I don't really care much where I go.'
> 'Don't you feel anything?'
> 'Yes, I feel something.'
> 'What?' she cried passionately.
> 'What?' he laughed, patting the water: 'why, lost!' (*OY*, p. 95)

The moment comes as a shock – Emily's body feels 'light and chilly' – as we realise that the figure she has constructed as an emblem of the security and fulfilment to which she aspires in fact feels none of these things. He too is a homeless inhabitant of the world of war and mortality and time (Emily has earlier noted the town hall clock with 'its hands like an enormous pair of scissors' (*OY*, p. 74)) and it is in this unstable world that she must make her life: 'There came a pounding vision of machinery, of voices unbroken by silence, into her ears and her closed eyes. The future . . .' (*OY*, p. 96).

The tranquillity which Emily associates with her aunt's riverside house, where she is currently staying and where she recalls living as a child, clearly draws on Evans's memories of Benhall.[11] At the same time there are undertones here that we do not hear in the glowing memories of 'The Immortal Hospital': 'Why did it all seem so near [. . .] and yet so irrevocably saddened? If one person dies, the past is altered. Uncle Donovan was dead. People she had loved were dead' (*OY*, p. 78). Even as Evans evokes the remembered place with which she most closely associates security and individuality, there is a shadow of vulnerability, of process and mortality. And it is worth observing that Evans does not ultimately sentimentalise childhood; in a late unpublished essay 'How do the children?' (*c*.1950–3) she challenges the notion that children are innocent: 'They are certainly not innocent of most of the faults adults have perfected. They are cruel and cunning and greedy as we are, and more so.'[12] Nor is childhood itself seen as being without its fear, anxieties, even its terrors, a word that is used more than once in these stories. The subtle, quietly elusive story 'Solomon' evokes a single ostensibly uneventful afternoon in the life of a middle-class family in their old rural home as a summer storm gathers: the mother goes riding, the children play outside.

Much of the story is narrated from the point of view of the little boy, nicknamed 'Barrabas'; it is he who has picked up, somewhat uncomprehendingly, the word 'Solomon' from being read St. Matthew's account of Christ's comparison of the lilies of the field with 'Solomon in all his glory'.[13] It has become something of a private, totemic word for the little boy: he associates it with the house itself (*OY*, p. 104) and 'Whenever he whispers it he is at *home*. [. . .] The word articulates in some enormous still sound, all that Barrabas feels for the house, the park, and the trees and even the sky that he lives in' (*OY*, p. 98, my italics). But notions of security are again shadowed by a sense of threat and vulnerability in this story. As the storm gathers, the light creates a sense of unreality and the countryside takes on 'the glassy darkness of an eclipse' (*OY*, p. 103). The father is concerned about his wife out riding and relieved when she gets home as the storm is about to break. He has previously been for a moment 'confused and terrified' (*OY*, p. 104) when he realises that he has left his gun propped up and accessible in the study ('he snatches it up and looks at it as if it had just shot one of the children' (*OY*, p. 105)). The mother, while out riding, worries about the family finances and the upkeep of the house; indeed there is a sense in which the family's occupancy of the house feels temporary, just a brief chapter in its long history. The family occasionally find old objects in the house and grounds, 'a silk purse with a black coin [. . .] the queer shrunken horseshoe. [. . .] [E]verything in the house has history' (*OY*, p. 100, p. 102). There is indeed an 'otherness' in the house – 'All is not known here. All will never be known' (*OY*, p. 106) – which runs counter to, and for the reader subverts, the security which Barrabas feels. And the story ends, again, on a note of anxiety as the mother experiences a pang of fear when she looks out of the window and sees little Barrabas outside as the storm is finally about to break.

On occasions in Margiad Evans's stories, childhood memories are associated with, embodied in, a remembered figure who herself had represented stability and continuity with an earlier past. In the unpublished 'The Equerry's House' the narrator remembers having come as a child to the 'midland town of H – ', having her hair cut and (in what was even then an old-fashioned process) singed by the local hairdresser, Miss Flute. With her pale make-up and old-fashioned clothes, Miss Flute is not merely a figure who had seemed to evade time and change, but one who evoked the actual impulse to remember:

It seems to me now that she preserved something [. . .] that was far less material than a comfortable living. Something that was for us and not for her. She was one of those even personalities which does not alter; and from this arose a changelessness in those who sat before her looking glass. Unconsciously as we sat absorbing that quietened view of ourselves, we made a memory of our looks. There is no reflection of myself that has ever seemed to me worth more than the moment I give it, except that one.[14]

But the memory is hedged with guilt – 'I betrayed her, and took my long plaits secretly elsewhere to be cut off. I never returned' – and, again, mortality: 'Miss Flute is dead and I live on in H—'.

The climax of the title story of *The Old and the Young* comes when the narrator, Arabella, remembers the lovely epiphanic scene when, some thirty years previously, as a little girl with the other village children, she had watched the fragile, eighty-nine-year-old Tilly Luce suddenly and uncertainly begin to dance with them in the sunshine. 'Long, long afterwards,' Arabella recalls, as she often has, 'everything became one' (*OY*, p. 162). Indeed so powerful to the child was this sense of harmony and at-one-ness that, again, it is *consciously* stored, a preserve against the flow of time: 'I'll remember this. [. . .] I'll *always* remember this' (OY, p. 162, emphasis in the original). Moreover, the steps that Tilly dances are themselves remembered, from 'some faded country dance' learned in her childhood, many decades before this scene of thirty years before. Tilly has become a part of the complex of memories which make Arabella who she is, part of Arabella's identity. Her memories having been stimulated by the sight of Tilly's old house, Arabella imagines (rather than remembers) Tilly pausing as she went shopping in the village thirty years ago, caught in a memory of her own: '[s]melling the wallflowers in her garden patch, the sight of her youth seemed to come back to her' (*OY*, p. 149).

But then, almost shockingly, as Arabella looks at the little old house, comes the realisation that not only has the village changed and 'Nobody there has ever heard of Tilly' (*OY*, p. 150), but that Arabella herself does not know what happened to her:

When did she die, and in which of our hayfield churchyards are her bones hidden? Again I don't know. Probably it happened when I was away from home on one of those miserable excursions into life which always ended (urgently) in a stampede for my own country. (*OY*, pp. 150–1)

One notices again that 'home', as well as the panicky retreat from wider events. But more crucially we realise from the outset – these thoughts

are in the opening pages of the story – how fragile is memory, and ultimately individual identity, in the flow of time and events – 'What has happened to us?'(*OY*, p. 150); one notes that, not insignificantly, it is precisely at this point that we get the single reference in the story to the war (as well as to time and mortality): 'The bridge has been widened for war traffic, and ruined, the eighteenth-century sundial has been carted away and left in a corner, a tomb without a grave' (*OY*, p. 150). The links with past times, the past that we feel to have been more secure, more stable, are fragile.[15] Tilly now only exists in Arabella's memory. And when Arabella herself dies, what then? The fact that this more sombre awareness comes near the beginning of the story gives the happy epiphanic moment of one-ness and security when Tilly dances, some ten pages later, even more poignancy, adds to the sense of both the value of memory and also to our awareness of the vulnerability of that remembering, conscious self.

On the opening page of 'Miss Potts and Music' the narrator quotes some lines from 'Logs on the Hearth: A Memory of a Sister' by Thomas Hardy, supremely the poet of memory, of a sense of the self unhomed in Time, and she comments: 'Many winds and winters are in those lines, which, like all real memories, hold much more of oblivion than remembrance' (*OY*, p. 107). That final phrase could almost stand as an epigraph to some of these stories. 'Miss Potts and Music' is one of the most structurally fluid in the collection, as the narrator's mind circles around the memory of Miss Potts, the supposed prodigy who was the niece of the spinster music teacher in the narrator's childhood. There is a deep sympathy for the seemingly lonely young Miss Potts, then cordially detested by the other children and, it seems, struggling to live up to her family's expectations. Miss Potts now exists for the narrator only as a fragment in her mind; albeit there is some suggestion of illness, perhaps breakdown, the narrator knows nothing of what subsequently happened to Miss Potts: 'I have never heard that Miss Potts *died*, nor for that matter that she lived. She has not become a celebrity' (*OY*, p. 114, emphasis in the original); like Tilly, she has become one of the lost. Indeed there is a sense in which the story is less about Miss Potts than about the action of the narrator's mind, about the uncertainty of memory, of what is true and what the mind itself has created, the ways in which the mind seeks to construct patterns of meaning in the face of the fluidity of time: 'I don't think I saw half of what I remember, and I may have dreamed or imagined it. Certainly it seems real' (*OY*, p. 111). In fact, in the last

lines of the narrative, 'Wind, tree, darkness and Miss Potts are all inscrutable' (*OY*, p. 115).

In two stories that darkness, inscrutable, even threatening, becomes a central element. While the narrator of 'The Boy Who Called for a Light' loved as a child to stand outside his rural home and gaze at the moonlight, what he also recalls – the whole story is again based on memory – is how he was 'terrified of the real whole dark. [. . .] It was not a shy, darting fear but a powerful, mature terror, shapeless and senseless. Only since growing up have I found even approximate words for it' (*OY*, p. 62). (The limited capacity of language to deal precisely with experience, be it the experience of a child, the elusiveness of recollection or those moments of mystical wholeness with the natural world in *Autobiography*, is a recurring concern in Evans's writing, including the stories.)[16] The germ of the story seems to have been given to Margiad Evans when a young local boy called at her door one night to ask for a light, but what is fascinating, given our present discussion, is the power with which she responded to that initial germ, the profound resonances which the notion of being fearfully alone in an ominous darkness seem to have set up in her imagination.[17] The night that continues to haunt the narrator as an adult is etched in his memory not just out of his deep fear of the dark but from the particular colouring which it is given by the neighbour who tells the boy of the ghostly 'visions' the man had seen on the road: '"Hundreds of 'em. Hundreds. [. . .] They look 1-1-like any other m-man you mid m-meet on the road. H-h-how be, be, be you to tell?" [. . .] His stammering increased my horror' (*OY*, p. 65). Even these fearful visions, though, are less terrifying to the boy than his fear of meeting 'an idiot man' who lives nearby, 'a certain old chap with a forgotten memory' (*OY*, p. 68); the man is an embodiment of disorientation, unable to make any sense of the world around him: to lose your memory, clearly, is to lose any sense of who you are. Kate Owen – yet another old lady recalled for the role she once played in a remembered childhood – offers the boy company and guidance on his journey home through the rural dark, but even she claims to have seen ghosts, in particular that of her dead brother, seen at dusk on the road in the village at the very time he is dying abroad in the First World War.

The narrator consciously meditates on the nature of memory and our relation to our pasts. His recollections of his home life, and his rather authoritarian mother, are not unambiguously happy; home for him does not represent the security of Benhall. But, again, he is

strikingly aware of the ways in which remembered and half-remembered recollections of home and its routines – 'To this day I shut my door when I turn on the light' – contribute to who we are: 'Well, that was the way home, and the queer thing is that after the first, the first one you remember, there's never another, not even when you're a man, married with your own children, living somewhere and going to work yourself' (*OY*, p. 62). But it is the journey through the dark with old Kate Owen that especially haunts him – 'I have never forgotten that night, never lost one single detail' (*OY*, p. 66). For the reader, perhaps the most striking thing in the story is again the recreation of the lonely, terrified consciousness of the boy surrounded by the menacing darkness. But what haunts the narrator, so many years after, what seems to bring the night recurrently to mind, is the way in which he feels that he had betrayed Kate and her kindness. For all the friendliness he knows she has shown to him – 'I felt that she was better than all of us' (*OY*, p. 70) – he not only impulsively leaves her without a word of thanks as he arrives home but he ingratiates himself with his parents, when he gets indoors, by joining in their mockery of the old lady. Like the memory of Miss Flute, the memory of the old woman is suffused with guilt.

'All Through the Night' is not concerned directly with memory, but it is striking that Evans creates another narrative which centres on children alone in the dark. When they miss their bus home, fourteen-year-old Helena and her younger brother, Augustus, initially see the twelve-mile walk home through the darkness of the countryside as something of an adventure; Helena indeed is happy to be walking in the dark at midnight since 'home was awful' (*OY*, p. 166): they have only just moved to the old rectory which is their new family home, and she is evidently unsettled. For the most part, they do not experience the continuous 'shapeless and senseless' terror which the narrator of 'The Boy Who Called for a Light' feels. However, the 'square black opening' in the floor of the barn in which they try to sleep is a focus for anxiety, and they flee in genuine fear from the old house into which they are taken in the middle of the night by the barn's owner: 'There was a smell. It was dreadful, and as they stood they seemed to feel it fixing them, as the light fixed them, in its solid whitey-yellow block' (*OY*, pp. 168–9). Having caught his breath after their running away from the house, Augustus is surprised by the sound of his voice when he asks his sister about the unexplained goings on in the house; his voice 'was like his mother's when she cut

her finger in the lawn mower and saw her own blood on the grass' (*OY*, p. 170). The boy unconsciously associates the fear he is experiencing with the unsettling memory of a parent who normally represents security being shocked and endangered.

When they get home (and the reader might share Helena's wonder that the parents have locked the door and gone to bed!), Helena is determined to write the experience down, presumably to memorialise it and thereby to make sense of it. In fact as she gazes out at the night she experiences something which – again – cannot be caught in words: 'It was something that had never happened to her before – something whole which took time and which could never be seen in glimpses "out of the window" as Augustus said' (*OY*, p. 172). The sensation is not developed further, as narrative attention moves to Augustus and his parents. In some ways we again sense the kind of intuition which Evans recalls from her time at Benhall, but what is striking is how much more fleeting, how much less secure Helena's intuition is. Again, what dominates the story is the darkness, and the vulnerability of the children.

'[W]e can never describe what we *are* as accurately as what we *were*', Margiad Evans writes in a late unpublished essay on 'Famous unknown children'.[18] In fact, what we are is ultimately bound up inextricably with what we were. Our individual identity is essentially created by a sense of the continuity of our consciousness through time. In *Autobiography*, Margiad Evans, partly in recollection of the sense of security and selfhood which to the end of her short life she always associated with Benhall, could feel herself almost mystically at-one-with, at home in, the rhythms and processes of the natural world around her. However, in the short stories written in the 1940s, many of them in the war years, such awareness may be yearned for but is very much less evident. The fragile thread of memory, and thus of identity, is surrounded by the indifferent flow of time and process which threatens its continued existence. In this, Margiad Evans manifests a very modern sense of human vulnerability and isolation.

Notes

[1] Margiad Evans, 'The Immortal Hospital or recollections of our childhood', unpublished autobiographical essay, National Library of Wales (hereafter NLW) 23369C.

2 Ibid.
3 Margiad Evans, *The Old and the Young*, ed. Ceridwen Lloyd-Morgan ([1948] Bridgend: Seren, 1998), p. 109. Further references are included in the text (*OY*). 'B.B.S.H.' is the narrator's nickname for her music teacher whose appearance she had seen as 'Combining Rossetti's Beata Beatrix and my own idea of Sherlock Holmes', a 'long, long throat, a big clever nose, a thin ethereal face with ascetic and romantic eyes' (*OY*, p. 108). The imaginative and associative nature of the narrator's mind is thus already evident.
4 Ceridwen Lloyd-Morgan, *Margiad Evans* (Bridgend: Seren, 1998), p. 103.
5 Margiad Evans, 'And Every Day of their Lives', NLW MS 23365D.
6 Barbara Prys-Williams, 'Writing it out: Margiad Evans (1909–1958)', in *Twentieth-Century Autobiography: Writing Wales in English* (Cardiff: University of Wales Press, 2004), pp. 33–4, p. 45. Prys-Williams notes that 'the picture that emerges of Margiad Evans's mother from "the Immortal Hospital" does not encourage any objective view of a close and loving bond' and points out Evans's reference to the parents' mocking of the clothes that Aunt Fran had bought for her; when Evans returned to the family home at the end of the year, 'the scrapping of those brilliant clothes in a bonfire of rather unkind laughter caused me pain. When they threw away certain things they were almost throwing me away. A *me* they could not recapture for myself: a peace like a summer's day [. . .]'.
7 Evans, 'The Immortal Hospital'.
8 Margiad Evans, *Autobiography* (Oxford: Basil Blackwell, 1943), p. 2. Further references are included in the text (*A*). The first section of the *Autobiography* is entitled 'A Little Journal of Being Alone'. Writing to Kate Roberts in 1946 in reply to a letter in which Roberts had expressed her loneliness (her husband had died that year), Evans writes '[. . .] don't fear it – everything durable, everything eternal comes out of loneliness'. For discussion of this correspondence and the distinction between 'loneliness' and 'aloneness', see Tony Brown, '"Stories from foreign countries": the short stories of Kate Roberts and Margiad Evans', in Alyce von Rothkirch and Daniel Williams (eds), *Beyond the Difference: Welsh Literature in Comparative Contexts* (Cardiff: University of Wales Press, 2004), pp. 21–37, pp. 25–6.
9 On this deepened sense of security with Michael Williams, see Prys-Williams, 'Writing it out', pp. 47–8.
10 The regular letters, hundreds of them, which she wrote to her husband while he was abroad, as Ceridwen Lloyd-Morgan points out, form a record of her state of mind, as well as her activities, parallel with the journal she was keeping. See Lloyd-Morgan, *Margiad Evans*, pp. 79–80.
11 The aunt and uncle are given the actual names of Evans's relations, Aunt Fran and Uncle Donovan, and the quiet bedtime hair-curling is also recalled (*OY*, p. 86).

[12] Margiad Evans, 'How do the children?', NLW MS 23372C.

[13] See Matthew 6.28–9. Cf. Luke 12.27. It is perhaps not irrelevant to the story, and to the mother's anxieties about the family finances, that Christ is of course urging his listeners to discount concerns for material things.

[14] Margiad Evans, 'The Equerry's House', NLW MS 23365D. Moira Dearnley has pointed out that the title of this story was included in Evans's journal (24 August 1948) in a list of titles for another collection of short stories, to be called *The Blessing of the Trumpets*. See Moira Dearnley, *Margiad Evans*, Writers of Wales series (Cardiff: University of Wales Press, 1982), p. 49.

[15] The insecurities of actual childhood are, once more, registered in the second section of the story. When Arabella, as a girl, suddenly has an intuition of fear: 'Something would happen [. . .] – and what – what was it? [. . .] To the child it was terrible – as if the deck of the lawn tilted over a big wave and the leaves reeled' (*OY*, p. 157). Although the child makes no connection, we note that a few lines later she and the other children meet Mr Spring who digs the graves in the village churchyard (*OY*, p. 157). Another gravedigger appears in 'The Boy Who Called for a Light' (*OY*, p. 61).

[16] Idris Parry comments on Evans's struggle to express her experiences of 'one-ness' in *Autobiography*, 'Margiad Evans and tendencies in European literature', *Transactions of the Honourable Society of Cymmrodorian* (1971), 224–36. Cf. the same author's 'Margiad Evans', *PN Review*, 15.3 (1989), 29–32.

[17] On the origin of the story, see Ceridwen Lloyd-Morgan's note in Evans, *The Old and the Young*, pp. 198–9.

[18] Margiad Evans, 'Famous unknown children, with a digression upon Wordsworth's psychological intuitions of childhood', NLW MS 23372C.

7

Margiad Evans and Eudora Welty: A Confluence of Imaginations

M. WYNN THOMAS

'I hate my writing and nearly every one else's.'[1] Margiad Evans's bull-ish comment, recorded in a brief profile of her as a writer that appeared in Keidrych Rhys's rumbustious magazine *Wales* in the summer of 1938, shouldn't be taken too seriously. After all, she proceeded to claim that her only reason for writing was so as to be able to buy paintings and to enjoy country pursuits, an explanation that is unlikely to survive even brief enquiry. Her provocative state-ment is very much in keeping with the tone of Rhys's *Wales*, a self-consciously outrageous publication. Anxious to cultivate a cava-lier image, it aimed to convey the ungovernable, irreverent spirit of a group of young Welsh anglophone writers uncowed by their elders and indifferent to the metropolitan judgements of the English estab-lishment. But the sharply discriminating reviews Evans occasionally contributed to periodicals of the period, such as *Wales* and the *Welsh Review*, confirm that hers was a fierce, demanding and finely discrimi-nating literary intelligence.

There were, though, writers who readily survived even her most searching scrutiny. Kate Roberts was one such and another, according to Ceridwen Lloyd-Morgan, was the great writer from the Mississippi delta, Eudora Welty. In noting that the 'writers who earned [Evans's] unconditional praise were from outside the English metropolitan circle', Lloyd-Morgan identifies Welty as 'one of her great favour-ites'.[2] She particularly relished the 'power and fury' of the Southerner's prose, and Lloyd-Morgan ventures to suggest that 'Welty may perhaps have had some influence on Margiad Evans's stories', noting possible 'stylistic affinities' between them and those by Welty collected in her 1943 collection, *The Wide Net*.

Lloyd-Morgan's point is well made, but that term 'influence' is often much too glibly applied to relationships between writers without any awareness being shown of the complex, irreducibly nebulous and incorrigibly problematical character of the *kind* of relationship towards which the word vaguely gestures. Writers' notorious shyness of being cornered by such a term is no doubt partly due to their understandable wish to 'cover their tracks' – like skylarks, they prefer to take flight at a distance from their precious nests. But equally, like any reflective person, they understand how difficult it is to determine where, when and how any deep, unforeseen impulse of affinity originates. Who could possibly tell, as Wordsworth powerfully enquires in *The Prelude*, what portion of the river of one's mind comes from what source? After all, as Paul Klee otherwise imaged it, the relationship between a creative work and its 'sources' resembles that of a tree to its manifold, tangled roots: who would ever claim to be able to trace any given branch back to its origins in a single root?

Eudora Welty herself had forceful and subtle things to say about such matters. Commenting on the structure and texture of her own writings in her revealing memoir, *One Writer's Beginnings*, she thoughtfully observed:

> Each of us is moving; remembering, we discover; and most intensely do we experience this when our separate journeys converge. Our living experience at those meeting points is one of the charged dramatic fields of fiction.
>
> I'm prepared now to use the wonderful word *confluence*, which of itself exists as a reality and symbol in one. It is the only kind of symbol that for me as a writer has any weight, testifying to the pattern, one of the chief patterns, of human experience.[3]

Elsewhere in the same essay, she further glossed that term 'confluence', explaining that by it she had in mind

> a writer's own discovery of affinities. In writing, as in life, the connections of all sorts of relationship and kinds lie in wait of discovery, and give out their signals to the Geiger counter of the charged imagination, once it is drawn into the right field. (*OWB*, p. 99)

Furthermore, she insisted that such 'confluence' occurred only at those deeply solitary points when a mind paradoxically descried echoes of its own singular uniqueness in the mind of another, and was thereby quickened into new creation. 'What counts', she wrote of herself as a writer, 'is only what lies at the solitary core' (*OWB*, p. 101):

only through the mysterious experience of confluence could such a core be penetrated and impregnated while somehow remaining virginal, pristine, inviolably itself.

In making such comments, Welty had in mind not only the kind of interconnective relationships within families and communities that she, as a writer, found herself exploring in her works, but also her analogous relationship with other authors, to whom she felt deeply indebted for enabling her own creative development. Two contemporaries whom she habitually called to mind in this context were William Faulkner and Virginia Woolf. And taking our cue from Welty's suggestive remarks, it would seem appropriate to consider Margiad Evans's interest in the Southerner's fiction under the rubric not of 'influence', but rather of 'confluence', as Welty interprets that term, because 'influence' is a concept that lends itself all too readily to the simplistic assumption that one writer passively absorbs what is 'learnt' from another, and is thus in danger of failing to take into account the shock of augmented self-recognition that is always a major aspect of a writer's unexpected, creatively responsive awakening to the work of a kindred spirit. Such, it seems to me, is the most interesting aspect of the relationship one perceives between the fiction of Evans and Welty.

In instancing what she means by Eudora Welty's 'influence' on Margiad Evans, Ceridwen Lloyd-Morgan points to a common concern with 'stories about working people in disadvantaged rural communities . . . told in a superb literary style' (*OY*, p. 4). But what I have termed 'confluence' operates at an altogether deeper and more radical level than that. It manifests itself in the singular manner in which both writers handle 'place' in their respective fictions. Both of them arrestingly, and indeed often disconcertingly, view human beings and their locales simply as different points on a single continuum: between them they constitute a single, highly distinctive, 'zone of consciousness' and it is this that both Welty and Evans recognise as constituting 'place'.

How instinctive this kind of vision was to Margiad Evans may be neatly illustrated by homing in on a small detail of a remark she made during the course of her otherwise routine review of *Old English Household Life*, an unremarkable study by Gertrude Jekyll and S. R. Jones. 'I have only to lift up my eyes to see one of the objects illustrated,' she observed, 'a white, earthenware horse who with us stands on the dresser, and is dusted every alternate Friday.'[4] This very

peculiar choice of the word 'who', rather than the customary 'that' or 'which' used to denote an inanimate object, is a signature feature of Evans's strange, distinctive, style of vision and of narration. Such a disorientating, or rather reorientating, use of 'who' prepares us to read the whole phrase – 'who with us stands on the dresser' – in a similarly unconventional way, understanding it now to be suggestive of the (earthenware!) horse's living, creaturely co-existence with its human 'owners': it is together and between them that ornament and people may be said to turn the house into a place of habitation. This offers us an insight into the peculiarity of Margiad Evans's 'places', where individuals repeatedly seem not so much alive to their world, or even alive in their world, but rather alive *with* their world, as their world, in its turn, seems alive with them.

Similar moments abound in Eudora Welty's classic 'autobiography of a writer', *One Writer's Beginnings*:

> In a children's art class, we sat in a ring on kindergarten chairs and drew three daffodils that had just been picked out of the yard; and while I was drawing, my sharpened yellow pencil and the cup of the yellow daffodil gave off whiffs just alike. That the pencil doing the drawing should give off the same smell as the flower it drew seemed part of the art lesson – as shouldn't it be? Children, like animals, use all their senses to discover the world. Then artists come along and discover it the same way, all over again. (*OWB*, p. 10)

Again, where others would distinguish between the inner world of human experience and the outer world of environment, Welty, like Evans, sees only a correspondence so intimate as to bind both together into a single complex, compound entity.

In such a context, it is not surprising to find her further noting that 'In my sensory education I include my physical awareness of the word' (*OWB*, p. 10). Elsewhere, in a review, she approvingly noted that 'the imprisonment of life in the word was as much a matter of the sense with Virginia Woolf as it was a concern of the intellect'.[5] 'Held in my mouth,' Welty recollected in *One Writer's Beginnings*, 'the moon became a word. It had the roundness of a Concord grape Grandpa took off his vine and gave me to suck out of its skin and swallow whole, in Ohio' (*OWB*, p. 10). A word here becomes an essential means of ingesting the world, and is thus central to the celebration of the communion of human beings with their intimate environment. And a similar aliveness to language is used to related effect in Margiad Evans's quirky writing. In 'Thomas Griffiths and Parson Pope', the

old gardener 'smoked all the time. The wind, passing him, went away with the swirling blue breath of his pipe. The wind would jump suddenly down into the garden and shuffle the yellow ivy leaves out of the side-paths . . . The sky looked through one blue eye' (*OY*, p. 27). The human being and his environment form a single, undifferentiated, animated environment and language is a veritable incarnation of this peculiar experience of 'location'.

For both Evans and Welty, words are the synapses, or vital connectives, of the single, composite consciousness shared by people and the objects, creatures, natural forces and growing things of a unitary, inter-animated world. To read their fictions is to enter a realm not so much of cohabitation as of 'coexistentialism'.[6] The term was coined by Gaston Bachelard, the remarkable French phenomenologist who understood that 'the imagination is ceaselessly imagining and enriching itself with new images. It is this wealth of imagined being that I should like to explore' (*PS*, p. xxxvi). To that end he wrote the suggestively entitled *The Poetics of Space* (first published as *La poétique d'espace* in 1958), declaring his concern to be with elaborating 'a phenomenology of the imagination' (*PS*, p. xviii). To study 'the onset of the image in an individual consciousness', he argued, 'can help us to restore the subjectivity of images and to measure their fullness, their strength and their transubjectivity' (*PS*, p. xix). Poetry was, for him, incomparably rich in such evidence, and a similar claim might usefully be made for the value of studying the compressed, 'poetic' short fictions of Eudora Welty and Margiad Evans.

While avoiding any sustained and systematic application of Bachelard's ideas, this essay will make occasional, adventitious use of his deeply suggestive insights. And it will do so not on the tacit assumption that these insights are somehow impartially authoritative but rather on the understanding that the climate of mind one encounters in Bachelard's influential work is, in a sense, that of a particular era, approximately the first half of the twentieth century, during which the minds of Eudora Welty and Margiad Evans were also decisively shaped and they were unconsciously developing their deep, mentally formative assumptions. These two writers seem to me to have shared with Bachelard the legacy both of Symbolism and of Modernism, with their respective disclosures about the processes of consciousness, and to have operated, like him, on the same wavelength as such powerful thinkers of the period as Henri Bergson, Karl Jung and the originator of phenomenology, Edmund Husserl. But

since the elective form of Welty and Evans was short fiction rather than Bachelard's poetry, to the love they shared with him for the mysterious potencies of symbol and image they added an excited addiction to story, tale, fable, legend, talk and myth. And whereas his subject was really the solitary soul – he rather effusively understood poetry to be 'a soul inaugurating a form' (*PS*, p. xxii) – their fascination was with the highly charged, dangerously electrified, web of 'community.'

Bachelard described his intention as being to conduct a 'topo-analysis', by which he meant 'the systematic psychological study of the sites of our intimate lives' (*PS*, p. 8). Central to his researches therefore was the figure of the house, because 'the house image would appear to have become the topography of our intimate being' (*PS*, p. xxxvi). Houses also figure prominently as psychic signifiers in the fiction of both Evans and Welty.[7] One notable instance is afforded by 'The Old Woman and the Wind', the short story that may surely be accounted one of Margiad Evans's most perfect accomplishments, beautifully shaped as it is to her compelling purpose and super-charged with several of her most intimate concerns. Through the vexed and varying relationship of the strange old hill-dweller Mrs Ashstone with the wind on the one hand and the villagers below on the other, Evans was able to explore the dialectical relationship between the wild and the domesticated, the contained and the boundless, between communal living and the solitary individual, and she herself no doubt oscillated between similar poles of her own, in her strange oddity of being a somewhat suspect female writer, semi-detached from the community around her and inclined to feel much closer kin to the natural world than to her immediate neighbours. Her ambivalent feelings about her imperious creative powers are mirrored in Mrs Ashstone's misgivings about her extraordinary relationship with the wind, and in the latter's allegedly 'witch-like' nature is suggested Evans's uneasy interest in the socially suspect powers of an unconventionally-minded female artist of her time.

The story is brimful of perfectly functional examples of her perpetually startling lyricism, faithful as the text is to the strange originality of her habitual angle of vision. Mrs Ashstone's house, like her very being, exists strictly in a dialectical relationship with the wind that is the presiding, defining presence of her life as it is the dominating presence in her environment. Its invisible plastic power is everywhere palpably apparent, as in 'the flattened smoke coming

down the chimney's neck in wisps like her own hair' (*OY*, p. 35). It even determines Mrs Ashstone's physical bearing, as 'her small, clutching hands' seemed always to be 'chasing the flying and broken things floating in the wind's wake' (*OY*, p. 36). From the vantage point of the village her remote upland house, distantly glimpsed 'where the greyness roamed the bracken,' resembles 'a white pebble that a boy had flung out of the river' (*OY*, p. 38). But such impression of impregnable solidity is contrary to the old widow's familiar experience of the house as an excitingly precarious, permeable dwelling-place, its porousness being the converse of the resolute solidity with which it stoically withstands 'the boulders of air the wind rolled against it' (*OY*, p. 38).

Bachelard writes at some length about poets' preoccupation with the relationship of house to storm. In evoking, as so frequently they do, the 'bestiary of the wind' (*PS*, p. 44), writers seem to him to focus figuratively on the destructive, animalistic side of the energies by which humans and universe are alike possessed. They turn the 'combatant house' (*PS*, p. 46) into a beleaguered fortress from which is exerted the 'counter-energy' of an individual's moral integrity. There is much of this in 'The Old Woman and the Wind', as the 'cruel rage and cruel envy' (*OY*, p. 37) that Mrs Ashstone feels for the villagers below finds expression through her relationship with the wind. Indeed, in describing a tempest, Evans accidentally echoes Bachelard *avant la lettre* when she says that 'a beast roared in the chimney' (*OY*, p. 38). But Evans also puts the wind to very different figurative use, such as is again touched on by Bachelard when he considers the ways in which, through its dynamic relationship to wind and storm, a house can become expressive of man's 'cosmic' positioning. 'The Old Woman and the Wind' is centrally concerned with this 'anthropo-cosmology' (*PS*, p. 470). Mrs Ashstone's cottage exists primarily as the site of a dialectical relationship evidenced in the alternation of the monstrous howl of the tempest and a correspondingly heightened, uncanny silence in which quieter powers make their mysterious presence known: 'she heard nothing except clock, kettle, and mouse. She felt that she lived in these stirrings' (*OY*, p. 39). When Mrs Ashstone finally throws in her lot with her exposed upland home, rather than opting to take the enticingly offered key to one of the trim houses in the village, she understands perfectly the reason for her choice:

Down there I couldn't hardly tell whether I were glad or sorry. I couldn't seem to *hear*, and that's the reason as I don't want to change my ways

now. I do like to hear even the mice in me cupboard, and the cock-roaches, I'm that curious and learned. (*OY*, p. 43, emphasis in the original)

And implicit in her decision is the determination to be absolute mistress of her own house rather than a mere 'home-keeper' for a husband, as the village women seem primarily to be. When Evans observes that Mrs Ashstone was so 'ignorant' and desocialised that she'd forgotten that the prefix 'Mrs' signified a woman's married status and now supposed it instead to be a first name, like 'Annie', she is implying a great deal. And when Mrs Ashstone claims a singular and unlikely 'learnedness' for herself at the end of the story, Margiad Evans fully respects the apparently anomalous application of such a term. Such superior 'learnedness' is the old woman's reward for her socially-perceived 'ignorance', her unregenerate, pagan independence.

Halfway through 'The Old Woman and the Wind', Captain Ifor, a pillar of the local village community, teasingly asks the visiting Mrs Ashstone whether she's 'down from [her] eyrie'. She is baffled: 'what was an ar-ray, and what had it do with her hill?' (*OY*, p. 37). Her maverick intelligence, resolutely uncomprehending of village ways, is as ever the strong solvent of established language, attuned as she is to the alternative idiom of wind, and stone, and mice, and grass, and rain. At the story's end, Captain Ifor repeats the word in his attempt to tempt her away from her hill fastness: 'Get you down from that eyrie of yours' (*OY*, p. 42). But in rejecting his proffered key Mrs Ashstone also refuses to speak his language, and as the conclusion of the story confirms, her instincts in this respect are true ones. Live in an 'eyrie' she may, from the villagers' point of view, but through her strange communion with her environment, her intimate relationship with the secret consciousness of place, the old woman knows her house to be 'eerie' in quite another sense: an 'uncanny' place in which she is at once safely at home and permanently 'unhoused', an unaccommodated dweller, along with mouse and boulder and wind and grass, in the cosmos itself. In 'The Old Woman and the Wind' the house thus becomes, in Bachelard's terms, 'an instrument with which to confront the cosmos' (*PS*, p. 46). 'A house that is as dynamic as this', he writes elsewhere, 'allows the poet to inhabit the universe. Or, to put it differently, the universe comes to inhabit his house' (*PS*, p. 51).

'The house', Bachelard further remarks, 'shelters day-dreaming, the house protects the dreamer, the house allows one to dream in peace' (*PS*, p. 6). Such indeed proves to be the case in Eudora Welty's 'June Recital', the remarkable long story that appears in her consummate collection of interconnected tales, *Golden Apples*.[8] All these stories are related, either directly or indirectly, to Morgana, a small Mississippi town named in part, as Welty repeatedly affirmed in interviews, for the *fata morgana*, or will-of-the-wisp, liable to lead humans into the realm of the equivocal and to leave them stranded in that chimerical place. A connoisseur of this disorientating oneiric realm, like Bachelard, Welty repeatedly mentioned dream time and dream states in her fiction and associated her art quite closely with reverie. Such a state dissolved the floor of memory, admitting human beings to the mysterious underworld of time which is paradoxically our real abode. Daydreams seemed to her naturally attuned to that understanding of our temporal existence that she identified in *One Writer's Beginnings*, an understanding born of the distinctively Southern sense of time she shared with her great contemporary and friend William Faulkner:

> [Living] is our inward journey that leads us through time – forward or back, seldom in a straight line, most often spiralling. Each of us is moving; remembering, we discover; and most intensely do we experience this when our separate journeys converge. Our living experience at those meeting points is one of the charged dramatic fields of fiction. (*OWB*, p. 102)

It is this dimension of time that is explored in 'June Recital'.

This substantial story interweaves the experiences and recollections of two youngsters, the boy Loch and his gawky adolescent sister, Cassie, via those dreams of yesterday that are triggered involuntarily in them by hearing the opening bars of Beethoven's Für Elise being played in the apparently empty house next door, a place unnervingly haunted for them both by the ghosts of their past. The difference between their recollections is due to a number of different factors, including their different gender, their contrasting ages and their respective temperaments. In addition, Loch's mental state is heightened by the malarial fever from which he is suffering while Cassie's disturbed equilibrium reflects in part the liminal state between adolescence and adulthood when personal identity, agitated not least by sexual awakenings, remains relatively fluid and undecided.

Riveting his attention on the house he can see from his sickbed, Loch responds to it as 'something very well known indeed. Its left-alone contour, its careless stretching away into that deep back-yard he knew by heart. The house's side was like a person's, if a person or giant would lie sleeping there, always sleeping' (*GA*, p. 21). Like Cassie he is readily inclined to see the house as a site of fantasy, akin to the magical places of fairy-tale and animated by a similarly exotic life. While Cassie aspires to a more dispassionate, 'grown-up' assessment of the property, she nevertheless finds her imagination becoming inexorably entrapped in its labyrinthine, infinitely recessive interiors and feels herself succumbing to its bewitchment, just like Hansel and Gretel in the witch's house. Drawn to the window, she stands there, her pale hair infested with paper curlers, her small head vulnerably balanced on her nakedly exposed frail neck, her feet bare, and looks 'pathetic – homeless-looking – horrible. Like a wave, the gathering past came right up to her. Next time it would be too high' (*GA*, p. 37). As her gaze becomes ever more fixated on the supposedly vacant building next door, she senses what she suspects to be 'agitation. Some life stirred through. It may have been *old* life . . . a life quicker' than the life of her own family, 'more driven probably, thought Cassie uneasily' (*GA*, p. 35). And for both Loch and his sister, the house (like the house in 'The Old Woman and the Wind') seems to mark a distinctive zone of consciousness where human life appears to be unified with, and thus inseparable from, the natural world. Indeed, in its decay, the house is in some respects 'maintained' by the natural cycle: 'Leaves and their shadows pressed up to it, arc-light sharp and still as noon all day' (*GA*, p. 35). As Loch's eyes scan a mattress in the old, semi-derelict property, 'A shadow from a tree, a branch and its leaves, slowly travelled over the hills and hollows of the mattress' (*GA*, p. 21). It is an example of what Bachelard had in mind when he spoke of '[the] coexistence of things in a space to which we add conscious-ness of our own existence . . . a very concrete thing' (*PS*, p. 203).

Gradually, both Loch and Cassie become aware of temporary inhabitants in the house – the old watchman who spends his days sleeping in one room; Virginia Rainey and her sailor boyfriend who use another room as their sexual trysting-place; and an eccentric old woman whose antics in the downstairs room which still houses the piano seem increasingly puzzling and bizarre. Onetime tomboy Virginia, it turns out, looms large in the charged narrative of Cassie's memories of her childhood. Ever socially untameable, a free spirit

scornful of the ways and opinions of others, the liberated Virginia was, and is, the pet hate and secret love of the inhibited Cassie. An inveterate worrier and social conformist, she yearns to emulate Virginia in her blithe insouciance and disregard for social *mores*. But at the centre of the story stands the nervous, awkward, unconventional figure of Miss Eckhart, an everlasting social outsider, indeed a virtual outcast, of German descent whose spinsterish occupation it was to teach Virginia and Cassie and other little girls how to play the piano that now stands abandoned and is the centre of the onlooking Loch's increasingly fascinated attention. It gradually becomes apparent that it is the eccentric Miss Eckhart's intention, in the derangement of her dotage, to set the piano alight and to burn the entire house down. However, while it is this act of arson that leads to the climactic action in the story, the real subject of the leisurely expansive and endlessly sinuous narrative is the whorl of the past and its infinite encroachments on the present. 'The space we love,' said Bachelard, 'is unwilling to remain permanently enclosed. It deploys and appears to move elsewhere, without difficulty; into other times, and on different planes of dream and memory' (*GA*, p. 53).

According to Bachelard, 'The oneirically definitive house . . . must retain its shadows' (*PS*, p. 13), and in 'June Recital' the old house preserves its mystery to the end, the mystery of man's temporal existence. Welty allows us to experience 'the house in its reality and in its virtuality, by means of thought and dreams' (*PS*, p. 5), and Margiad Evans performs a similar miracle in stories like 'Into Kings'. This wondrously intense and exquisitely wrought tale is self-confessedly one that entices us, like 'June Recital', to step out of the world of ordinary place and time. Little five-year-old Harry, we're told at the outset, 'neither lived nor remembered in sequence, and life and his dreams appeared without reason. He was a busy visionary' (*OY*, p. 44). It is courtesy of his consciousness that we are able to enter the twilit world of enchantment that is the living-room of Peewit Castle, a little cottage – whose strange misfit of a name mystifies him – occupied by elderly Mr and Mrs Lackit and their disabled daughter. And Harry's adventuring secretly over their threshold is also an enactment of the little boy's discovery of his own mysterious interiority: 'He began to be aware he was a being – a *private* being, and that he need not tell' (*OY*, p. 46).

The living room's dim interior is a magical zone of restlessly metamorphosing forms, like the face of the invalid asleep in the chair,

whose eyes and mouth seem to be twitching monstrously as the fire-light plays over her features. The most dominant feature in this fairy-tale realm is the tall gilded mirror, in the 'poetry' of whose glass all the objects in the surrounding space seem to be strangely stilled, 'compacted [. . .] into a tilted but solid peace' (*OY*, p. 48). Indeed, in this living-room the whole domestic world seems set permanently slightly askew. For the little boy Harry, epiphany comes in the form of a 'cheap round shaving glass' (*OY*, p. 49). Caught in its reflection, a vulgar golden wreath from the cheap, tired old pier-glass is transformed before his enraptured gaze into the golden crown he would have expected to find in a cottage otherwise so puzzlingly called a castle. And once he discovers the crown, Harry instinctively garbs the old Lackits in the gorgeous glamour of regal regalia:

> Hadn't he always wanted to know why they lived in a castle? It was the greatest of marvels, the most delicious answer [. . .] The most real of stories seemed about to begin. He saw Mrs Lackit as queen with a great yellow ring around her brows. And driving her, in the little black tub, Mr Lackit, the king. Poor drab old Nellie the donkey disappeared, and in her place in the shafts trotted a circus pony with red harness . . .
>
> He didn't believe in the crown, any more than he believed that the excited heart he could feel was alive in the mirror. Yet, like the heart, it existed *outside*. Perhaps, yes, somewhere? (*OY*, p. 49, original emphasis)

Little Harry has, then, stumbled wonderingly on what is for Margiad Evans, like Eudora Welty, the real source of story: his entry into that shabby little living-room crammed full of tasteless bric-a-brac is actually his entry into the very womb of narrative, as Evans and Welty understood it. What makes it so, is that it is the realm of what E. M. Forster, in a famous phrase, termed 'the twilit vision'. It is a region where things and people alike both are and are not as they seem. As critics regularly point out, at the very heart of Welty's fiction lies her consciousness of this doubleness, and the same could be claimed for Evans's stories. She points to this in the concluding line of 'Into Kings'. After the wonders of mirror and 'crown', the little boy next literally awakens in the invalid a wholly unexpected, clumsy and inarticulate tenderness, and is caught by old Mr and Mrs Lackit at the very moment this melting happens. Gruff Mrs Lackit is moved to quiet tears, leaving her husband as the only one who has not been turned by the affecting scene into something rich and strange. 'He', writes Margiad Evans, 'was the only person of the four to whom nothing could possibly have been otherwise than as it was' (*OY*, p. 50).

Literalist to their 'visionary', he stands there, searching for his pipe, to remind us that the world is, indeed, mundane as well as magical. The true artist's genius lies, of course, in granting equal 'reality' to the scene in both its transfigured and its untransfigured states, and Evans was faithful to this 'double vision' in every detail of her writing. 'It was November,' we learn at the beginning of 'Into Kings', 'the brown winds were visible with leaves. Yellow and tortoiseshell, grey and lacquer red, mahogany and gingerbread colour, they span and skimmed' (*OY*, p. 46). The first sentence, that remarkably views the leaves as a visible incarnation of the wind, is counterbalanced by the second, where the simple reality of the leaves in all the variegated colours of their ordinary, rich leafiness is reasserted.

For both Evans and Welty, it was art that frequently brought out the 'inscrutable' mystery, the unsuspected 'otherness', of people. The word 'inscrutable' comes from the concluding sentence of 'Miss Potts and Music'. Rather like 'June Recital' it is a story that pivots on the astonishing transformation that happens when an otherwise nondescript young girl sits at a piano and begins to play. And similarly in 'A Modest Adornment', who could possibly have dreamt that Miss Allensmore, ostensibly a 'fat black cauldron' (*OY*, p. 117) of an old 'hag', finds secret ecstatic – and indeed erotic – fulfilment by playing the oboe with breathy, sensuous lyricism. Similarly, at the climax of the collection's title story, 'The Old and the Young', the young girl Arabella stumbles on a scene where the old woman, Tilly, dances to the vigorous popular tunes being played by robust Josephine, in her gardening breeches. The scene is an idyllically communal one, embracing both the old and the young, but earlier in the same story, as little Arabella thinks wistfully of Josephine's magical playing, she suddenly recalls how her violin could suddenly change its tune. First, to Arabella's distress, would come the breakdown of melody into seeming cacophony – 'her legs would straddle and stiffen and out of the violin came the screams of a parrot in the rage. To the child it was terrible – as if the deck of the lawn tilted over a big wave and the leaves reeled' – and then the instrument would settle to an entirely different key: 'The tune would fall, would drop half a tone as if the horizon had darkened, as if the sun had been lowered like a lamp – and Arabella knew it was Beethoven' (*OY*, p. 157). The change of key signifies, of course, the music's explorations of complex, subtle moods and experiences unknown to childhood and thus foreshadows the conclusion of the story, when little Esther – younger even than

Arabella – breaks the charm of the innocent moment by enquiring, with semi-conscious pertness, where babies come from.

As for the otherness, the secret selves and 'virtualities' of localities, what better language could there be for exploring such uncanny dimensions of familiar 'reality' than that afforded by fairy-tale, legend and myth, a narrative vocabulary in which both Evans and Welty were fluent. Such tales 'reflect upon forces and signs', as Bachelard put it (*PS*, p. 41). The interconnected stories in Welty's *The Golden Apples* make particularly powerful use of such rich psychic materials. The hints are already there in the very title of the opening story, 'The Shower of Gold', where the part of Zeus is taken by the elusive King MacLain, who, floating free of his family and from all the moral constraints of provincial Morgana, roams the countryside at will, mysteriously materialising on fleeting occasion like the incarnation of some amoral, sexually potent and predatory force of forest life. The very stuff of legend, MacLain is a figure ancient and distant as classical mythology yet familiar and local to Mississippi folk culture, the stories about him naturally resembling the tall tales of the south-west frontier on which Welty modelled her notable early novel *The Robber Bridegroom*. King MacLain is flesh-and-blood yet also exists as a figment of the feverish imaginations of the locals in whose circulating tales he looms so menacingly yet enticingly large. In this latter respect he is the means whereby Welty implicitly reflects on the origins and functions of tale-telling (and its close relative gossiping) in the 'economy' of communal existence.

His unpredictable appearances in the wood are mirrored by his unexpected appearances in the tales themselves. He returns, for example, in 'Sir Rabbit', as a kind of king of the woods entitled to exercise his seigneurial rights over all those who venture into his kingdom. When Mattie Will goes hunting with her frightened husband, aptly named Junior, and his young black helper, the party is from the outset much more apprehensive about running into MacLain than it is intent on shooting a rabbit. And when MacLain does lazily appear, drifting between and behind the trees like a stalking ghost, he has only to fire a load of buckshot vaguely in Junior's direction to scare him into a dead faint, leaving Mattie entirely at MacLain's disposal. Zeus to her Leda, he complacently has his will, and as he saunters off, so 'a dove feather came turning down through the light that was like golden smoke' (*GA*, p. 108). No swan he, nor shower of gold, but

nevertheless he has all the attributes of a Zeus, divinely careless of human ties and obligations.

Welty's interest in communal tales is paralleled by Margiad Evans's fascination with the stories she heard on the lips of local villagers. In the footnotes to her edition of *The Old and the Young*, Ceridwen Lloyd-Morgan consistently demonstrates what an appetite Evans had for recording such materials, out of which she regularly compiled her own fictions. And, again like Welty, she was concerned to capture the actual words used by her unconscious 'informants', sensitive as both were to the fact that there could be no successful separation of oral story from the exact manner, as well as occasion, of its utterance. Evans and Welty were both connoisseurs of dialect, of inflection, of the very pace and rhythm, sound and texture, of narrative that actually constituted the very marrow of story; its core substance and meaning. And both writers placed storytelling at the very epicentre of their art. Welty, for example, stated that

> Family stories are where you get your first notions of profound feelings, mysterious feelings that you might not understand till you grow into them. But you know they exist and that they have power.[9]

While, reviewing a book on the Welsh border country, Evans could admire the photographs but very much regretted 'that there is not just an inch for the scraps of story belonging to the places they illustrate.'[10]

The interest of Evans and Welty in such matters seems to have been intensified by a melancholy intuition that such tales, in their experience, were the exhalations of a dying world. In 'The Boy Who Called for a Light', a story that is, to some extent, like some of Welty's, so constructed as to reflect on its own character as a tale, the adult narrator finds his narrative spontaneously invoking for him the vanished circumstances of its own origins:

> I'd no idea of remembering that much. It all fits in so that it is difficult to take out the pieces I need. I seem to be back there in the moon-blanched lane, standing under the tree, hearing the sounds drop out of the sky, falling clearly, with a starry stillness and shapeliness on the fields of hills. (*OY*, p. 63)

As is clear from a number of stories in *The Old and the Young*, the recurrent elegiac note is due, in part, to their being the anxious product of a time of war and therefore of a period of profound, and potentially cataclysmic, change. Measured in terms of its damage to the intimate

relationship between young woman and fiancée in 'The Ruin', this wartime world of change leaves its physical mark, in 'The Old and the Young', on the pre-war layout that so suited slow and leisurely village life. 'The village has changed,' notes Arabella. 'The bridge has been widened for war traffic, and ruined, the eighteenth-century sundial has been carted away and left in a corner, a tomb without a grave' (*OY*, p. 150).

Arabella's worried, bewildered, question – 'Where's everybody? And what has happened to us?' (*OY*, p. 150) – is one with which Welty may very well have sympathised. She was, after all, one of the nostalgic Southern generation of writers and intellectuals whose unease about the new, post-bellum South was so arrestingly voiced in the classic 'Agrarian' manifesto *I Take My Stand* (1930).[11] Although never committed, like her distinguished contemporaries John Crowe Ransom, Allen Tate and Donald Davidson, to its socially conservative agenda, Welty certainly sympathised with its concern to defend traditional, rural, communal values from the destructive encroachments of the aggressively individualist and functional ideology of the victorious, heavily industrialised Northern states of the Union. Along with her other contemporaries in what was a brilliant constellation of talents from across the diverse regions of the South – writers like William Faulkner, John Crowe Ransom, Allen Tate, Robert Penn Warren, Flannery O'Connor, Tennessee Williams, Cleanth Brooks, Katherine Anne Porter and Erskine Caldwell – Welty developed her own rhetorical strategies (instanced, for example, by her preoccupation with time, memory and the past, and by the value she placed on collective imaginative enterprises such as the tale) for addressing the crisis of her South. Indeed, the very ambivalences of her 'double vision' were very much in keeping with the famous and influential concern with paradox of other Southern writers and critics of her time – a concern that spawned what became known as 'the New Criticism'.

Underlying this conspicuous privileging of creative equivocation – and the related appreciation of the pregnant indeterminacies of image and symbol (what Bachelard called 'the coalescence of images that refuse an absolute anatomy' (*PS*, p. 29)) – lay Southerners' conviction that Northern culture was so single-minded and monomaniac in its pursuit of 'progress' that it had completely lost the capacity to appreciate the rich complexities and insoluble enigmas of human existence. Believers in the straightforwardly open road to

ever-increasing prosperity, the materialistic Yankees were deemed indifferent to Welty's dominant sense of 'spiralling time' and the brooding omnipresence of the past. In this context, 'the double vision' was very much understood by the Agrarians and others to be, in the US context, the unique gift of traditional Southern culture; a legacy of inestimable value to the arts. In Welty's work (as, most famously, in Faulkner's) this cultural climate is powerfully inscribed in an original style that often seems also to be evocative of the torrid body heat of the South and the miasmic quality of vision it so readily generates:

> [Like the physical climate, the style creates] an evanescent medium in which things are constantly melting into one another or dividing their identity between different levels of experience. The mind absorbs the landscape and then the landscape absorbs the mind . . . Everything . . . is animate and apparently capable of numerous metamorphoses: so much so that the metaphors lacing the description hardly seem like metaphors at all, but literal accounts of a magical environment. All is shifting, all is clear and yet somehow fluid, intangible.[12]

And while Margiad Evans's style is, of course, as markedly different from that of Welty as the climate of the Welsh border country is different from that of the Mississippi delta, it nevertheless – or so this essay has been suggesting – possesses in its own answering way many of the salient characteristics of the style of Welty so accurately characterised in this passage by Richard Gray.

Also like Welty, Evans is resistant to the ironing out of life to a bland 'Yankee' flatness. Again like Welty, she is temperamentally inclined to think of life instead as an elusive, ephemeral function of the space-time complex. The defining characteristic of 'the space we love', according to Bachelard, is that it 'is unwilling to remain permanently enclosed. It deploys and appears to move elsewhere without difficulty; into other times, and on different planes of dream and memory' (*PS*, p. 53). In 'Solomon', Evans uses the fantastical consciousness of a little boy, Albert (known in the family as Barrabas), to illustrate how a cavernous house, 'filled with the green air of the trees' but with 'too few people in it' (*OY*, p. 97), proves to be exactly such a space as Bachelard specifies. So large and time-scarred is the house that 'nobody can number what's in it or guess who dropped and hid the things they find' (*OY*, p. 100). And just as its endless multiplicity of rooms is for Albert suggestive of its labyrinthine history, so, when he joins his sisters for an imaginary tea-party in the grounds, he informs them – 'in a voice that seems to come through the back of his

head' – that '"I'm listening to where all the little paths go to"' before selecting from the 'skein' 'one he thinks wants to go home' (*OY*, p. 102). Living as he does in a world in which everything has a will and secret purpose of its own, he laughs and then 'turns to see which way the laugh went' (*OY*, p. 102). And when he looks up, he 'gazes amazed at some sky which is coming round the corner of a steamy cloud' (*OY*, p. 102). There is, therefore, no fixed centre, no commanding 'point of view' in his universe, which resembles a post-Einsteinian universe of relativity complete with time-warped space through which it is impossible to travel in any straight line of understanding. As an electric storm gathers overhead, little Albert makes his way out of doors to join the old gardener, Meffy, and notices that from the back the great house 'is ponderous age. Compared with the façade it is earthenware compared with porcelain' (*OY*, p. 104). The story he demands from Meffy is 'part of the house', and the old man's 'memory is inseparable from the place' (*OY*, p. 104).

The violent storm proves to be the destabilising force that radically unsettles the 'normality' in which Albert's parents habitually dwell, so that they, too, are not so much drawn as harassed into sharing his vision. His father panics at the thought that one of the children may have got hold of his gun, with fateful consequences. His mother, returning at a wild gallop from her visit elsewhere, roams the rooms of the house closing windows against the tempest, becoming ever more uneasy. Even the candle she holds in her hand turns sinister, and seems to release unquiet presences wherever it goes:

> And then she sees it is not light she is bringing with the candle, but only a yellow smirk like fog.
>
> She hears the voices in the kitchen, she hears a moan of thunder and her own shadow twirls about her as she returns. It's as though some loosened entity of the house were revolving wherever she moves, now dancing as in a cage, now fitfully concealed within her own body. (*OY*, pp. 105–6)

Hastening to a window, and throwing up the sash, she is transfixed by the site of little Albert sitting in the yard exposed to the lightning and stirring the embers of a fire. Suddenly he seems to her a sinister, foreign creature: 'For a moment she hardly recognizes him. That's what frightens her' (*OY*, p. 106). On the verge of hysteria she screams at him to come in and as he lifts his face in acknowledgement it is unnervingly caught in the 'white flash of light to earth', while thunder breaks overhead like an avalanche (*OY*, p. 106).

It is an eerie story steeped in a sense of the uncanny. By increasingly infectious degrees that reach their zenith when the house becomes complicit with the storm, home is inverted into a hostile, unsettling place, and intimate family ties become a source of terror rather than of consolation. Knowing that the story was written in October 1945, immediately after the conclusion of the war in Europe, I find it difficult not to associate it with the atmosphere of a period of profound dislocation, when it was clear that old ways, old values, old relationships could not simply be resumed because everything had irrevocably changed. The deep resultant sense of unease was the shadow side of the enthusiasm for change that found historic expression in the unexpected election of a Labour government at that precise juncture. In that sense, 'Solomon' may be read as capturing the last phase of an extended period of disorientation beginning with the nightmarish anxieties of the pre-war years, and continuing through wartime experiences such as those of the Blitz, when many observers were shocked and bewildered by eviscerated houses whose most intimate interiors were suddenly exposed to casual public view. A classic text of the first, pre-war, phase would be Vernon Watkins's 'Ballad of the Mari Lwyd', with its invocation of the ghosts that come ominously knocking at doors and windows on New Year's Eve and press most peremptorily for admission to the domestic hearth:

> Out in the night the nightmares ride;
> And the nightmares' hooves draw near.
> Dead men pummel the panes outside,
> And the living quake with fear.
> Quietness stretches the pendulum's chain
> To the limits where terrors start,
> Where the dead and the living find again
> They beat with the selfsame heart.[13]

As for the second phase, what text is there that more powerfully evokes the stunned air of the London streets at dawn following an air-raid than 'Little Gidding', when T. S. Eliot encounters ghosts of the distant past released by the chaos onto the streets of the present. And it is in the company of texts such as these that I feel 'Solomon' naturally belongs as it uses a rural setting to suggest the way in which the heart of war-shocked, post-war England broods on its new strangeness to its old, familiar self.

One possible reason, therefore, for the 'confluence' of the imaginations of Margiad Evans and Eudora Welty may be their common

source in an experience of radical social and cultural change. But, as this essay has already intimated, there are many more reasons than one for the uncanny mutuality of their minds, and the enigma of their creative correspondence must ultimately be allowed to remain insoluble. What is clear, however, is that although Welty's talent had considerably more reach and range than that of Evans – allowance having first been made, of course, for the fact that the American outlived the Welsh border writer by more than half a century – the creative imaginations of the two writers were, nevertheless, joined at the hip, unique though their respective achievements indisputably were. 'Art, then,' wrote Bachelard, in another of his resonant apothegms, 'is an increase of life, a sort of competition of surprises that stimulates our consciousness and keeps it from becoming somnolent' (*PS*, p. xxxiii). And it is precisely for the remarkable power they both held in common to 'increase life' in this irreplaceable way that we should value the haunting fictions of both Margiad Evans and Eudora Welty.

Notes

1. 'Bibliographies of modern Welsh authors: no. 4 Margiad Evans', *Wales*, 5 (Summer 1938), 181–2, 182.
2. Margiad Evans, *The Old and the Young*, ed. Ceridwen Lloyd-Morgan (Bridgend: Seren, 1998), p. 15. Hereafter *OY*.
3. Eudora Welty, *One Writer's Beginnings* (Cambridge, Mass.: Harvard University Press, 1983), p. 102. Hereafter *OWB*.
4. Margiad Evans, 'Book reviews: *Welsh Border Country* and *Old English Household Life*', *Wales*, 10 (October 1939), 285–6, 285.
5. Eudora Welty, *A Writer's Eye* (Jackson: University of Mississippi, 1994), p. 26.
6. Gaston Bachelard, *The Poetics of Space*, tr. Maria Jolas (Boston: Beacon Press, 1994), p. 201. Hereafter *PS*.
7. Dr Kirsti Bohata has drawn to my attention the following intriguing entry from Margiad Evans's journal for August 22, 1943: 'One of my strange house dreams, about mother. Big rooms, big beds & black staircases, the moonlight like curtain's [?] rods. All these things I must remember.' (NLW, Margiad Evans MSS 34).
8. Eudora Welty, *The Golden Apples* (New York: Harcourt, Brace and World, Inc., 1949). Hereafter *GA*.
9. Quoted in Jan Nordby Goetland, *Eudora Welty's Aesthetics of Place* (London and Toronto: Associated University Presses, 1994), p. 364.

[10] Evans, 'Book reviews', 285.

[11] The most comprehensive and authoritative introductions to Southern culture during the period in question are Richard Gray, *The Literature of Memory: Modern Writers of the American South* (London: Edward Arnold, 1977) and Richard Gray, *Writing the South* (Cambridge: Cambridge University Press, 1986).

[12] Gray, *The Literature of Memory*, p. 178.

[13] Vernon Watkins, *Collected Poems* (Ipswich: Golgonooza Press, 1986), p. 47.

8

The Apparitional Lover: Homoerotic and Lesbian Imagery in the Writing of Margiad Evans

KIRSTI BOHATA

On 14 November 1935, Margiad Evans recorded the first anniversary of her 'wedding day'. Writing in her journal, wearing 'the scent that Ruth chose for me, for our first anniversary', she lamented, as she would often do during the course of their relationship, that Ruth herself was absent.[1] Evans's affair with Ruth Farr began in April 1934 and lasted several years, but the two women remained close friends into the 1940s.[2] An important if often difficult figure in her life, Ruth Farr has been pushed into the background in studies of Margiad Evans's life and work in a manner typical of the historical 'ghosting' described by Terry Castle in *The Apparitional Lesbian*.[3] Margiad Evans's short story about a lesbian triangle, 'A Modest Adornment', is well known and Arabella's homoeroticism in *The Wooden Doctor* has been discussed in an excellent essay by Sue Asbee,[4] but there has been no wider study of the homoerotic and lesbian content of Evans's writing. The present essay draws on the journals and letters of Margiad Evans to outline the biographical context of Evans's interest in depicting women's same-sex love and attraction in her fiction. Its primary aim, however, is to discuss the homoerotic imagery and metaphors repeatedly used by Evans in her work. Of central importance to her oeuvre, I argue, is a modern reworking of the paradigmatic figure of the apparitional lesbian, but Evans also uses metaphors of music, illness and an array of lesser images to articulate homoerotic or lesbian dimensions in her writing.

Ruth Farr entered Margiad Evans's life in February 1934 (Evans was nearly twenty-five and Ruth was twenty) when Evans's mother, Mrs Whistler, brought her home to Lavender Cottage. It was not love

at first sight. Evans's journal records with cruel glee how she and her sister hid, 'Nancy behind Betty's door & me under Nancy's bed with my feet sticking out'.[5] But by the end of April, an intense emotional and physical relationship had begun: 'I'm in flames and burning. Run Arabella, run. A physical tie connects us so that we can hardly tear ourselves apart.'[6]

From the beginning, the two women had to contend with opposition and setbacks, including maternal disapprobation on both sides, periods of enforced absence, as well as Farr's (unspecified but long-term) ill-health. The early months of their relationship were shattered by Ruth's infidelity with Nancy (Evans's younger sister), yet Evans and Farr eventually exchanged rings although they would never live together as Evans wished.[7] The fragmentary journal for the months and years following their trip to Iceland in June 1936 does not include a record of how or when their sexual relationship ended, but Ruth remained an important presence in Evans's life long after she married their mutual friend Michael Williams in 1940. In letters to her husband, Evans describes scenes of domestic harmony when Ruth occasionally stayed with her at Potacre during the war. By 1942, however, Evans was aware of a growing divide. In a letter to Michael in November, she wrote:

> I told Ruth that just where I part from everybody else *I meet you*. Don't ever worry. [. . .] Poor dear Ruth. Whether she's aware of it or not our old intimacy is finished. . . . It's inevitable.[8]

At just this time, in fact, Ruth was embarking on a new life and new intimacies of her own, in the orbit of the Christian visionary and healer, Dorothy Kerin.[9]

This essay cannot offer a detailed biographical narrative, still less a psychological study, of Margiad Evans. The discussion that follows does comment on how Evans represents her sense of sexuality and sexual identity in her journals with reference to the historical context of post-1928 Britain,[10] but it specifically resists attempting to foist a sexual identity upon her. Indeed, Evans herself resisted available categories. Although she once combatively referred to herself in French as a '*déviant*'[11] she did not name herself lesbian even though she describes Ruth as such. Neither did Evans see herself in terms of the androgynous bisexual favoured by Virginia Woolf[12] and others (in whom the two genders coexist) although she was clearly attracted to both men and women before she fell in love with Ruth Farr.[13] Evans's

account of the start of her relationship with Farr is one of reluctant seduction, a 'deadly pursuit I had endured without help or relenting',[14] followed by a rapidly intensifying love, and it is love that Evans uses to 'justify' her physical relationship with Ruth. Outraged that Nancy had falsely suggested Evans had first slept with Ruth 'for experience', she defended herself and justified her actions in a long diary entry:

> Experience? As I'm a woman with two breasts and a waiting womb I swear that I was terrified to sleep with Ruth because I didn't know what she would do to me. I loved her. In love I slept with her. I never denied my love when it was there: I never lied about it. As it grew I confessed it.[15]

Her approach is firmly personal and she sidesteps labels of sexual identity altogether. Nevertheless, we can locate her representation of relentless pursuit and eventual seduction in the context of contemporary sexology.

Evans's understanding of Ruth, in the early days at least, chimes with Havelock Ellis's categories of masculine and feminine female inversion. Ruth is pictured as a masculine invert (the congenital or 'true' invert) – Evans declares: 'Ruth is a man'; she has a 'male mind'.[16] Intriguingly, in trying to understand the nature of a woman who loves women, Evans constructs an image which essentially represents the lesbian, or invert, as a female body haunted by a male soul: 'If Ruth's female body can't affect her male mind in life, why should it in death? But has she a female brain? If not, then it seems to me is proof of survival, or at any rate of their [*sic*] being something within us that is unphysical and detached.'[17]

Alongside passionate love and desire for Ruth, Evans's personal journals include registers of loathing and repulsion, including the imagery of morbidity long associated with homosexuality (from the 'deathly pursuit' quoted above, to her 'sick self' which longs for Ruth in 1939).[18] Significantly, perhaps, this negative language appears mainly in the periods before and after their love affair, during which images of warfare and embattlement are common. But Evans was also capable of mobilising homophobic stereotypes against Ruth when hurt: Ruth as a wrecking sexual predator, leaving behind a string of conquests at school,[19] and this virulent description of 3 July 1934, written at the height of her anger at Ruth's infidelity:

> In Ross today my eyes were gladdened by the sight of a real seedy Lesbian of Ruth's tribe, walking with her sweetie, a woman in a frilly dress whose scarlet under lip hung over her chin. The Lesbian was sickly

pale; she wore a squashed felt hat and a linen suit: her gait was at once idle and feeble. She drooped, she sagged, she was mouldy and sulky, brow beaten and vicious. Her inert gaze expressed the same cloudy suffering. She slouched weakly and indifferently beside the woman who strutted beneath her picture hat and gazed around possessively.[20]

Evans seems to have seen herself as the 'sweetie' in her relationship with Ruth: the feminine invert – the accidental, pragmatic or seduced homosexual – one of the women who, in Havelock Ellis's formulation, were 'the pick of the women whom the average man would pass by', women who would be in a heterosexual relationship had a man made an offer.[21] In the first, ambivalent days of their relationship Evans wrote, 'So, I have discovered that we must go apart or live together. If the latter, she will lose me to the first man who casually attracts me [. . .]'[22] Having perhaps communicated this view, she writes two days later that 'Ruth was harsh. On what grounds, of good or bad, has she a right to judge me? She has behaved naturally to herself, why not I also?'[23] Thus, Evans sees her sexuality as different from Farr's, but equally 'natural'.

Ruth, according to Evans, was a 'confessed' lesbian[24] but, sadly, she was not, it seems, free from self-doubt. In December 1935, whether prompted by self-loathing or a desire for affirmation of her sexual identity, Ruth appears to have sought professional intervention – to the dismay of Evans:

Perhaps the psychologists will separate Ruth and me. I feel sick. [. . .] When she told me I looked at her with utter terror as if she contained me and was going to be destroyed. The next moment I seemed to be filled with her. I could not tell of us two which was single.[25]

This was a period in which the pressures on their relationship from without were multiple and Evans imagined 'A council of fiends [. . .] sitting over us',[26] writing that 'Present and future have no hint of Ruth. I adore her – she worships me and the word they yell is wrong wrong wrong . . . '.[27] A welcome reprieve was apparently delivered by Ruth's doctor: 'Dr Francis said that it was all a nonsense. He gave her names of men whom he said would help us. I was delirious with relief',[28] and on 15 December Evans noted that 'Havelock Ellis has written to Ruth'.[29] Despite these external pressures and the frequent absences for which Evans berated Ruth, the couple remained together. Nor would Evans disown her homosexual past once committed to a

heterosexual marriage. In a letter to Michael Williams in March 1943, Evans wrote:

> There are a good many bitter feelings re our friend Miss Ruth [. . .] there being such a person at all reminds me of a past which I am beginning woefully to regret. Not from the moral point of view but because it was unsuitable. So unsuitable & I might have done so many things. In Iceland for instance – I was a good swimmer almost as good as the Icelanders – and I never swum [*sic*] with them in their hot pools. [. . .] Burn this letter – don't add it to your packets. It's my one wish now that Ruth should not seem [to] assume a false value in my life.[30]

Whatever Evans's regrets, this is a disavowal that explicitly avoids repudiation of the 'moral' (i.e. lesbian) dimension of their relationship even as she wishes to marginalise Ruth's place in her biography.

Despite Evans's words in 1943, Ruth Farr was an important part of Margiad Evans's life during the period when she was writing *Creed* (1936) and she was also a presence when she was compiling some of the material that would become *The Old and the Young* (1948). Evans's interest in lesbian relationships continued well beyond this period, however, as seen in 'The Haunted Window', an unpublished short story dated 1953. While I do not wish to suggest that all her interest in women's relationships and homoerotic representations of female forms are purely autobiographical in conception, what is fascinating about Ruth's presence in Evans's life is that Margiad describes her contact with Ruth in her private writing using images and metaphors which reappear in work intended for public consumption.

Music, apparitions and illness are metaphors used to suggest lesbian relationships or create a homoerotic subtext in Evans's fiction, along with a scattering of other tropes including birds, flowers, gardens and orchards, jewellery, witches and a primitivist representation of racial otherness. This essay will concentrate on just the first three major metaphors, beginning with Evans's use of the spectral. In *The Apparitional Lesbian*, Terry Castle outlines a literary history in which the lesbian was primarily imagined as a dysphoric 'absence, as chimera', as a ghost (*AL*, p. 30). In the eighteenth and nineteenth centuries, she argues,

> lesbianism, or its possibility, can only be represented to the degree that it is simultaneously 'derealized,' through a blanching authorial infusion of spectral metaphors. [. . .] One woman or the other must be a ghost, or on the way to becoming one. Passion is excited, only to be obscured, disembodied, decarnalized. The vision is inevitably waved off.' (*AL*, p. 34)

111

Ironically, as Castle suggests, 'the case could be made that the meta-phor meant to derealize lesbian desire in fact did just the opposite' (*AL*, p. 63). The ghost will not be laid to rest and haunting suggests a relentless presence. Rather than obliterating 'the disturbing carnality of lesbian love', the 'ghostly figure [. . .] was inevitably a notion of reembodiment: of uncanny return to the flesh' (*AL*, pp. 62–3). In the twentieth century the apparitional lesbian as a device of disavowal is overtaken by the reappropriation, or 'seductive permutation' (*AL*, p. 60), of the metaphor of haunting as a prelude to or extension of a more corporeal lesbian connection. The possession of Stephen Gordon, at the end of Radclyffe Hall's *The Well of Loneliness* (1928), by the spectral voices of past and future women demanding 'affirm-ation of existence', marks a turning point in the 'repossession' of the spectral metaphor by lesbian writers (*AL*, p. 52). Margiad Evans's use of spectral imagery belongs for the most part to this modern use of the apparitional lesbian to encode a lesbian desire which nevertheless remains unnamed for her characters as well as her readers. Significantly, however, Evans's imagery treads a borderline between a coded affirmation of same-sex relationships and a dysphoric ambiva-lence that is represented in language of morbidity and death, images that also have a long semantic connection with homosexuality.[31]

In Evans's journals, Ruth is imagined as a powerful and erotic spec-tral presence. In hospital in March 1936, waiting for an operation to remove her tonsils, Evans imagines the effects of the anaesthetic: 'My mind will be undressed and they will hear its naked footsteps pacing in the dark . . . Coming towards them heedlessly passing them, haunt-ing the name of Ruth . . . The name of Ruth . . . the face of Ruth [. . .] Ruth far off on the hills with the wind at Tretire . . .'[32] Elsewhere Ruth's 'lips [are] like candle flames which blown out stay spectrally painted in their own close form! How to describe those two lips, not shining, not glowing, languid and sickly reflections, yet so insuffer-ably alluring that mine must cover them to hide them?'[33] Yet, as these quotations show, this erotic spectre is also associated with images of illness. Evans's bed becomes a haunted sickbed:

> Her ill health sits on my pillow, her cowardice at my feet, her suffering lies beside me, her love is a weight on my chest, but worst of all her charm [illeg.] under my eyelids and I lie there thinking of her as I have thought on and off all day. So my bed is possessed, my thoughts are seized, even my dreams and there seems to be no rest and no refuge.[34]

As late as 1942, Evans records the end of a week-long visit from Ruth:

Last night – the first after Ruth had gone I dreamed I was a ghost. I don't know whether I was my own phantasm only that a sort of consciousness & sight with me behind it slid across sideways & covered the outline of a [illeg.] We stood there, my self and the stranger and I saw the hands stretched out, laid flat with the thumbs tucked in on an ebony grand piano . . . or a coffin.[35]

This ambivalent mixture of erotic spectre and troubling illness appears in an unpublished short story, 'The Haunted Window', in which Evans uses apparitions to bring two psychic women together, implying that their visionary abilities are signs of a lesbian sexuality, while suggesting that the union of the two women will ultimately result in the illness and death of one. In fact, there are many ways in which this story reveals its lesbian subtext – from the disingenuous opening line, 'Miss May Hill was ordinary',[36] to her 'frighten[ing]' dreams of a nightingale singing in the willow tree in her 'neglected' but luxuriant garden, to the way the story can be read as a parable of sexual repression and glib medical 'cure' of sexual difference (HW, f. 58). But most important are the visions of ghosts which Miss May Hill sees on the occasion she 'did commit eccentricity for once' (HW, f. 58) by going into the garden at night after a disturbing dream of mundane existence. Looking into the lighted living room window, she sees a terrifying apparition of a grotesque woman bloated and distorted by illness, sitting in her living room accompanied by an unfamiliar yapping dog. When she looks through the living room window from the inside, she sees a funeral cortège waiting outside her house. May Hill develops an uncontrollable fascination with the visions in the window, 'and a purely malicious hatred' (HW, f. 63) and terror of the dog (which it is tempting to see as an ironic shadow of the sexually symbolic fox of her earlier novel *The Wooden Doctor*). Miss Hill is hospitalised after a policeman finds her collapsed on her garden path one night, overcome by fear. Miss Hill has confided her abnormal visions to her closest friend, the widow Mrs Flora Vickson – a psychic who confirms what May Hill can see – and while in hospital May invites Flora to move in with her. Meanwhile, a self-satisfied but not unkindly Scottish doctor eventually takes an interest in the case and takes May Hill home. After gaining her trust by pretending to see the apparitions too, he smashes the living room window, fracturing the view of the funeral outside. The doctor thinks he has broken the delusion when May Hill finishes off the job, shattering the remaining glass and thereby destroying the ghostly image,

only for her friend to move in the following week, bringing with her the very mongrel terrier puppy she has seen in her vision.

Miss Hill's vision of her future self in 'The Haunted Window' is reminiscent of the portrait of Miss Allensmore, in 'A Modest Adornment' (and indeed Mrs Trouncer, the slatternly character in *Creed*, who dies on the steps of a mouldy cellar, wanting someone to love her). The apparition has:

> a very large, fat face like a dropped plum with a whitish bloom as of powder or sheer decay over the purple features. It was leaning on a plump fore-arm, on a cushion, at the end of *her* sofa. A thermometer stuck out of the lips. Beside it, a yellow and white curly mongrel terrier stood with its forepaws on the cushion. From its open jaws came the movements of barking, but no sound from the ghost dog disturbed Acacia Avenue. Such a face as this woman's is only seen when the person is surely near death. (HW, f. 59, emphasis in the original)

A repulsive and terrifying sight, this spectre nevertheless provides the impetus for May Hill to invite her friend to move in, and she admits, frankly, that she would not be ashamed to let her friend witness her extraordinary secret: 'Oh Flora, come and live with me. You've seen it too – I should be quite easy with you seeing it' (HW, f. 66). That this is more than a practical living arrangement is manifest in Mrs Vickson's reaction to the proposal:

> there would have been silence in the room, if it hadn't been for Mrs Vickson tapping her marquise ring on the locker until she said: 'I can't commit myself yet May. It might work. The lease of the flat is up – and there's an intense, but not too intense sympathy between us – and we're both psychic too. I must say that once your attitude to our Helpers on the other side – was – was – or would have been – against it. But that's different now. Thank you May. I'll think it over. Cheer up dear.' (HW, ff. 66–7)

Flora sees their shared spectral visions as a necessary prerequisite for their cohabitation, while the tapping of her ring hints that the invitation is a symbolic marriage. Interestingly, the marquise (a pointed oval-shaped) ring worn by Mrs Vickson recalls one of Margiad Evans's own dreams recorded in a letter to her husband around March 1943:

> I had a strange dream last night that Miss Harrington took off my rings – my wedding ring & the worn one – & put one of her own on my finger instead. I saw it clearly – a ring of pale gold & set in it a very odd, beautiful semi-clear green stone, oval & convex. Such a queer green – not

emerald but pale & yellowish. This must be some underground reverberation of Peg Leg's remark that Miss H[arrington] & Miss Trevor were *sweet hearts*.

I saw them walking. We met by the gate at the bottom of Panbrook pitch. I forgot to ask her if she had such a ring.[37]

Miss Harrington and Miss Trevor have been suggested as a model for Miss Allensmore and Miss Plant, and here we see a much more personal imaginative response to the idea of two female sweethearts, as Margiad Evans imagines her wedding ring replaced by Miss Harrington's green ring. This dream ring, with its curious green stone, and the implicit symbolism of infidelity in Evans's dream, might also be seen as inspiring the green gloves Mrs Webb gives to Miss Plant as a token of her love and her attempt to usurp Miss Allensmore in 'A Modest Adornment'.

Published in *The Old and the Young*, 'A Modest Adornment' is an accomplished story about the 'secretly weary' relationship between fat Miss Allensmore and emaciated Miss Plant, as the latter lies dying of heart disease, and the attraction of a third woman, a villager named Mrs Webb, to Miss Plant. The construction of Miss Allensmore as a lesbian is based on her portrayal as a glutton, a witch and a cannibal, as I have discussed elsewhere, and much more positively as a musician (discussed below).[38] But the apparitional is central to Mrs Webb's attraction to Miss Plant, as is the circumstance of Miss Plant's terminal illness. Mrs Webb's fascination is expressed through a series of powerful visions in which she imagines Miss Plant's fabled romantic walk to London – 'a superstitious long way' – and believes that Miss Plant has remained there 'in spirit' (*OY*, p. 127), which of course she has in the sense that London is the place she announced her love for Miss Allensmore. On a trip to the city, Mrs Webb imagines Miss Plant visiting the same places, until at the site of an execution at the Tower she imagines not 'some great man' but 'poor Miss Plant [. . .] She saw her. She seemed to quaver across the air, across the sunshine, weaving herself, as it were, *behind* the April light' (*OY*, pp. 127–8, emphasis in the original). On the journey home, she dreams that Miss Plant is asleep in the next seat, 'leaning on her' (*OY*, p. 128). And recalling Miss Plant on her deathbed, Mrs Webb makes the connection between her sick profile and the ghost she may yet become: 'Remembering [. . .] the hair like glass or rice, and the strange fluttering eyes, the shape of which was an intensity in itself, Mrs Webb felt how easy it would be to see Miss Plant's ghost' (*OY*, p. 130).

If Mrs Webb's desire is evoked through apparitions of Miss Plant, Miss Allensmore's feelings are expressed through her oboe. Indeed, music (often Beethoven) is a recurring theme in Evans's depictions of same-sex attraction, from the dancing Mrs de Kuyper in *The Wooden Doctor* to the musicians in 'Miss Potts and Music' and the violin-playing Josephine and dancing Tilly who so fascinate the child Arabella in 'The Old and the Young'. Miss Allensmore's 'educated' and incomprehensible music sets her apart from the villagers as Miss Potts's music sets her apart from the other children. More important than a simple marker of difference, however, music is used in 'A Modest Adornment' to reveal the contours of the relationship between Miss Allensmore and Miss Plant, specifically their disconnection in the present: 'When Miss Allensmore played in her presence, Miss Plant would sit looking desultory, like a person who is taking part in a hopeless conversation' (*OY*, pp. 116–17). In life, Miss Plant's silence 'hadn't the length or loyalty needed for music' (*OY*, p. 116), but in death, she embodies a powerful silence to which Miss Allensmore responds:

> Silence. With her instrument ready, Miss Allensmore turned to face it. [. . .] [S]ilence was transparent to Miss Allensmore. The musicians' dawn she called it. And now she was face to face with the biggest silence she had ever known and all the time the nurse was gathering up this and that she was longing to breathe across it the first dangerous phrase. (*OY*, p. 118)

Margiad Evans creates a chiaroscuro in which sound and silence are contrasted in place of, and sometimes as extensions of, lightness and darkness – where the silent Miss Plant's dead eyes become the darkness outside the cottage window. At the end of the story, suddenly believing Miss Plant to have betrayed their 'profound, if secretly weary, fidelity', Miss Allensmore faces internal uproar as she becomes filled with the awareness of her own 'quaint affection' and again, the music of the oboe is linked to a profound expression of love between women:

> She could not speak: her outcry was mental only. There, leaning on her umbrella, she stood, speechless, as when, with her oboe, she turned towards the silence with the first low summons to the hordes of sound, as when, all those years ago, Miss Plant had come to London just to say to her, 'I can no longer bear to live away from you.' (*OY*, p. 135)

Music is the key to Miss Allensmore's emotional register as well as a metaphor for her sexuality, and even the more muted rhythms of the

Christian Litany lead to a moment of intimacy between Miss Plant and Mrs Webb as they recite the 'rhythmic words' together (*OY*, p. 130).

The compelling power of music is used to express same sex desire and attraction in its most positive shades in Evans's writing. In 'The Old and the Young', Arabella's fantasy of playing 'the violin so violently and romantically that everybody in the world wanted to hear her' (*OY*, p. 156) merges with her erotic, possibly orgasmic, vision of Josephine playing her violin in the garden:

> [Arabella] stopped dead in the middle of the path when she thought of Josephine playing [. . .] And then – how awful it was – Josephine – Something would happen – she would be walking about the lawn in all the bright green plumage of the garden, playing, playing, the mouth, the eye, the fingers and the heavenly strings all singing – and what – what was it? She would stop – her legs would straddle and stiffen and out of the violin came the screams of a parrot in a rage. To the child it was terrible [. . .] then the tune would fall, would drop half a tone as if the horizon had darkened, as if the sun had been lowered like a lamp – and Arabella knew it was Beethoven. (*OY*, p. 157)

Later, Josephine, in her 'gardening breeches', plays her violin – described as a 'boy's whistle' – to accompany the old woman, Tilly, who has inexplicably started to dance. Arabella is 'entranced' by the sight of Tilly dancing, and as she watches her face, she becomes a wraith, leaning 'hard against the house until it seemed the old stones were sinking in and softly overlapping her bones' (*OY*, p. 162). Self-consciously, as she has done throughout this story, Arabella is aware of fixing the moment in her memory.

Apparitions, music and memory intersect in the hauntingly suggestive story 'Miss Potts and Music' in which the spectral figure of the musically gifted but tormented Miss Potts haunts the narrator. The story draws on Dante Alighieri's *La Vita Nuova* (1295) in which the poet describes his profound love for Beatrice, his muse and a woman whom he has seen only twice – the first time when they were both children.[39] 'Miss Potts and Music' is composed in a dreamlike prose which slips back and forth across time, the narrator's memory and fancy coalesce to conjure the story of the mysterious, compelling, twelve-year-old Constance Potts. An accomplished violin and piano player, Miss Potts is dominated by her female relatives and she is seen (in a sinister and homoerotic echo of Dante's Beatrice) 'always between two women as though the world were a slender path endlessly

enclosed' (*OY*, p. 114). In this story, music sets Miss Potts apart. That music is linked to a female sexuality which does not reach out to men is suggested by the portrait of the piano teacher, Miss Potts's aunt. Miss Amy Holman, or B.B.S.H. as our narrator nicknames her because she 'combines Rossetti's Beata Beatrix and my own idea of Sherlock Holmes' (*OY*, p. 108), is one of the three female relatives who watch over Miss Potts. Her androgyny and otherworldliness, with 'thin ethereal face', is counterbalanced by the very feminine and physical sexual symbol of the 'unfurling rose in a silver vase' (*OY*, p. 108) which she keeps on top of the piano, and the matching 'damson dark rose' (*OY*, p. 110) she wears on her grey dress.

Miss Potts's music signals her difference but is also the means by which she leaves a profound impression upon the narrator in a singular moment of revelation comparable to Arabella's entrancement with Tilly and Josephine described above. In 'Miss Potts and Music', the narrator's heightened response to Miss Potts's playing is described in a passage which adopts the imagery of dreams, ghosts and visions:

> When she began to play I found no one to look at. And suddenly I wanted a face who would meet my eyes and my astonishment. For without premonition how could I have been prepared? *Astonished –* I was so astonished that I might have been picked off the bench and set down in the middle of the churchyard without noticing I'd moved. And my chest felt blank, not uncomfortable, but simply empty, as if I had no breath and no need to breathe. [. . .] Miss Potts might have been thinking it to me as she played it. It seemed as if I could see the arch of the notes in the air through the thick red panels of the door, definite and lovely as the swallows strung on the telegraph wire, but of some unknown spirit colour resembling white gold . . . (*OY*, pp. 112–13, emphasis and ellipsis in the original)

At the sound of Miss Potts's music, the narrator herself is transformed into a ghostly or spiritual being, with no need for breath, as comfortable in the churchyard as on a bench, seeing the 'spirit colour' of the music which the other children seem not to recognise. The imagery is also deeply sensuous and erotic, arched notes emanating through the thick red panels, and a communion of two minds in the music.

It soon becomes apparent that this is a story concerned not with the reality of Miss Potts – indeed, the narrator fears 'probably there was nothing, nothing at all interesting, one way or the other' (*OY*, p. 114) about her. Rather, it is the narrator's sense of something unnamable, something 'inscrutable' (*OY*, p. 115) about Miss Potts that drives

– haunts – this story. The narrator's fascination with Miss Potts is infused with images of haunting and death. The story is inspired because the narrator half believes she has seen a ghostly child in a tree, a vision that becomes the recollection of Miss Potts. In the memories and remembered daydreams recounted in the narrative, Miss Potts is repeatedly associated with graveyards, tombstones and coffins: a graveyard is the view from the window of B.B.S.H.'s teaching room; on an imagined social call 'I saw [Miss Potts and B.B.S.H.] with the little black coffins that held their fiddles' (*OY*, p. 110); the narrator imagines B.B.S.H.'s 'peculiar ecstatic smile, holding Miss Potts by the hand as I had sometimes seen her do when they walked quickly across the churchyard to wherever they were going' (*OY*, p. 110); Miss Potts is remembered – or imagined – 'jumping off a tombstone, and running along the churchyard wall as far as the iron lamp . . .' (*OY*, p. 111); the narrator 'hear[s] again her *spirited* voice' (*OY*, p. 111, my emphasis). And the narrator's memories of Miss Potts are compared to her memory of witnessing a ghostly car, 'one of those intense psychic impressions' children conceive of as real:

> I can believe that she did these things and I saw her. But who can tell me? I don't think I saw half of what I remember, and I may have dreamed or imagined it. Certainly it seems real. Terribly noticeably real. But then so does the dark red car going swiftly along without a driver, but containing a man asleep in the back with his head on a white bolster. (*OY*, p. 111)

Moreover, her memories of Miss Potts are explicitly configured as a haunting: 'Yet she did that once come back. When I read the letter which was going to be burned on my bonfire. She came, as she has come to-night, abruptly, not with a speech, but with a certain astounding brevity, like a ghost story in a newspaper' (*OY*, p. 114).

In this story the narrator's complex desire and resentment of Miss Potts is expressed in her wish to appropriate the latter's musical abilities. She is hurt when B.B.S.H. will not allow her to play Beethoven's Moonlight Sonata which Miss Potts has mastered and fantasises (like Arabella in 'The Old and the Young') about being given a violin which she will play better than Miss Potts and will keep all her life and be buried with upon death, leading a friend to identify her morbidity: '"You always talk about being dead", cried Marian' (*OY*, p. 110). Miss Potts leaves the town and the narrator becomes obsessed with what happened to this intriguing girl in later life. Knowing her to have

been taken to Weymouth for her health, she imagines her locked in an endlessly repeated ghostly walk:

> growing unobtrusively older between them [her mother and grand-mother]: walking along the esplanade in that kind of seaside rain which seems to oil the roofs and the waves, glancing occasionally aside uneas-ily and rapidly at the swishing, dishevelled beach, the whorls of clinging, shining shells . . .' (*OY*, pp. 114–15)

In an alternative vision, the narrator imagines Miss Potts has given up music and selected 'lipstick and dancing and marriage', the implied opposite. Consequently, the violin is stored on top of a wardrobe and her life 'allow[s] the women a pension of moderate affection only. Nothing lonely, slow or wistful after all . . .' (*OY*, p. 115). The loneli-ness, the difference, the dedication to music – and the stifling presence of those guarding women – is contrasted with a prosaically disap-pointing heterosexual life. But Miss Potts may just as easily be dead (*OY*, p. 107) – her health is poor but 'Constance is so devoted to her music that there is no holding her back' (*OY*, p. 114). There is an implicit connection between her pursuit of music and her illness, and thus illness, music and the apparitional reinforce each other in a lesbian interpretation of this story.

Illness, as I have already suggested, is a common feature of Margiad Evans's 'lesbian' stories. Miss May Hill's spectral self in 'The Haunted Window' is an unhealthy shade of mauve and sits with a thermometer in her mouth (and a coffin waiting outside). Miss Plant, with 'gaunt cheeks and brows' (*OY*, p. 126) is dying of heart disease, while her illness offers the excuse an 'invalidish' (*OY*, p. 122) Mrs Webb needs to initiate their intimacy. Miss Potts's aunt, B.B.S.H., is admired not only for her music but for her 'brilliant ill-health' (*OY*, p. 111). Sue Asbee has discussed how illness in *The Wooden Doctor* is bound up in a complex and ambiguous way with Arabella's developing sexuality; her bouts of abdominal pain summon the comforting presence of her beloved doctor, but Asbee also points out that Arabella's illness provides the opportunity for homoerotic encounters, such as when a nurse, who 'move[s] like a person dancing a slow sensual tango' is granted permission to examine the mysterious patient.[40]

In her journals, Evans introduces images of illness in homoerotically-charged scenes. In April 1934, Ruth walked out on her mother after an argument and became a troublesome and rather needy guest, initially resented by Evans, who felt both encumbered and self-conscious, as a beautifully composed paragraph for 15 April conveys:

> I light my cigarette and then forget to draw at it and it goes out. It's a hot night after the warmest day for April we've had these 40 years: seventy five degrees in some places. We have a red [fire?], the windows are open, and the curtain hanging loose from the hook. The room smells of smoke. Ruth Farr sits by the fire absently rubbing her hands. N[ancy] sits on the coal box casually drawing, me at the table, and we both feel Ruth who is a confessed & obvious Lesbian. I'm hot, but I can't take off my jumper because I'm afraid, because my breast is beautiful & she would look at it, perhaps think of it afterwards. In the corners of our lazy & warm conversation I remembered how I lay in my bed when I was 16 & was sick all over my own face & the bedclothes. 'I wonder what my brother would say if he knew I was a lesbian' says Ruth & odds & ends of her sex keep cropping up in [illeg.]. Now N. is shading heavily – the charcoal scrapes across the cardboard.[41]

The scene is sensuous and uncomfortably charged, as conveyed by the use of the present tense. Evans's awareness of the erotic beauty of her body in the eyes of another woman is implicitly linked with her memory of being sick, which presumably necessitated removing her night-clothes in a way she contemplates but resists in the present. The language of disease is similarly employed when their relationship was nearly derailed in May 1934. Evans condemns Ruth and bewails her hurt:

> Ruth has made our love homeless. There's nothing left of her but the recollection of the ghastly[?] fire in my chest which craved her touch; a cancer on my lips and in my breast like mother's lopped and bitter bosom on whose poisoned veins I would perversely lean my head, feeling the same vindictive corrosive blood pour through me, as if I were in her womb.[42]

The cancer is both Evans's hurt and a 'perverse' metaphor for her unquenched desire, represented by vampiric imagery and a transformation of Ruth into a mother whose womb Evans would inhabit. In a monograph which compares the social taboos surrounding lesbianism and cancer, Jackie Stacey has discussed how lesbianism is imagined as a disturbing return to the mother – as a desire for 'non-differentiation' resulting in a 'symbolic death'. Using Julia Kristeva's model of abjection, she sees lesbianism and cancer as being figuratively and culturally linked in the abject disgust and fear they both evoke.[43] In Evans's profoundly unmaternal image, the destruction of her bond with Ruth is figured in terms of disease and her remaining desire is thus transformed into sickness, a longing for a

return to a mother whose nurturing (and erotically desirable) breast is poisoned and disfigured, even absent (lopped), the cancer spreading from the lips to the breast to the poisoned 'vindictive' veins.

Breast cancer is used in *Creed* to bring two women together in a homoerotic scene in which Florence Dollbright shows a lump on her breast to her friend Emily in a carefully prepared bedroom, complete with welcoming fire. Summoned by Florence

> Mrs. Jones, in her husband's coat, ran with Florence to the Dollbrights' house. They went up to the bedroom where, to her surprise, a fire was burning. Florence banged the window. Her hand was lying on her breast.
>
> 'Emily I don't want you to tell anybody,' she pulled down her dress.
>
> 'My good God, you haven't found anything there!'
>
> Florence nodded feebly. Her hands would settle on the venomous centre of her fear. [. . .]
>
> She knelt in front of Emily, and took her by the wrist.
>
> 'Feel there. You can press your hand in. I never feel any pain.'
>
> Emily pressed her fingers into the undercurve of the breast. Beneath the flesh she felt a hard, seemingly movable substance. She gave an hysterical sob, and hid her face in Florence's shoulder.[44]

Just as in *The Wooden Doctor*, cystitis gives the nurse access to Arabella's vulva, in *Creed* breast cancer allows for an intimate scene with homoerotic undertones that are linked with the sharing of a secret between two women.[45] The scene in which the cancer connects the two women in *Creed* is echoed through the novel in multivalent echoes of frustrated erotic, emotional and spiritual desires. In a preceding scene, Florence's husband clasps her hand to his chest in a sterile adumbration of this scene: 'He felt an actual pain in his chest as if part of him had been torn away' (*C*, p. 30) before he relinquishes it, believing it a temptation of the flesh. Later, he will recoil in dismay at the sight of the hospital matron who has just assisted in Florence's mastectomy: 'Her apron was actually marked all over the front with the blotches of his wife's blood, from fresh pink to deathly scarlet' (*C*, p. 124). The links between the journal entry and the fictional imagery are striking and underline the relevance of reading Evans's fiction alongside her personal writing.

Readers familiar with Evans's oeuvre, and indeed her private journals and letters, will be aware of her recurring and multivalent uses of the imagery and metaphors I have discussed here in a specifically lesbian context. Illness, music and her use of apparitional metaphors,

while often referring to sexuality, extend beyond straightforward representations of lesbian desire. But rather than trying to divide her work into lesbian and 'other' writing, perhaps it would be more helpful to study the intersections of meanings in these recurring images, looking for the overlap between her interest in same-sex attraction and other concerns, much as Evans's relationship with Ruth Farr overlaps with her marriage to Michael Williams. In a more extensive study, one might also be able to extend lesbian readings of Evans's work, particularly when one notes the frequency with which some of her central images (the wind, gardens, flowers, dreams, witches, darkness, her sense of difference and mystery) appear in lesbian texts by other contemporary writers, alongside which Evans's work demands to be read.

Thus there is clearly more work to be done in analysing the rich lesbian content and subtexts of Evans's writing and in reading her work within contemporary traditions of 'Sapphic modernism'.[46] As I have tried to show, Evans's complex and often autobiographical explorations of female sexuality are both sophisticated literary constructions and important experiments in representing and resisting modern categories of sexual identity in the first half of the twentieth century.

Acknowledgements

I am profoundly thankful for Cassandra Davis's permission to quote from the journals and letters of Margiad Evans. I am indebted to Ceridwen Lloyd-Morgan for her great academic generosity and comradely support. Her expertise has allowed me to navigate a manageable path through the extensive archives at the National Library of Wales. Any omissions or errors are mine, of course, as are the opinions offered in this discussion.

Notes

1   National Library of Wales (hereafter NLW) MS 23577C. Ruth Farr was in fact 'driving Liberals to vote for that ass A. E. Farr', since 14 November 1935 was also election day.

2   Although it would be more correct to speak of 'Peggy Whistler' when discussing the journals, I use the literary alias Margiad Evans throughout in the interests of consistency and to avoid generating the impression that

her private and public selves were completely separate: in many instances the private and public writing overlap.

[3] Terry Castle, *The Apparitional Lesbian: Female Homosexuality and Modern Culture* (New York: Columbia University Press, 1993), p. 5. Hereafter *AL*. Margiad Evans's journals and letters in which she describes her relationship with Ruth were donated to the National Library of Wales by her husband, but biographers have chosen not to discuss this important relationship in any detail. Ruth Farr appears in Moira Dearnley's 'Writers of Wales' monograph as a 'friend' with whom Margiad Evans travelled to Iceland (Moira Dearnley, *Margiad Evans* (Cardiff: University of Wales Press on behalf of the Welsh Arts Council, 1982), p. 26). She is treated more suggestively but still somewhat obliquely in Ceridwen Lloyd-Morgan's biography which holds back from revealing the full extent of the relationship (Ceridwen Lloyd-Morgan, *Margiad Evans* (Bridgend: Seren, 1998), p. 55). Barbara Prys-Williams is a little more direct in a chapter on Margiad Evans in her PhD thesis 'Variations in the nature of the perceived self in some twentieth-century Welsh autobiographical writing in English' (unpublished PhD thesis, University of Wales Swansea, 2002), but the published version skims over the nature of their intimacy (Barbara Prys-Williams, *Twentieth-Century Autobiography: Writing Wales in English* (Cardiff: University of Wales Press, 2004), p. 44). In the thesis, Prys-Williams is dismissive of Evans's relationship with Ruth, describing it as a 'largely unhappy' episode on the way to a 'mature' heterosexual marriage (p. 42).

[4] Sue Asbee, 'Margiad Evans's *The Wooden Doctor*: illness and sexuality', *Welsh Writing in English: A Yearbook of Critical Essays*, vol. 9 (2004), pp. 33–49.

[5] NLW MS 23366D, 18 February 1934.

[6] NLW MS 23366D, 26 April 1934. This is the journal entry in its entirety. Arabella is one of Evans's alter egos.

[7] There is no journal for the year between July 1934 and September 1935, the period during which the 'wedding' would have taken place, on 14 November 1934. A journal entry for 20 January 1936, however, mentions that Peggy wears Ruth's ring (NLW MS 23577C).

[8] Margiad Evans MSS 121 (29 November 1942), emphasis and second ellipsis in the original.

[9] Ruth Farr was born on 9 October 1913, the youngest of five sisters and a brother. She attended Sibford School, an enlightened Quaker establishment that taught technical skills to girls and domestic skills to boys. She left in 1928 and after a largely unsuccessful attempt to develop a career as a writer, she trained in furniture design at the Central School of Arts and Crafts before entering a furniture-making firm in Worcestershire, a career quickly interrupted by war work. For a time Farr had found 'a desirable escape' in agnosticism, but later she began to search for religious meaning.

In November 1942 she was admitted to Chapel House (in Ealing, west London) a place of Christian healing – although it is not clear from what ailment, physical or mental, as well as spiritual, she was suffering. After three months she started to work in the Home for four hours a day, as Michael Williams records in a letter to Evans after paying a visit to Ruth (Margiad Evans MSS 170, postmarked 24 March 1943). Farr had found her spiritual and emotional home and would spend the rest of her life devoted to the Christian hospital and its founder, the visionary and healer, Dorothy Kerin (1889–1963). Writing in 1970, Ruth Farr records how she, like so many who came into contact with Kerin, felt a 'love which came from God but was somehow merged with the thought of Dorothy' (Ruth Farr, *Will You Go Back?* (Tunbridge Wells: The Dorothy Kerin Trust, 1970, new edn 1977) p. 58). And in an article for her old school magazine, Farr wrote, 'Though I did not know it at the time, Ruth had met her Naomi' (Ruth Farr, 'Healing and making whole', reprinted in *Burrswood Herald* (Spring 1984), 50–3, 51). Farr became Dorothy Kerin's god-daughter and continued to work (as a technician, car driver, assistant editor and more) and to live at Burrswood (the new premises of Kerin's hospital from 1948 to the present) until her death on 28 November 1986. I am very grateful to John Taylor, Burrswood Archivist, for his invaluable help in tracing Ruth Farr's history and supplying copies of articles from the *Burrswood Herald*.

[10] In 1928, Radclyffe Hall's *The Well of Loneliness* was published, with a short 'commentary' or endorsement by the sexologist Havelock Ellis. The book, a portrait of lesbianism heavily reliant on Krafft-Ebing's theories of sexual inversion which Ellis himself had adopted and developed, was prosecuted under the Obscene Publications Act 1857. The trial ensured notoriety for the book and its author with her carefully cultivated mannish style as 'the media circulat[ed] a visible embodiment of a specimen "invert"' (Laura Doan, *Fashioning Sapphism: The Origins of a Modern English Lesbian Culture*, New York: Columbia University Press, 2000, p. xv).

[11] NLW MS 23366D, 20 July 1934.

[12] Virginia Woolf, *A Room of One's Own* ([1929] Orlando, VA: Harcourt, 1989), pp. 97–9. See also Virgina Woolf's *Orlando* (1928).

[13] As well as the fictional(ised) homoerotic encounters in *The Wooden Doctor* discussed by Asbee, a suggestive entry in Evans's diary records her erotic-ally charged reaction to Greta Garbo in the iconic film Queen Christina ('a lesbian actress, portraying a notoriously lesbian queen' (*AL*, p. 2), as Terry Castle summarises the film). 'Mother took us to see Greta Garbo as Queen Cristina. Her movements are full of sharp dignity; she is amazingly tall, straight and narrow. She has no bum and no hips and little pointed breasts very far apart and her face is long, hollow, spiritual with expressive, mystic badly made up eyes. Her hair is very beautiful – straight, fine, soft, a darkish blonde. The film rotton [*sic*] . . .' (NLW MS 23366D, 1 March 1934).

[14] NLW MS 23366D, 24 July 1934.

[15] Ibid. It is difficult not to hear in this impassioned statement an echo of the end of Radclyffe Hall's *The Well of Loneliness*, in which Stephen Gordon's 'barren womb became fruitful', possessed by teeming millions of past and future female voices, in a throbbing description somewhere between orgasm and the throes of labour. See Castle, *The Apparitional Lesbian*, pp. 51–2.

[16] NLW MS 23366D, 17 April 1934 and 16 April 1934 respectively.

[17] Ibid., 16 April 1934.

[18] NLW MS 23577C, n. d. (August 1939), f. 125.

[19] NLW MS 23366D, 20 June 1934.

[20] Ibid., 3 July 1934.

[21] As Lucy Bland, citing Havelock Ellis, explains: 'Assuming only opposites attract, the "masculine" aspect of the female invert compelled the attraction to a "feminine" woman – not to another (mannish) "true" female invert, but an "artificial" homosexual, "a class in which homosexuality [. . .] is only slightly marked". [. . .] Because such women could equally well turn to heterosexuality, congenital female inverts were presented as both predatory and the sexual rivals of men.' (Lucy Bland, *Banishing the Beast: English Feminism and Sexual Morality 1885–1914* (London: Penguin 1995), p. 263).

[22] NLW MS 23366D, 29 April 1934.

[23] Ibid., 1 May 1934. Although later Evans would briefly make 'A vow to her and a vow to myself. A vow against it. Against ever saying 'love' to any man again' (NLW MS 23577C, 'August' 1936), this declaration comes as the relationship is beginning to show signs of strain. It is also worth noting that for much of the time she loved Ruth, Evans remained intermittently infatuated with Basil Blackwell to whom, along with Ruth, one of her journals is bequeathed.

[24] NLW MS 23366D, 15 April 1934.

[25] NLW MS 23577C, n.d. (early December 1935), ff. 25 and 25 verso.

[26] Ibid., n.d. (early December 1935), f. 26

[27] Ibid., 10 December 1935, ellipsis in the original.

[28] Ibid., n.d. (early December 1935), f. 26.

[29] The nature and content of the letter is unrecorded and Evans reports only that 'I feel as if there were no words in me good or bad' (NLW MS 23577C, 15 December 1935). Farr's, and perhaps Evans's, continuing pursuit of information or confirmation of other lesbians is suggested by a glimpse of 'Ruthie reading the Ladies [of Llangollen]' while staying at Potacre (Margiad Evans MSS 115 (2 November 1942)). In other letters to Michael Williams, Evans references or quotes from the Ladies of Llangollen to describe 'A day of Sweetest most contained and Exquisite retirement' (Margiad Evans MSS 85 (1–2 September, 1942); see also Margiad Evans MSS 60 (1 August 1942)). Presumably, Evans had a copy of *The Hamwood*

Papers of the Ladies of Llangollen and Caroline Hamilton, ed. Mrs G. H. Bell, which was published by Macmillan in 1930. I am indebted to Ceridwen Lloyd-Morgan for the identification of the quotation and the passages cited here.

[30] Margiad Evans MSS 169/7, emphasis in the original. The letter is undated, but Ceridwen Lloyd-Morgan has suggested March 1943. By this time, Ruth Farr was living and working in Chapel House.

[31] Martha Vicinus describes how by the end of the nineteenth century, the word 'morbid had become a provocative euphemism for homosexuality' (*Intimate Friends: Women who Loved Women 1778–1928* (Chicago and London: University of Chicago Press, 2004) p. xxii). She shows its continued use into the twentieth century, for instance in one critic's description of Romaine Brooks's studies of Ida Rubenstien as 'exercises in morbidity' (p. 200). As Vicinus argues, 'this key word, indicative of physical disease, tied an emotion (same-sex desire) to a bodily condition (sickness)' (p. xxii). On Havelock Ellis, morbidity and homosexuality see Vicinus, *Intimate Friends*, p. 206.

[32] NLW MS 23577C, n.d. (March 1936), f. 52 verso. Ellipses in original except where in square brackets.

[33] NLW MS 23366D, 4 July 1934.

[34] Ibid., 14 May 1934.

[35] Margiad Evans MSS 34, journal entry for 3 November 1942, ellipsis in the original. Evans records distress the cause of which she says she will never write down, but in the entry for 17 November, she writes, 'After my talk with Mike I slept most peacefully. It was exorcism – the sleep of the lightened.' It is not clear whether the exorcism of the talk is related to Ruth, but the language as well as her dreams of ghosts suggests a connection.

[36] Margiad Evans, 'The Haunted Window', NLW MS 23365 D, 57–71 (May 1953), ff. 57. Hereafter HW, with folio references to this typescript given in the text.

[37] Margiad Evans MSS 169/2 (*c.*March 1943, see note 27), emphasis in the original.

[38] See Kirsti Bohata, 'Apes and cannibals in Cambria: images of the racial and gendered Other in Welsh Gothic writing', in *Welsh Writing in English: A Yearbook of Critical Essays*, vol. 6, (2000), 119–43 and Kirsti Bohata, 'Excessive appetites: cannibalism and lesbianism', in Wojciech H. Kalaga and Tadeusz Rachwal (eds), *Spoiling the Cannibals' Fun?: Cannibalism and Cannibalisation in Culture and Elsewhere* (Frankfurt am Main: Peter Lang, 2005), pp. 81–91. In addition to the primitivism of Miss Allensmore, Evans uses class difference to describe the power dynamic in their relationship and to bring into focus yet more lesbian figures in this important story. When Miss Plant stops to ask directions at a big house on her way to London she finds an eccentric 'servant' woman who directs her to her mistress. 'I've often thought she might have been me', she remarks. 'I'm

sure there were only two of them living there and they both ate their meals in the kitchen together.' Margiad Evans, *The Old and the Young*, ed. Ceridwen Lloyd-Morgan (Bridgend: Seren, 1998), p. 131. Hereafter *OY*.

[39] Evans might also have drawn upon Elizabeth's Bowen's short story 'The Apple Tree' (1934). In this story, as Emma Donoghue explains, the newly married Myra is haunted by 'the nightly apparition of an apple tree' which is 'eventually revealed as standing for the intense bond' she had aged twelve for a '"queer-looking"' schoolfellow, Doria. Having formed a pact with Doria, the two unpopular girls hide up in the branches of the apple tree, '"quite proud of ourselves, of being different"'. But Myra betrays Doria as soon as she makes other friends 'joining in the others' mockery' until one night Myra finds Doria hanging by the neck from the apple tree. Explaining her nightmares to a third woman who eventually releases Myra from her haunting, Myra depicts the relationship as compelling, innate and debilitating: '"I have to go after her; there is always the apple tree. Its roots are in me. It takes all my strength."' Emma Donoghue, *Inseparable: Desire Between Women in Literature* (Berkley: Cleis Press, 2010), pp. 134–5. Donoghue is quoting from Bowen's *The Collected Stories* (London: Jonathan Cape, 1980), pp. 468–70.

[40] Asbee, 'Margiad Evans's *The Wooden Doctor*', p. 47.

[41] NLW MS 23366D, 15 April 1934.

[42] Ibid., 21 May 1934. In transcribing this passage it is not possible to be absolutely sure that the word is 'ghastly' rather than 'ghostly' fire; similarly, the apostrophe in mother's is floating and could conceivably be *mothers'*.

[43] Jackie Stacey, *Teratologies: A Cultural Study of Cancer* (London and New York: Routledge, 1997), pp. 85–7.

[44] Margiad Evans, *Creed* (Oxford: Basil Blackwell, 1936), pp. 40–1. Hereafter *C*.

[45] On the dynamic between breast cancer, lesbianism, secrecy and femininity see Stacey, *Teratologies* and Eve Kosofsky Sedgwick, *Tendencies* (London: Routledge, 1994). On cancer and repression, see Susan Sontag, *Illness as Metaphor and Aids and its Metaphors* ([1978 and 1989] London: Penguin, 1991). On Arabella and the nurse in *The Wooden Doctor*, see Asbee, 'Margiad Evans's *The Wooden Doctor*, p. 47.

[46] On Sapphic modernism (a term which includes writers such as H. D., Djuna Barnes and, in some analyses, Virginia Woolf, among others, see, for instance, Laura L. Doan and Jane Garrity, *Sapphic Modernities: Sexuality, Women, and National Culture* (Basingstoke: Palgrave, 2006); Robin Hackett, *Sapphic Primitivism: Productions of Race, Class, and Sexuality in Key Works of Modern Fiction* (Piscataway, NJ: Rutgers University Press, 2004).

9

A 'Herstory' of Epilepsy in a Creative Writer: The Case of Margiad Evans

A. J. LARNER

Introduction

Margiad Evans was diagnosed with epilepsy in her early forties following the occurrence of generalised epileptic seizures, although it is possible that she may have had partial seizures for some years prior to this. Following consultation with a neurologist, her seizures were initially ascribed to a (hypothetical) scar on the brain resulting from a mild head injury in childhood. Epilepsy had a profound impact on Margiad Evans both as a woman, in terms of pregnancy and child care, and as a writer. Treatment with the then-available anti-epileptic drugs was problematic: their sedative adverse effects impacted on her ability to concentrate, and her published output undoubtedly declined (although a number of unpublished manuscripts were produced). Despite treatment, her seizures did not settle, eventually prompting further investigation, including brain surgery, with the discovery of an underlying malignant tumour. This eventually caused her death before the age of fifty.

Margiad Evans's accounts of epilepsy, *A Ray of Darkness* (1952) and 'The Nightingale Silenced' (an unpublished work written probably 1954–5), constitute two of the earliest patient accounts of the disease. For this reason alone, Evans is of interest to neurologists. Her experience also addresses the fascinating question of what the relationship might be between epilepsy and artistic creativity. Although any current analysis risks the potential errors of retrospective diagnosis, nonetheless it may be worth recording her clinical history in hopes of enlightening an appreciation of her art.

Epilepsy defined

The brain may be conceptualised physiologically as an electrical organ. Epileptic seizures result from abnormal electrical activity within the brain. In pathological states, brain cells (neurones) discharge in highly rhythmic and coordinated (hypersynchronous) patterns which override normal physiological brain activity and function to produce the phenomena which are witnessed and/or experienced as epileptic seizures. Many types of epileptic seizure may be delineated according to either seizure characteristics, known as the seizure semiology, or underlying mechanism. Seizures may include motor, sensory, autonomic (relating to the automatic homeostatic mechanisms of the body, for example control of blood pressure, breathing, sweating), or psychic phenomena.

Broadly epileptic seizures may be classified according to either aetiology (i.e. cause) or neurophysiology (i.e. mechanism). Aetiologically, seizures may be either *idiopathic/primary* (i.e. cause unknown) or *symptomatic/secondary* (cause identified, e.g. brain tumour, infection, neurodegeneration such as Alzheimer's disease). Neurophysiologically, seizures may be either *generalised* (abnormal electrical activity throughout the brain at seizure onset) or *partial/localisation-related* (focal abnormal electrical activity at seizure onset, which may remain localised or spread to other brain areas, sometimes becoming generalised and resulting in a secondarily generalised seizure). Generalised seizures may take various forms such as grand mal (or generalised tonic-clonic seizures) and petit mal, and partial seizures may be *simple* if consciousness is preserved or *complex* if consciousness is impaired.[1]

A distinction may be drawn between epileptic seizures and epilepsy. Epilepsy may be canonically defined as an enduring predisposition of the brain to generate epileptic seizures, a definition which may be operationalised to mean the occurrence of two or more unprovoked seizures.[2] Margiad Evans gave a graphic account of her second seizure in *A Ray of Darkness*:

> One morning in our cottage [the Black House, Elkstone, Gloucestershire] I got up fairly early out of bed and went down stairs to make tea. I carried the tray upstairs, put it down by the bed and the next moment it seemed heard my husband saying to me as my head lay on the pillow: 'How do you feel, dearie?'
> Astonished, I answered drowsily that I felt very well, why? 'Because you have just had another attack,' he said. With those words an

amazement entered into me which has never left me. Ever since I have been incredulous of all things firm and material. The light has held patches of invisible blackness, Time has become as rotten as worm-eaten wood, the earth under me is full of trap-doors and the sense of being, which is life and all that surrounds and creates it, a thing taken and given irresponsibly and without warning as children snatch at a toy. Sight, hearing, touch, consciousness, torn from one like a nest from a bird!

Of course it was only slowly I realised the truth as my eyes discovered a blood-stained pillow-case, my senses a tongue bitten through at the edge, for it seemed he had had as little warning as myself. It had been a swift performance. One kick, he said, as I lay down, and he cried 'What are you doing?' and turned and saw. It had lasted twenty minutes. He had changed the pillow-case under my head. Twenty minutes! and less than a blink to me, for this time, as I had been lying in bed and was not hurt apart from my tongue, I felt no illness afterwards. In fact the tea was still hot and we drank it quite as usual. This was my second major or total attack of epilepsy.[3]

This seizure probably occurred at some time in late July or early August of 1950, when Margiad was forty-one years of age. It followed her initial seizure of 11 May 1950 (her husband, Michael Williams, had not witnessed this event, having been away from home at the time) and her first consultation with Professor Frederick Golla (1878–1968), an expert in the diagnosis and treatment of epilepsy, at the Burden Neurological Institute near Bristol (8 June 1950). Golla confirmed the diagnosis of epilepsy and had remarked that Evans might never have another fit, stating that her epilepsy was caused in all likelihood by a small scar on the brain, clinical opinions which were both proved wrong with the passage of time. By the time of the second attack, Margiad was two to three months pregnant, a situation known to lower the threshold in some symptomatic epilepsies, probably due to the hormonal changes of pregnancy.[4]

Irrespective of professional clinical definitions of epilepsy, the second seizure was, according to her written account, a watershed for Margiad: 'My security was gone' (*RD*, p. 123). She had already acknowledged herself to be an epileptic. The 'adventure of body and mind' which was to prompt the writing of 'the story of my epilepsy' (*RD*, p. 12) had begun, a journey which was to produce a novel literary account. Although she evidently experienced other neurological phenomena distinct from epileptic seizures,[5] it is the latter which form the subject of this account, as well as a consideration of the effect of epilepsy on Margiad Evans as a creative writer.

Epilepsy in literature

Shakespeare used the word 'epilepsy' only once in his plays. In *Othello* (IV, i, 51), the Moor collapses as Iago goads him into believing Desdemona is unfaithful:

My lord is fallen into an epilepsy;
This is his second fit; he had one yesterday.

Othello's rapid recovery and the circumstances of the attack suggest (to this clinician) that this was not an epileptic seizure,[6] as some commentators have seemed willing to accept,[7] but syncope or a vasovagal attack (in lay parlance, a faint), a much more frequent cause of loss of consciousness. This is a common, and often challenging, differential diagnosis in clinical practice even today, based on the clinical history and often requiring an eyewitness account of the episode, rather than any sophisticated diagnostic testing.[8] Indeed, Margiad Evans reports that her relatives suggested to her that her first attack was simply a faint, but she was able to rebut this from her own experience of the difference between the two. Of course there is a least one definite account of epilepsy in Shakespeare, although it is not named as such, in *Julius Caesar* (I, iii, 253–6) when Casca and Brutus discuss Caesar falling in the market place and foaming at the mouth, diagnosed by Brutus as the 'falling sickness'.[9] Elizabethan 'falling sickness' almost certainly equates to modern epilepsy.

Such seizures were familiar in ancient medical literature, the earliest treatise devoted to the subject probably being that of Hippocrates of Cos, *On the Sacred Disease*, dating from the fourth century BCE. Hippocrates was clear that this was not a supernatural phenomenon:

It is thus with regard to the disease called Sacred: it appears to me to be nowise more divine nor more sacred than other diseases, but has a natural cause . . . like other affections.[10]

The term 'epilepsy' derived ultimately from ancient Greek, meaning to be seized upon or attacked. However, the *Oxford English Dictionary* lists only one usage of 'Epilepsie' prior to that of Shakespeare (1604), dating from 1578, in the *Niewe herball or historie of plantes* by Henry Lyte (1529?–1607), a botanist and antiquary, this being a translation of the Flemish physician and botanist Rembert Dodoens's (1516/17–85) *Cruydeboek* of 1554, an extensive herbal which became a standard in English through Lyte's translation, and which had a dedication to

Queen Elizabeth. A familiarity with botany was at that time a key element of medical training and practice.[11]

A definitive literary history of epilepsy has yet to be written, but a few examples of literary accounts of seizures may be given here. The plot of *Silas Marner, the Weaver of Raveloe* (1861) by George Eliot (another Evans, this time by birth rather than pseudonym) hinges upon a theft occurring during the protagonist's fit, later described thus:

> he saw that Marner's eyes were set like a dead man's, and he spoke to him, and shook him, and his limbs were stiff [. . .] just as he had made up his mind that the weaver was dead, he came all right again [. . .] and said 'Good-night', and walked off.[12]

This has features compatible with a complex partial seizure.[13] Fyodor Dostoevsky (1821–81), himself an epileptic, described seizures in many of his works, notably as a key plot device in *The Brothers Karamazov* (1881). Freud suggested that Dostoevsky's seizures were hysterical in origin, but the evidence is against this, as first pointed out by E. H. Carr, for example in his 1931 biography of Dostoevsky. Dostoevsky's own experience of epilepsy may have directly informed the portrayal of seizures experienced by Prince Myshkin in *The Idiot* (1868).[14] Examples of epileptic seizures may also be noted in films, many focusing on 'possession' as the cause of convulsions.[15]

Despite these artistic presentations of seizures, first-hand accounts of the experience of epilepsy were few prior to Margiad Evans's *A Ray of Darkness*, which gives insights into one woman's consciousness of the phenomenality of epilepsy.

Margiad Evans's epilepsy: personal and professional accounts

Margiad Evans's epilepsy has necessarily been described in biographical works focusing on her as a writer, albeit in passing,[16] and also by neurologists who were personally involved in her clinical care in the 1950s, specifically Frederick Golla[17] and William Lennox.[18] However, her illness and its effect on her as a writer has attracted relatively little clinical interest until recently.[19]

What was the nature of her epilepsy? Clinical clues may be drawn from *A Ray of Darkness* (1952) and from the unpublished manuscript of 'The Nightingale Silenced' (1954–5).[20] Since the latter is addressed

specifically to medical professionals, it behoves us to examine this work critically.

Whereas the first two epileptic attacks Evans suffered occurred without any appreciable warning (see above for the description of the second attack), in later attacks there was a ghastly awareness of fading consciousness, associated with overwhelming psychic phenomena. Indeed many later seizures comprised solely the latter: some 'convulsions were confined to mental sensations only', in which fear was the predominant and overriding feeling. Without such feelings ('panic without cause'), the seizures may not have troubled her greatly: 'Could Fear [. . .] be wiped away, the seizures would not matter very much'. But when attacks occurred these sensations were overwhelming:

> I was [. . .] incapable of controlling the sudden panic [. . .]. Every object became impregnated with terror. [. . .] The term 'restless horror' is nearer to an approximation of the utterly evil, utterly causeless, panic I was in [. . .]. There was not the slightest outward sign of an epileptic state [. . .] except this causeless fear and a certain blurring of the consciousness as though the brain had been wiped over with a dirty wet rag. [. . .]
>
> [A]n appalling terror amounting to panic seemed to emanate from every piece of furniture, every book, every saucepan. [. . .] These things might have been dangerous animals, only I knew that they did not want my body: it was my mind they wanted to destroy.
>
> As soon as the attacks began to subside the panic disappeared [. . .].
> (NS)

This change in the nature of the seizures is clearly reported following the initiation of anti-epileptic drug therapy. First treated with Luminal (phenobarbital), Evans also subsequently received Epanutin (phenytoin) and, when the seizures were particularly frequent, Mysoline (primidone). Although effective for the suppression of seizures, all these medications have unwanted adverse effects and none would be considered as first-line anti-epileptic drug treatments today.

Some epileptic attacks were also accompanied by motor phenomena, always affecting the left side of her body: there was a 'strange stiffening of the left side of my body', and after a severe fit 'I was very slightly paralysed in the left side and hand'. Speech difficulty was also noted on occasion: 'I was silent [. . .] for nearly two minutes'. Of particular note to a writer, she could not write during attacks: 'To continue to write is impossible even though I am right handed and the right hand is not usually disabled.' Possible autonomic features were

also mentioned: 'It was as though a ghost walked through me chilling every chamber of my body'; 'I feel as if the hair on my head was whitening [. . .] and my body withering' (NS).

The subjective phenomena so graphically described by Margiad Evans (although she was fully aware of the difficulties of rendering these phenomena intelligible to others: 'My task is to be the very difficult one of giving an outside inside story' (NS)) would suggest to a clinician that her seizures were of partial rather than generalised onset, and hence possibly associated with focal brain pathology. The motor phenomena (left-sided) are clearly lateralising, suggesting a right-sided brain lesion, whereas the psychic phenomenon of ictal fear (i.e. fear as part of an epileptic attack), although also of focal onset, does not permit clear lateralisation.[21] Speech arrest is also recognised as an ictal phenomenon, typically associated with pathology in the left frontal lobe of the brain.[22]

Hence the seizure semiology is suggestive of focal, rather than generalised, seizures, with the possibility of multifocal onset of seizures. Today, such an account of epileptic seizures would mandate structural brain imaging, preferably with the technique of magnetic resonance imaging. Such technology lay over thirty years in the future at the time of Evans's presentation, with electroencephalography (EEG; 'brainwaves') being the only non-invasive investigative technique readily available at the time.[23] Hence no criticism can be leveled at Golla's original diagnostic formulation. It was only with the passage of time (an important investigation in many neurological conditions), and the evident progression of disease, that more invasive investigation, namely surgical exploration, was undertaken, no doubt after very careful consideration and with some misgivings. In his textbook, Lennox states of Margiad Evans that 'a gliomatous brain tumour [. . .] lay behind both seizures and, after a dozen years [sic; in fact eight], death. The temporal lobe was not involved'.[24] The exploratory surgical intervention which allowed this diagnosis rendered Margiad Evans partially paralysed on her left side.

As previously mentioned, Margiad Evans was pregnant by the time of her epilepsy diagnosis. Her observations on this subject (in A Ray of Darkness) retain a resonance for women today: 'Epilepsy and pregnancy. The shock of waking every morning to such a grim problem of life' (RD, p. 125). Although there was no family history of epilepsy, Margiad was concerned, understandably, that the condition might be hereditary, and evidently contemplated abortion, then still illegal:

People who could help me have written to me and asked me why not have it quietly removed and I have replied that since the second fit that is my wish and that if they knew of any one who would do it, please help me. (*RD*, pp. 124–5)

Her general practitioner, Dr Y, however, maintained all would be well, visiting Margiad to read

a passage from *Nervous Diseases* by the Professor of Neurology at London University [neither book nor author identified], which he said was the last and most up-to-date work on epilepsy. [. . .] there was in reality only the very slightest danger of its being hereditary. (*RD*, p. 128)

The child was born uneventfully, but after a post partum fit concerns about safety meant that Margiad 'was never again able to feed my child' (*RD*, p. 153).

Epilepsy and creativity: is there a link?

Margiad Evans's epilepsy raises a number of questions and dilemmas which continue to challenge epilepsy management today, not least the issue of pregnancy and epilepsy mentioned above.[25] However, for scholars of literature, possible links between epilepsy and creativity may be of more interest. The neural substrates of creativity remain a subject of mystery, although new techniques in neuroscientific research may help to uncover some of them.[26] There is increasing interest among the faculty regarding the effects of neurological disorders in famous artists.[27]

Whether brain disorders such as epilepsy may enhance or diminish creative faculties has also been a subject of interest for many years. In the visual arts, Vincent van Gogh (1853–90) was at one time thought to have suffered from temporal lobe epilepsy, but in recent times there has been a move away from this idea to suggestions of borderline personality disorder and bipolar affective disorder.[28] Other examples of visual artists thought to have epilepsy and whose art may have been influenced by seizure activity include Kyffin Williams, Edward Lear, Charles Altamont Doyle (father of Arthur Conan Doyle) and Giorgio de Chirico.[29] In the verbal arts, Caesar wrote (in the third person) his histories of *The Gallic War* and *The Civil War*, epilepsy nothwithstanding. Dostoevsky not only transcended his epilepsy but capitalised on it as a device in his fiction. Could it be possible that

inspiration itself is 'some unknown form of epilepsy'?[30] Frederick Golla may have thought so: 'Where writers of genius have been sufferers [of epilepsy], it is fascinating to trace how greatly their sensibility and creative activity have been enhanced by the liability of their nervous system to respond as a whole [. . .] [T]he expression of her [Margiad Evans's] total personality has been facilitated by the malady.'[31] He may well have had Dostoevsky in mind, since according to *A Ray of Darkness* he suggested to Margiad Evans that she read the works of 'Dostoëffsky', presumably because he was another author with epilepsy, who had managed to incorporate his knowledge of epilepsy into several of his novels. Evans apparently declined Golla's suggestion, at least initially, although Dostoevsky is mentioned in both *A Ray of Darkness* and 'The Nightingale Silenced', being described in the latter as 'the greatest descriptive writer of epilepsy'. Of her own writing, Evans mentions 'an older incomplete fragment of a novel about an epileptic man'. This has not been identified, although there is a passage in *Turf and Stone* (1934) in which a female character has episodes from childhood in which 'something like a telephone rings in my head, and then my neck seems to go numb [. . .] I have walked quite a long way and come to myself and wondered how I did it, for I couldn't remember a thing.'[32] Although this is far from a typical description of an epileptic seizure, there are a number of features in it which are suggestive to a clinician, namely episodic, stereotyped events with loss of awareness and for which there is subsequent amnesia.

At times, Evans herself seems to concur with the possibility that epilepsy facilitated creativity in her own work: she speaks of writing 'many poems in the hospital ward' not to mention 'hundreds of letters'. 'In my writing [. . .] words and phrases [. . .] began to race over the pages without stopping' (NS), although she notes a 'fatal voluminousness' in her output (hypergraphia may be one feature of complex partial seizures, often associated with temporal lobe pathology).[33] She speaks of a 'quickness of mind', and of an 'intuitive imagination' as an attribute of 'horror-stricken sufferers' (NS).

In contrast, the adverse effects of epilepsy on cognition are now well recognised. These may be multifactorial, related to epileptic seizures per se, to the underlying brain pathology responsible for the seizures, and to anti-epileptic drug treatment, as well as to concurrent depression and anxiety occasioned by the illness itself.[34] Indeed, the effects of medication were all too apparent to Margiad Evans:

> [S]ince taking drugs I cannot keep awake for those free quiet hours which were my most creative. True my power of concentration is lost also.

> [T]he drugs I have to take to prevent the discharges of the epilepsy make me apathetic, have faded and dulled and dimmed the powers of imagination and concentration. (NS)

Although 'grateful for the treatment', she also acknowledges that she 'cannot work against drugs [. . .] although I should perhaps have died mentally last summer without [. . .] these drugs, it is better to die than to continue so wearily, dulled, blunted, stricken' (NS).

If the 'cloud of epilepsy' affected her poetry favourably, itself a questionable contention, its effect on her prose was undoubtedly adverse. Empirically, she published no books after *A Ray of Darkness*, and despite the 'many poems' written she states that 'the only poem I wrote in the hospital I really liked I lost', possibly the one entitled 'Cassandra desolated'. A projected work on Emily Brontë, an author for whom Margiad Evans had a long-standing interest, was abandoned.

Furthermore, William Lennox's encomium of *A Ray of Darkness* (it 'carries the bonus of being beautifully and deftly expressed')[35] could not be applied, even by the most generous critic, to 'The Nightingale Silenced', a less coherent work, difficult to read and interpret, and with many repetitions, some almost verbatim (possibly representing two drafts of the same work). This may explain why 'The Nightingale Silenced' remains unpublished more than fifty years after the author's death.

Conclusion

A Ray of Darkness and 'The Nightingale Silenced' manifest the author as witness of her own subjectivity, writing an 'adventure of body and mind' which was 'the story of my epilepsy', a mental journey ('The Margiad', perhaps?)[36] which produced a novel literary account. This history or, perhaps more correctly, 'herstory' of epilepsy ends tragically, the inescapable conclusion being that the progressive nature of the brain pathology underlying her seizures robbed Margiad Evans of her creative powers as well as, eventually, her life. Epilepsy was perhaps just one more facet, along with gender, sexuality, and a border identity,[37] of 'the isolation and the inevitable

"otherness" of the artist'[38] which characterised the oeuvre of Margiad Evans. Nevertheless, her works on epilepsy remain as a bridge between the discourses of the humanities and the sciences.

Acknowledgements

Thanks are due to Jim Pratt, Peggy Williams's nephew, for permission to quote from his typescript of 'The Nightingale Silenced', and to Kirsti Bohata of the Centre for Research into the English Literature and Language of Wales (CREW), Swansea.

Notes

1   C. P. Panayiotopoulos, *The Epilepsies: Seizures, Syndromes and Management* (Chipping Norton: Bladon Medical Publishing, 2005).
2   R. S. Fisher, B. W. van Emde, W. Blume et al., 'Epileptic seizures and epilepsy: definitions proposed by the International League Against Epilepsy (ILAE) and the International Bureau for Epilepsy (IBE)', *Epilepsia*, 46 (2005), 470–2.
3   Margiad Evans, *A Ray of Darkness* ([1952] London: John Calder, 1978), pp. 122–3. Hereafter *RD*.
4   A. J. Larner, S. J. M. Smith, J. S. Duncan and R. S. Howard, 'Late-onset Rasmussen's syndrome with first seizure during pregnancy', *European Neurology*, 35 (1995), 172.
5   A. J. Larner, '"Neurological literature": headache (part 4)', *Advances in Clinical Neuroscience & Rehabilitation*, 7/6 (2008), 17; A. J. Larner, 'Illusory visual spread or visuospatial perseveration', *Advances in Clinical Neuroscience & Rehabilitation*, 9/5 (2009), 14.
6   Idem, 'Has Shakespeare's Iago deceived again?', *www.bmj.com/cgi/letters/333/7582/1335*, 2 January 2007.
7   R. Lawson, 'The epilepsy of Othello', *Journal of Mental Science*, 26 (1880), 1–11; K. W. Heaton, 'Faints, fits and fatalities from emotion in Shakespeare's characters: survey of the canon', *BMJ*, 333 (2006), 1335–8; Jeannette Stirling, *Representing Epilepsy: Myth and Matter* (Liverpool: Liverpool University Press, 2010), p. 4.
8   A. J. Larner, 'Syncope', in T. M. Cox et al. (eds), *Oxford Textbook of Medicine* (5th edn) (Oxford: Oxford University Press, 2010), pp. 4838–41.
9   Idem, '"Neurological literature": epilepsy', *Advances in Clinical Neuroscience & Rehabilitation*, 7/3 (2007), 16.
10 G. E. R. Lloyd (ed.), *Hippocratic Writings* (London: Penguin, 1978), p. 237.

[11] A. J. Larner, 'Demise of botany in the medical curriculum', *Journal of Medical Biography*, 16 (2008), 1–2.

[12] George Eliot, *Silas Marner: The Weaver of Raveloe*, ed. Terence Cave (Oxford: Oxford World's Classics, 2008; reissue edn), p. 6.

[13] Larner, '"Neurological literature": epilepsy'.

[14] C. R. Baumann, V. P. Novikov, M. Regard and A. M. Siegel, 'Did Fyodor Mikhailovich Dostoevsky suffer from mesial temporal lobe epilepsy?', *Seizure*, 14 (2005), 324–30; I. Iniesta, 'On the good use of epilepsy by Fyodor Dostoevsky', *Clinical Medicine*, 8 (2008), 338–9; A. J. Larner, 'Dostoevsky and epilepsy', *Advances in Clinical Neuroscience & Rehabilitation*, 6/1 (2006), 26.

[15] S. Baxendale, 'Epilepsy at the movies: possession to presidential assassination', *Lancet Neurology*, 2 (2003), 764–70; S. F. Ford and A. J. Larner, 'Neurology at the movies', *Advances in Clinical Neuroscience & Rehabilitation*, 9/4 (2009), 48–9.

[16] Moira Dearnley, *Margiad Evans* (Cardiff: University of Wales Press, 1982); Ceridwen Lloyd-Morgan, *Margiad Evans* (Bridgend: Seren Press, 1998); Barbara Prys-Williams, *Twentieth-century Autobiography: Writing Wales in English* (Cardiff: University of Wales Press, 2004), pp. 32–57.

[17] Frederick Golla, 'This is a work of great importance', *John Bull Magazine*, 18 October 1952, 8.

[18] W. G. Lennox and M. A. Lennox, *Epilepsy and Related Disorders* (London: J. A. Churchill, 1960), pp. 182, 191, 192, 269, 297, 711.

[19] Jim Pratt, 'Margiad Evans: centenary of an artist with epilepsy', paper delivered to the 28th International Epilepsy Congress, Budapest, 28 June–2 July 2009; A. J. Larner, '"A ray of darkness": Margiad Evans's account of her epilepsy (1952)', *Clinical Medicine*, 9 (2009), 193–4; A. J. Larner, 'Margiad Evans (1909–1958): a history of epilepsy in a creative writer', *Epilepsy & Behavior*, 16 (2009), 596–8; I. Iniesta, 'Epilepsy and literature', *Medical Historian*, 20 (2008–9), 31–53 (31–2, 36–8).

[20] Margiad Evans, 'The Nightingale Silenced', National Library of Wales, MSS 23367B. All quotations are taken from the typescript prepared by Jim Pratt, dated 17 April 2009. Hereafter NS.

[21] V. P. Rosa, G. M. A. Filho, M. A. Rahal, L. O. S. F. Caboclo, A. C. Sakamoto and E. M. T. Yacubian, 'Ictal fear: semiologic characteristics and differential diagnosis with interictal anxiety disorders', *Journal of Epilepsy and Clinical Neurophysiology*, 12 (2006), 89–94.

[22] U. C. Wieshmann, L. Niehaus and H. Meierkord, 'Ictal speech arrest and parasagittal lesions', *European Neurology*, 38 (1997), 123–7.

[23] Clare Morgan showed a slide depicting a handwritten poem by ME on what appeared to be EEG paper on which calibration traces are seen, presumably thrown out as scrap paper. Clare Morgan, 'Margiad Evans: a writer in her time', Margiad Evans Centenary Conference, National Library of Wales, Aberystwyth, 15 May 2009.

24 Lennox and Lennox, *Epilepsy and Related Disorders*, p. 711.
25 Larner, '"A ray of darkness": Margiad Evans's account of her epilepsy (1952)'; Larner, 'Margiad Evans (1909–1958): a history of epilepsy in a creative writer'.
26 T. D. Griffiths, 'Capturing creativity', *Brain*, 131 (2008), 6–7.
27 J. Bogousslavsky and F. Boller (eds), *Neurological Disorders in Famous Artists*, part 1 (Frontiers of Neurology and Neuroscience, vol. 19) (Basel: Karger, 2005); J. Bogousslavsky and M. Hennerici (eds), *Neurological Disorders in Famous Artists*, part 2 (Frontiers of Neurology and Neuroscience, vol. 22) (Basel: Karger, 2007); J. Bogousslavsky, M. Hennerici, H. Bazner and C. Bassetti (eds), *Neurological Disorders in Famous Artists*, part 3 (Frontiers of Neurology and Neuroscience, vol. 27) (Basel: Karger, 2010).
28 Larner, '"Neurological literature": epilepsy'.
29 R. H. Thomas, J. M. Mullins, T. Waddington, K. Nugent and P. E. M. Smith, 'Epilepsy: creative sparks', *Practical Neurology*, 10 (2010), 219–26.
30 Yevgeny Zamyatin, *We* ([1924] London: Penguin, 1993), p. 18.
31 Golla, 'This is a work of great importance', 8.
32 Margiad Evans, *Turf or Stone* ([1934] Cardigan: Parthian, 2010), p. 104.
33 A. J. Larner, *A Dictionary of Neurological Signs* (3rd edn) (New York: Springer, 2011), p. 184.
34 R. Blake, S. Wroe, E. Breen and R. McCarthy, 'Accelerated forgetting in patients with epilepsy: evidence for impairment in memory consolidation', *Brain*, 123 (2000), 472–83; D. W. Loring, S. Marino and K. J. Meador, 'Neuropsychological and behavioural effects of antiepilepsy drugs', *Neuropsychology Review*, 17 (2007), 413–25; A. J. Larner, *Neuropsychological Neurology: the Neurocognitive Impairments of Neurological Disorders* (Cambridge: Cambridge University Press, 2008), pp. 115–24.
35 Lennox and Lennox, *Epilepsy and Related Disorders*, p. 711.
36 M. Atwood, *The Penelopiad* (Toronto: Knopf, 2005).
37 K. Gramich, *Twentieth-century Women's Writing in Wales: Land, Gender, Belonging* (Cardiff: University of Wales Press, 2008).
38 Clare Morgan, 'Exile and the kingdom: Margiad Evans and the mythic landscape of Wales', *Welsh Writing in English: A Yearbook of Critical Essays*, vol. 6 (2000), 89–118 (90).

10

Warding off the Real: The Recreation of Self in Autobiography *and* A Ray of Darkness

KAREN CAESAR

A Ray of Darkness is Margiad Evans's response to the physical calamity which befell her on 11 May 1950. Alone in the Black Cottage at Elkstone between 11 p.m. and midnight she suffered her first epileptic fit. She regained consciousness to discover that she was lying on the floor; she had lost control of her bladder and her head was cut and bleeding: her body had failed her, cutting loose from her mind's control with the result that she felt that she had fallen through 'Time, Continuity and Being'.[1] She could see by the clock that she had lost time: seventy minutes between 11.10 p.m. and 12.20 a.m. and with it the continuity of her life had been disrupted. At 11.10 p.m. she was sitting at her table with a cup of tea and at 12.20 a.m. the tea was spilt, time had been lost and her very being compromised. For Evans, 'being' was intensely associated with physicality, as is evidenced in her entire 'corpus'. She experienced herself and others as embodied beings. *A Ray of Darkness*, her last published book, can be read as the meditation of a sufferer on what happens when the embodied self can no longer be controlled by the will.

Evans makes many references in *A Ray of Darkness* (1952) to her earlier autobiographical work entitled *Autobiography* (1946),[2] remarking that the later work is a continuation of the first. In *Autobiography* the author had two main preoccupations: the relationship between her embodied self and nature and the difficulty of what she describes in *A Ray of Darkness* as 'the continuous effort to put into language what was in reality a deeply relaxing experience' (*RD*, p. 66).

What emerges in *Autobiography* is her perception that her body and nature are inseparable:

I see and contain the muscular growth of the hawthorn and the descent of a plover. (*A*, p. 119)

I'm tired, but the touch of the ground heals my hand [. . .] I can *be* the field, the trees – the movement of the branches in the breeze is like my own blood going through and round my life-centre – the earth is the lung by which I breathe – the earth is my greater flesh. (*A*, p. 88)

The earth contains her and her body encompasses the earth: the hawthorn's growth is 'muscular'; the breeze is like the circulation of her blood; the earth is her lung – essential to breathing and life. Her connection with the earth revitalises her; it has the power to heal. But it is not only her body which is intimately tied to the earth, her thoughts and feelings are also reflected back to her by her environment:

I saw an outward resemblance to my thoughts in the clammy ground, blear hedgerows and foggy trees whose faint colour was the blue of veins. (*A*, p. 33)

Here the landscape reflects her thoughts, which are vague and melancholic but the image also suggests the reciprocity between animate and inanimate: the trees have the bluish tinge of veins. At times the connection is so strong that her perception is of the external becoming absorbed into her very being, constituting her thoughts: 'I feel all that I see, entering and becoming part of my existence – the shape, the colour – the black ivy trails, the wild strawberry flower' (*A*, p. 86). Her communion with the natural world brings a sense that her body is entirely constituted of thoughts and feelings:

To stand outside in the warmth, to breathe and look was to feel the body made of thought. (*A*, p. 52)

Shutting my eyes I became the thought of what I had seen. Not a part of my body but has its brain [. . .] The brain is the earth, the body is the universe, strung planet to planet by impalpable communicating threads. (*A*, p. 101)

Her sense of unity with the earth can be described as that of the 'nature mystic' in the tradition of Henry Thoreau and Richard Jefferies, both of whose writing she admired.

William James refers to Thoreau and Jefferies as 'naturalistic pantheists'[3] who have in common a mystical sense of 'enlargement, union and emancipation' inspired by their response to nature. James in his lecture on Mysticism also quotes the 'alienist' Sir James

Crichton Brown's theory of 'dreamy states'. This is the description he gives to 'sudden invasions of vaguely reminiscent consciousness', the feeling of having been there before often reported as part of mystical experiences. According to Crichton Brown these bring

> a sense of mystery and the metaphysical duality of things, and the feeling of an enlargement of perception which seems imminent but never completes itself.[4]

These words aptly describe the state Evans struggles to convey in *Autobiography:*

> The divisions of time fail. As I sit here I don't know whether it's today or yesterday, and I don't believe the rooks do either. I seem to have a part in each and nothing to join them together with. There's a memory in me like a landscape full of my first delight. (*A*, p. 16)

Dr Crichton Brown connects these feelings with 'the perplexed and scared disturbances of self consciousness which occasionally precede epileptic attacks'.[5]

For over a hundred years neurologists have been studying and recording the altered states produced by the abnormal discharges in the brains of epileptics. In a 1983 article in *Epilepsia*, the Journal of the International League against Epilepsy, Norman Geschwind suggests that: 'Common behavioural alterations associated with epilepsy include an increased interest in philosophical and religious concerns and extensive writing of a cosmic or philosophical nature.'[6] He hypothesises that this behaviour is the result of an 'intermittent spike focus in the temporal lobe' which affects the response of the limbic system, the area of the brain which controls emotion and emotional response as well as mood and sensations of pain and pleasure. This alteration caused by the abnormal discharge in the brain of an epileptic may result in heightened emotional responses to many different stimuli. D. F. Benson has since suggested that these behavioural traits amount to a personality disorder he has named Geschwind's Syndrome.[7] Although the existence of such a syndrome remains controversial the fact that clinicians treating epileptic sufferers have recognised such characteristics in numbers of their patients points to the complex relationship between the anatomical and the psychological.

Although in *Autobiography* Evans is describing sensations experienced ten years before her first major fit and the diagnosis of epilepsy, it is possible that Evans's mystical experiences, her sense of being

haunted, her meditations on the relationship between mind, soul and body, her sense of the irrelevance of time and union with nature had a neurological base, especially in view of her remark in *A Ray of Darkness* that she has experienced 'absences' for as long as she can remember:

> I cannot recall when I was without moments of separation from my consciousness – moments when I was quite literally conscious and unconscious at the same time. (*RD*, p. 38)

Finding a language to express these mystical moments of perception is the central preoccupation of *Autobiography*. Language can be seen as occupying a position at the interface between body and mind: it is where thought must become tangible and communicable. However, she struggles to express her sense that her 'meaning grew in the earth and the firmament' (*A*, p. 39), but words literally fail her. Her thoughts cannot be expressed. She says, 'I think in a language I cannot speak' (*A*, p. 117) and, 'I understand without words the thought that is in me: but without words what may be *testified?*' (*A*, p. 86). The urge to communicate is strong; she records her desire to 'reproduce and retain some record tangible' of what she sees and loves in the earth, but the right words will not come: 'The air and the light will not get into the paper' (*A*, p. 61). She feels that her language, rather than connecting her to others, sets her apart:

> Wherever I go I must carry speech in my mouth and brain which is as incomprehensible to the other kinds of being as the sparrows' jangling is to me. (*A*, p. 61)

Hence she must work hard to acquire a common language but she is ambivalent about this project because she fears that in acquiring this language she will lose the very thing she seeks to express – her sense of communion with the earth. She cannot name all the flowers and creatures she observes in her garden on a May morning, still less can she find words to convey her feelings of 'beauty and joy, rest and energy':

> And I cannot tell of them without our having a common symbol between us, and so I must learn more, twisting away from them, to a closer understanding with people risking the infinite loss of the direct and wordless touch of the earth. (*A*, p. 62)

She is intensely frustrated by her attempts, convinced that her writing is 'tedious' and 'inadequate':

I must use words which I loathe when I would go beyond words, write beyond print, show more of moments, days, of life, than paper can take. (*A*, p. 61)

Evans's struggle to find a language to voice her deeply felt perceptions recalls Virginia Woolf who, twenty years before, was expressing similar sentiments in her diary:

and still I say to myself instinctively, 'What's the phrase for that?' and try to make more and more vivid the roughness of the air current and the tremor of the rook's wing.[8]

Woolf concluded that the very form of the sentence did not fit her because it was a sentence made by men,

too loose, too heavy, too pompous for a woman's use [. . .] And this a woman must make for herself, altering and adapting the current sentence until she writes one that takes the natural shape of her thought without crushing or distorting it.[9]

The difficulties experienced by both Woolf and Evans in finding an appropriate language to express themselves can be explained with reference to the Lacanian idea that language is necessarily slippery and ambiguous and can only ever offer an approximation of what it seeks to articulate. Thus, when human beings are in extremis, experiencing feelings of fear, pain or love they become inarticulate, even speechless. As Bernard puts it in *The Waves*,

What is the phrase for the moon? And the phrase for love? By what name are we to call death? I do not know. I need a little language such as lovers use, words of one syllable such as children speak [. . .] I need a howl, a cry [. . .] I need no words [. . .] I have done with phrases. How much better is silence?[10]

Evans comes close to the same conviction: there simply is no language to express her thoughts and that, therefore, silence comes closer to truth: 'I have failed to describe it because language cannot form the thought, because it is wordless and unimaginable and pictureless' (*A*, p. 96).

Lacanian theory also illuminates Evans's conviction that language simply fails her when she attempts to describe her relationship with the natural world. For Evans, nature was the mirror in which she saw herself reflected. It constituted a return to what Lacan describes as the Imaginary stage, which is one of phantasised wholeness and plenitude. In this sense nature for her was *Mother* Nature, reflecting back

to her a self which was whole and in harmony with itself and its surroundings. As Terry Eagleton describes it, Lacan's Imaginary is a condition in which the self seems to pass into objects and vice versa in a ceaseless closed exchange: the image a pre-linguistic child sees in the mirror is somehow the meaning of itself.[11] This can be compared with Evans's observation in *Autobiography*:

> I stood leaning on a gate. I was behind the sky. I was in the ground. I was in the space between the trees. My meaning grew in the earth and the firmament. (*A*, p. 39)

From the full imaginary possession of the mother's body and the illusion of wholeness reflected back to the child in the mirror she is propelled into the empty world of language. It is empty because the sign presupposes the absence of the object it seeks to describe. Language, according to Lacan, is motivated by loss and desire and this goes to the heart of Evans's problem. As soon as she introduces language into her relationship with nature, then the harmony and sense of unity is lost. Because language stands in for absent objects and nature is so intimately present to her, her attempts to capture it in words are bound to fail; language cannot render the object fully present. Language itself creates desire by severing the individual from the mother's body. The more Evans attempts to use language, the more she perceives a separation between herself and what she is trying to describe. By attempting to order her perceptions in an autobiography Evans shows herself again to be striving for the sense of wholeness, the misleadingly harmonious image in the mirror. The mirror can therefore be seen as an analogy for the self-reflective process which is autobiography. As Shari Benstock suggests, autobiography 'reveals the impossibility of its own dream: what begins in the presumption of self-knowledge ends in the creation of a fiction that covers the premises of its construction.' The subject, through autobiography, strives towards the 'false symmetry' of the mirror, a 'unified self which can only ever be a fiction.'[12]

For Lacan the 'I' is also elusive and its unity illusory. The unity between the speaking 'I' and the 'I' described in speech is imaginary; according to his famous reworking of Descartes: 'I am not where I think, and I think where I am not.'[13] Again, Evans anticipates this in *Autobiography*: 'Such is the power of life over me then that I lose language and think only by being' (*A*, p. 152). She expresses her sense of a self that is fragmented and dispersed:

the stems that touched my hands, the ant hills, the crickets that jerked, and the silent clouds had my mind in them. I could not write: I could not concentrate, for my being was in everything. (*A*, p. 152)

But, paradoxically, she produces her book; she perceives that, for her, 'being' *is* writing. This is the only means she has of creating herself: 'Each time I take hold of a pen it's like being born – and the spirit hangs back *knowing* the greater joy of unconsciousness' (*A*, p. 24). Writing brings her into being, but it is painful, like birth, so much so that she resists and avoids it, but even when too ill to write she feels the 'guiltiness of the infant to be stillborn who will not enter the struggle' (*A*, p. 24). When she does manage to write she feels that some of her thoughts do transfer to the page: they are pressed on the surface as her thoughts press on her brain: 'At last this white oblong half covered with words, pushed into a shut book and apparently disregarded, has become almost an inner part of me' (*A*, p. 61). She *incorporates* the writing; it becomes herself.

Ten years later, following the diagnosis of 'major epilepsy', Evans again takes herself as the subject of a book, *A Ray of Darkness*, in which she returns to many of the same themes which had preoccupied her in her earlier autobiographical text. However, there is a crucial difference: the new book will be a 'pathography': an account of her illness. As with *Autobiography*, Evans draws on her contemporary diaries for material for *A Ray of Darkness* and at the end of the intro-ductory chapter offers this as proof of the truthfulness of what follows: 'It is the truth, most of it exactly as it was written down at that time, for I have my diaries' (*RD*, p. 12). Many theorists of auto-biography agree that in writing the story of the self, not only is that self elusive but its past is rearranged and even recreated in the telling. Roy Pascal in *Design and Truth in Autobiography* discusses how 'the past is not simply recorded in the autobiographical act but given a structure, a coherence, a meaning.'[14] However, Anne Hunsaker Hawkins suggests that pathography differs significantly from other forms of autobiography because it is about the self in crisis. The consequence is that readers of narratives describing illness and death are 'repeatedly confronted with the pragmatic reality and experiential unity of the autobiographical self. The self that is sick is in some way a concentration of other versions, fictions and metaphors, an essence, a "hard" defensive ontological reality.'[15]

For the sufferer from epilepsy, however, the nature of the disease itself disrupts the sufferer's ontological reality. Evans experienced her

seizures as a loss of self. Regaining consciousness after her first major seizure and failing to recognise her surroundings she asks herself, '*Who was I?*' (*RD*, p. 80). This is repeated after another severe attack: 'I could not remember who or where I was' (*RD*, p. 152). This loss of self seems to her a rehearsal for death, a subject that had preoccupied her even before the onset of her last illness. She quotes the critic Derek Savage, who in his analysis of *Autobiography* included in his book of critical essays, *The Withered Branch* (1950), points to 'the inner sadness, hollowness and final despair' of the 'nature cult' and the 'death wish' he discerns in her writing (*RD*, p. 63). She corrects him saying this was more of an obsession, which she has 'associated with epilepsy' (*RD*, p. 63). The falling into unconsciousness, she says: '*can* teach. It can gently, and as it were, by steps or a staircase, show us the probable darkness of death, and remove our fear of that descent' (*RD*, p. 11).

In the desperate days following her first seizure, she turns again to nature for solace as she described in *Autobiography*, sensing that her 'long passion for earth life and its study, was as healthy and protective, as spiritual, as any religion could be' (*RD*, p. 88), but although there is some comfort in the springtime it is not the same: 'Death, more death, had entered me through unconsciousness' (*RD*, p. 89). In a quoted journal entry for 23 May, she reflects poignantly back to the time when her body had seemed to her a microcosm of the great earth with which she had felt such a close communion. Now she says the necessity of death seems natural to her because just as she had learned about 'natural life and death' from the great earth, now the little earth, her body, may reveal through 'its storms and physical complexes, the mystery of its cessation' (*RD*, pp. 92–3). The identification she makes between her body and the earth is strengthened by the use of the word 'storm' to describe her body's vulnerability, its complete passive subjection to the violent physical manifestations of the fit she has suffered.

She links body and earth again when she describes the slow return to consciousness after her first fit. There was 'a feeling that the soul didn't know whither it had returned, to the right earth or to an unknown one' (*RD*, p. 81). The idea of her soul returning to a body, which feels as if it might be alien territory, is a powerful metaphor for the dislocation she feels between body and mind.

In the diary entry for 23 May, she again links her experience of falling into unconsciousness with death:

I don't think a lot about the other night now. The horror has certainly passed. I don't think it was a fit – oh I don't know! It might have been. But whatever it was physically – and it was total blackness, a hole in the self – to me, it was a glimpse. Some have them in visions, some in prayers, some come to them through entreaty, through disappointment, or weariness, some through sainthood. Death is the soul's delight. Death is God, Death grows to be our daily appetite. Give us our necessity. (*RD*, p. 92)

Evans describes her experience in terms that go beyond the physical: the total darkness of the seizure created 'a hole in the self', which can be compared only to death. With the loss of the self in unconsciousness, she approaches 'the real' in the Lacanian sense of that which exists beyond or outside of meaning and signification. 'Nothing was seen', she says, but it was 'just the separation from the will, so entire, so instantaneous, so involuntary, that seemed to illustrate for me what is inevitable to come to be' (*RD*, p. 93). The seizures, which occur in a space beyond language, are a rehearsal for death: the ultimate truth. As she remarks in a contemporary letter, 'I know now and shall know again what it is not to exist'.[16]

The second fit plunges her 'deeper into the darkness of epilepsy' (*RD*, p. 122). It occurs just as she is setting down a tray of morning tea by the bedside. She comes round to hear her husband telling her she has had another attack:

With those words an amazement entered into me which has never left me. Ever since I have been incredulous of all things firm and material. The light has held patches of invisible blackness, Time has become as rotten as worm-eaten wood, the earth under me is full of trap-doors and the sense of being, which is life and all that surrounds and creates it, a thing taken and given irresponsibly and without warning as a child snatches a toy. Sight, hearing, touch, consciousness, torn from one like a nest from a bird. (*RD*, p. 122)

Here, she conveys a sense of the precarious state in which she now lives. All the things she depended upon: the earth, her senses, time and light are now pierced with gaps and spaces which threaten to draw her in, to give way beneath her, leaving her homeless, adrift and insecure.

She speaks about the effects of the seizures as creating 'numb patches' in her thought (*RD*, p. 81). When she is struggling back to consciousness, trying to remember who and where she is, she reports that messages from her brain trying to bring her that information, 'kept flashing to me and then fading again leaving blanks in my mind

that were like the air under flight' (*RD*, p. 152). These blanks are paradoxical in that they are invisible; they appear to be static, empty spaces containing nothing but they are also dynamic, powerful and freighted with significance. Evans tells her nurse, 'I'm sure I've had a fit because of the blanks in me' (*RD*, p. 153).

According to Lacan, our unconscious desire for our mothers reappears in the spaces between words. Words paper over the cracks, plug the gaps in our being: language is the way we manage loss. Deprived of speech by the seizures, Evans experiences a foretaste of the Real, that which is beyond language, but her experience of gaps and spaces in her self can be seen as the cracks reappearing when language is lost, manifestations of the unconscious desire which, according to Lacan, is at the centre of our lived experience.

This idea is reinforced by her sense of being haunted. In the quoted diary entry for 23 May, twelve days after her first seizure she writes:

> For several days afterwards if I turned my head quickly, something, some unusual, some significant shape seemed just to avoid me, just to run out of the corner of my eye [. . .] Maybe it would be a stone, a post, which just one breath away had been a human shape, a ghost. The world was populated with vanishings. (*RD*, p. 93)

Ghosts disturb our sense of a separation between the living and the dead so are appropriate companions for the sufferer from epilepsy, a condition which locates her in a liminal space where while alive she can experience the loss of consciousness which mirrors the negation of death. Like a ghost, she is both there and not there. The ghostly space, like the air under flight is another blank weighted with significance.

In 'The Nightingale Silenced' she describes how she feels during the seizures, which have become much more frequent: 'It was as if a ghost walked through me, chilling with a faint draught every chamber of the body.'[17] Here the blanks she has described, the patches of blackness in the light are represented as a ghostly figure wandering through the mansion of her body (this image has also appeared before). The metaphor is effective because it conveys the fear of the sufferer. It also refers back to old ideas of epilepsy as Possession and links to her sense that she is 'possessed by restlessness and vacancy' (*NS*, p. 90). 'Ghost' is the shape in which she sometimes conceives that vacancy. In a letter to her friend Bryher (26 October 1950) she writes: 'It's like a ghost in yourself and say what commonsense will

and mind doctors, you are haunted and you are different.'[18] As Virginia Woolf comments in her essay on Henry James's ghost stories: 'Henry James's ghosts . . . have their origin within us. They are present whenever the significant overflows our powers of expressing it; whenever the ordinary appears ringed by the strange.'[19] Beth Torgerson, discussing ghosts in *Wuthering Heights*, comments: 'Images of ghosts render visible "dispossession" and the powerlessness of the dispossessed.'[20] In Evans's case, her ghosts represent her sense that she is no longer in possession of herself.

As has been discussed, the epileptic seizures deprived her of speech for their duration. The central paradox of *A Ray of Darkness* is that the disease that silenced her also unleashed words on to the page. Deprived of language, she responds with writing. Quoting from her diaries, she describes finding a mouse and her young while out gardening and then comments, 'I have a hope that it will help to straighten out the disorder in me if I write down such things as mice and thunderstorms' (*RD*, p. 90). And 'I must start again on my Emily Brontë book. I must do something to keep myself calm and decent' (*RD*, p. 87). She has a clear sense that writing might be her salvation and, despite finding it difficult, her output at this period was considerable. She wrote letters, articles, poetry and the journals which form the basis of *A Ray of Darkness*. Even as the disease progressed and the fits became more frequent she continued the narrative of her illness in the unpublished *The Nightingale Silenced* which exists in several manuscripts hand written compulsively while confined to bed in hospital in Tunbridge Wells. Reading these narratives give the sense that, by writing, Evans is attempting to impose order on her world threatened by chaos.

Arthur Frank writes of 'chaos stories' as a type of pathography. He points to a difficulty with this type of narrative, which is the impossibility for those who are living chaos to tell it in words because reflective grasp and distance are needed to tell the story. 'The chaotic story cannot be told, but the voice of chaos can be identified and a story reconstructed.'[21] In these reconstructed stories life is imagined as never getting better. At the opening of the last chapter of her book, which she dates 30 December 1951, Evans describes how she has entered a state of 'miserable impatience and mental velocity' similar to the one which tormented her for so many years before 'the great wave of the disease parted me perhaps forever from the land of normality' (*RD*, p. 181). She is marooned in the kingdom of the sick

for all time. Chaos narratives also lack narrative order and coherent sequence. Evans's text moves backwards and forwards in time. 'I am not now writing chronologically', she says. 'In the state which writing now induces in me, it is doubtful if I could' (*RD*, p. 112). She describes the act of trying to capture her thoughts in writing as chaotic: 'And I find that in writing so hurriedly my thought is flung down like water upon a floor and dashed in all ways at once and wasted without channel' (*RD*, p. 157). Her choice of image provides a link between her chaotic thought processes and the domestic physical life, which at times she has blamed for her disease: 'And once I thought it was the Muse herself in rage turning on one who had neglected her for years of common tasks and common existence' (*RD*, p. 11).

Although Frank describes the hurry and repetitious jumble of words employed by people attempting to convey their chaotic stories he concludes that:

> Ultimately, chaos is told in the silences that speech cannot penetrate or illuminate. The chaos narrative is always beyond speech, thus it is always *lacking* in speech. Chaos is what can never be told: it is the hole in the telling [. . .] chaos is the ultimate muteness that forces speech to go faster and faster, trying to catch the suffering in words.[22]

Evans's thoughts spill out in a flood all over the floor because her writing is so hurried. She also records how, at the beginning of her illness, her diary is full of nature jottings, but these are suddenly interrupted by 'brief incomprehensible mental ejaculations, to which the key is lost' (*RD*, p. 110). She gives an example:

> The black currants were ripe, the moon was thin, the summer house door was ajar . . . would I rather be me, sane, in the secret way Ophelia was? And like Ophelia, dragging wild flowers with her through the dew? But I didn't touch them – the mallow, the ox-eye, the – oh, I forget words.
> (*RD*, p. 110)

Here are 'holes in the telling' which even the author cannot fill and finally at the end of the entry a fading away into mute wordlessness. On the final pages of the book, Evans asks what to do with this 'dark, restless, pining life'. But she expects no answer 'for my silent disease has no reply for me' (*RD*, p. 190). There is no hope of recovery or restitution of health. The end again is silence.

In 'The Nightingale Silenced' Evans records how in the minutes leading up to a fit she feels the urge to get out of bed, but she knows that she must not follow this urge because if she did, '[t]hings would

disintegrate. I should be chaos' (NS, p. 131). Chaos would not only constitute the horrific space she inhabits because of her disease; she would actually become part of chaos herself. This vision of chaos almost renders her silent, but her story is her resistance to silence: the epileptic seizures interrupt her life and dislocate her sense of self but turning these experiences into a story is her attempt to neutralise the chaos. The story is made to substitute for her ailing, chaotic body.

Elaine Scarry points to the examples of the suffering figures of Sophocles' Oedipus, Shakespeare's Lear and Beckett's Winnie, for each of whom 'the voice becomes a final source of self extension; so long as one is speaking, the self extends beyond the boundaries of the body, occupies a space much larger than the body.'[23] Evans felt her body's unreliability and feared the disintegration of her mind so she, like Lear and Winnie, 'speaks' unceasingly and like them with great virtuosity, signifying her perhaps unconscious realisation that as long as she has a 'voice' she cannot be confined by the body's limitations. As Scarry says of Oedipus, Lear and Winnie, '[t]heir ceaseless talk articulates their unspoken understanding that only in silence do the edges of the self become coterminous with the edges of the body it will die with.'[24] Echoing this, Evans writes on the opening page of 'The Nightingale Silenced': 'Illness is very like a longing to die. Yet there remains in me something obstinate, instincts which want to speak, to testify, to reason, to raise up myself' (NS, pp. 1–2). The nightingale may be silenced, but not quite yet.

Arthur Frank suggests that the ill person not only loses a sense of herself but also loses the 'destination and map' that had previously guided her life. He quotes a letter from Judith Zaruches, a sufferer from chronic fatigue syndrome, in which she writes, 'The destination and map I had used to navigate before were no longer useful.' She now needed 'to think differently and construct new perceptions of my relationship to the world'.[25] One of the ways of doing this, Frank argues, is for the ill person to tell her story; the story itself then becomes part of the new map. *A Ray of Darkness* is Evans's story; its writing is performative in that it re-establishes the relevance of the old map and destination: that guiding Margiad Evans, poet and author. The importance of this map to her is conveyed in her letters to Bryher. Writing in February 1951, and employing a similar metaphor, she says – referring to her literary persona in the third person – 'Margiad Evans is lost and may never find her way back ever'.[26]

The circumstances in which she was writing this letter are crucial: she was in hospital, thirty-five weeks pregnant and suffering from oedema and a worsening of her epilepsy. *A Ray of Darkness* describes in parallel the birth of itself, the book, and her daughter, Cassandra. In her earlier autobiographical writing she describes the bringing forth of a book in intensely physical terms. Of *The Wooden Doctor* she writes that she has 'wrought bones, muscles, a beating heart': a living book.[27] Writing, she gives birth to words and to herself through the text. A sense of her desperate struggle to give birth to herself through writing is expressed again ten years later in *Autobiography*: 'Each time I take hold of a pen it's like being born' (*A*, p. 24). This identification of herself with the body of her work, her corpus, is made explicit in her journal of 1949. On 6 August, frustrated that she cannot write her 'great wild book',[28] she says, '[b]ut I have always been a silly diary, not a great book', and on 20 December, 'I am a text of myself.'[29] But the text is not only herself, it is also her child; it is what she will leave behind after her death. In a letter to her husband, Michael, she refers to her recently published *Autobiography* which is dedicated to him, 'To you I owe *Autobiography* – it's more than dedicated; it's our own child.'[30] *A Ray of Darkness* is an account of her illness, but it is also a narrative about its own birth and, in parallel, the birth of a flesh and blood child.

The extent to which these two are inextricably linked for her can be seen in the language she uses to describe her feelings about her pregnancy. In the letter quoted above where she feels afraid that 'Margiad Evans's may be lost' she also writes, 'I think longingly of my dear unwritten book and the poems one loves more than any flesh. And I think all lost if I die, and to die for this . . .'[31] Her priorities are clear: words mean more to her than flesh. Death in childbirth, even if this means giving life to a child, would be no compensation for her lost words. She repeats this sentiment in *A Ray of Darkness* when describing her feelings when her pregnancy was confirmed:

> Triumph I did feel, inseparable from the fulfilment of the purpose for which I was a woman: but I confess that it was a lesser one than I had already had in finding a child in the womb of my brain. (*RD*, pp. 120–1)

The book and the child are representatives of the split between the intellectual life and the domestic life that she feels may have led to her illness. She characterises this as a battle: 'the brain and the womb are enemy cities, and the inhabitants of them are born to strive with one another' (*RD*, p. 121).

Evans interprets the discovery that she has conceived a child, despite her illness, in terms of her body making a choice for life rather than death but she identifies as the child's twin rather than its mother:

> The woman who is carrying her child, although she feels an adult and maternal responsibility for it, and a charming friendliness towards it, is not as yet so much its *mother as its twin*. (*RD*, p. 120, original emphasis)

Later in the text she refers to the baby as a 'mysterious twin', an image which reflects Evans's perception that she is involved in a double gestation: that of her child and herself embodied in a book. The twin imagery also echoes the central perception of her text that her illness, one that divides her body from her brain, has given her insight into the dualities and divisions that pervade life. The image reappears in the final pages of her text where she offers her concluding insight into the nature of her disease: her suffering is caused by the presence within her brain, body and mind of 'two or more *complete* entities' (*RD*, p. 181, original emphasis): 'To use a simile of birth, the individual is not with child of Siamese twins but with unbound twins wrestling for the opening to life' (*RD*, p. 181).

Linda Anderson suggests that 'one of the desires that is encoded by autobiography [. . .] is that of becoming, within the realm of the symbolic, one's own progenitor, of assuming authorship of one's own life.'[32] As I have shown above, Evans's text is about her own rebirth as an author as well as the birth of her child. Vladimir speaking to Estragon at the end of Becket's *Waiting for Godot* powerfully links birth and death: 'Astride of a grave and a difficult birth. Down in the hole, lingeringly, the gravedigger puts on the forceps. We have time to grow old. The air is full of our cries.'[33] Evans was losing confidence that she would have time to grow old, so her book about birth is simultaneously a textual challenge thrown down against the silence of death, the Real. And these words are what ensure her immortality; they allow her to cheat death by providing her epitaph.

She will live on also in her daughter, whom she named Cassandra. The significance of the name for her is illustrated by her use of it in a simile in which she identifies herself with the mythological Cassandra: her illness is a result of her, '[g]enie or Muse . . . turning on me as Apollo turned his rage upon his seer Cassandra' (*RD*, p. 173). She, like Cassandra, suffers at the hands of the beloved who believe themselves betrayed. There is another suggestive layer in her choice of name. Cassandra was cursed by Apollo so that her prophetic words would never be believed. For a woman whose whole existence centred

on language, who in extremis turns to words, to name her daughter after a prophetess whose words were powerless reveals perhaps her most profound unconscious fear.

The final chapter of *Ray of Darkness* is haunted by her fear of annihilation. While in the process of writing the book her disease has taken a stronger hold and she returns to her voyage metaphor to express her conviction that 'the great wave of the disease [has] parted me perhaps forever from the land of normality' (*RD*, p. 181). From her position on the other side of the wave she reiterates her intimation of the possibility of being conscious and unconscious at the same time; both there and not there, when the epilepsy seizes her. In these final pages she concludes: '[t]he opposite of each thing makes the outline of the other' (*RD*, p. 185). Things are defined by what they are not, in the same way as Saussure theorised linguistic signs as having meaning only by virtue of their difference from other signs. The book's title, *A Ray of Darkness*, refers to this central vision: 'for when is light so expressed as at midnight, or darkness so clear as at noonday?' (*RD*, p. 185).

This is a text which, in its insistence on a world characterised by ghosts, hauntings and divisions, paradoxes and ambivalence, perfectly articulates the absence and loss at the heart of language. 'To enter language is to be severed from what Lacan calls the "real", that inaccessible realm which is always beyond the reach of signification, always outside the symbolic order.'[34] The real, illuminated for Evans by her ray of darkness, is glimpsed by the reader through the silences in her text.

Notes

[1] Margiad Evans, *A Ray of Darkness* (London: John Calder, 1978). Further references are to this edition, hereafter *RD*.

[2] Margiad Evans, *Autobiography* (Oxford: Basil Blackwell, 1943). Further references are to this edition, hereafter *A*.

[3] William James, *Varieties of Religious Experience: A Study in Human Nature*, centenary edn ([1902] London and New York: Routledge, 2002), p. 329.

[4] Crichton Brown is quoted by James on p. 298. Crichton Brown was first published in *The Lancet*, 6 and 13 July 1895 and reprinted as the Cavendish lecture 'On Dreamy States' (London: Bailliere, 1895).

[5] James, *Varieties of Religious Experience*, p. 298.

6   N. Geschwind, 'Interictal behavioural changes in epilepsy', *Epilepsia*, vol. 24: S4 (1983), S23–S30.

7   D. F. Benson, 'The Geschwind syndrome', *Advanced Neurology*, 55 (1991), 411–21.

8   Virginia Woolf, entry for Sunday, 12 August 1928, in Anne Olivier Bell (ed.), *The Diary of Virginia Woolf, Vol. III: 1925–30* (London: Penguin, 1982), p. 191.

9   Virginia Woolf, 'Women and fiction', in *Virginia Woolf on Women and Writing*, selected and introduced by Michèle Barrett (London: The Women's Press, 1979), p. 48.

10 Virginia Woolf, *The Waves* (Oxford: Oxford University Press, 1998), p. 246.

11 Terry Eagleton, *Literary Theory: An Introduction*, 2nd edn (Oxford: Blackwell, 1996), p. 144.

12 Shari Benstock (ed.), *The Private Self: Theory and Practice of Women's Autobiographical Writings* (Chapel Hill and London: University of North Carolina Press, 1988), pp. 11, 12.

13 Jacques Lacan, *Écrits* (Seuil, 1966), pp. 517, 166.

14 Roy Pascal quoted in Anne Hunsaker Hawkins, *Reconstructing Illness: Studies in Pathography* (West Lafayette: Purdue University Press, 1993), p. 15.

15 Hunsaker Hawkins, *Reconstructing Illness*, p. 17.

16 Letter to Bryher, 26 October 1950. Bryher Papers. General Collection, Beinecke Rare Book and Manuscript Library, Yale University. MSS 97.

17 Margiad Evans, National Library of Wales (hereafter NLW) MS 23367B, p. 41. Further references to 'The Nightingale Silenced' are given in the text, hereafter NS.

18 Bryher Papers. General Collection, Beinecke Rare Book and Manuscript Library, Yale University. MSS 97.

19 Virginia Woolf, *Collected Essays Vol. 1* (London: The Hogarth Press, 1966), p. 291.

20 Beth Torgerson, *Reading the Brontë Body: Disease, Desire and the Constraints of Culture* (New York and Basingstoke: Palgrave MacMillan, 2005), p. 16.

21 Arthur Frank, *The Wounded Storyteller: Body, Illness and Ethics* (Chicago: Chicago University Press, 1995), p. 98.

22 Frank, *The Wounded Storyteller*, pp. 101–2.

23 Elaine Scarry, *The Body in Pain: The Making and Unmaking of the World* (Oxford: Oxford University Press, 1985), p. 33.

24 Ibid.

25 Frank, *The Wounded Storyteller*, p. 1.

26 Letter to Bryher, 23 February 1951. Bryher Papers. General Collection, Beinecke Rare Book and Manuscript Library, Yale University. MSS 97.

27 Evans, NLW MS 23366D, p. 141.

28 Evans, NLW MS A1982/89.
29 Ibid.
30 Evans, NLW File 12, Michael Williams Letters, 17 October 1944.
31 Letter to Bryher, 23 February 1951, in Bryher Papers. General Collection, Beinecke Rare Book and Manuscript Library, Yale University. MSS 97.
32 Linda Anderson, *Autobiography* (London and New York: Routledge, 2001), pp. 67–8.
33 Samuel Beckett, *Waiting for Godot* (London: Faber and Faber, 1956), pp. 90–1, cited in Daniel Gunn, *Psychoanalysis and Fiction: An Exploration of Literary and Psychoanalytic Borders* (Cambridge: Cambridge University Press, 1988), p. 71.
34 Eagleton, *Literary Theory*, p. 145.

11

'The Human Tune'[1]: Margiad Evans and the Frustrating Fifties

CLARE MORGAN

At the end of the 1940s Margiad Evans's fortunes as a writer seemed to hang in the balance. She had published her collection of stories, *The Old and the Young*, in 1948 and these had been generally well received, despite the contention that some of them exhibited tendencies that were 'quite mad'.[2] As late as 1950, the momentum she had established with her four earlier novels had not wholly dissipated. D. S. Savage, in *The Withered Branch*[3] compared her writing to Woolf, Forster, Huxley, Joyce and Hemingway (or at least considered her equally among them). And yet, as the twentieth century turned on its mid-point and the post-war world awoke to the atomic age, Margiad Evans was finding increasing difficulty in securing publication for her fiction. Among the rejection letters she received was one from John Lehmann, in which he finds himself 'unable to publish [her] work at this present'.[4] The frustration she feels spills over in a notebook entry: *'Oh meaning, you elude me* – oh genius, profound pulse of my soul *you mock my life and entangle me in endless dreams and avenues of shadows'*.[5] By her own admission her 'prose deteriorated into a scurry and a tediousness'.[6] It seemed she was badly in need of a new direction for her work.[7]

Critics are divided as to what new direction she may have been attempting. Ceridwen Lloyd-Morgan traces a shift, in the forties writing, away from 'narratives of her own psyche',[8] while Katie Gramich believes that in her later work 'Margiad Evans grew increasingly mystical'.[9] It is certainly true that in *Autobiography* at least, Evans's attention is very much 'on the natural world'[10] and it is also clear that the poems in her late collection *A Candle Ahead* contain strong elements that could be considered mystical.[11] However, it is also well

known that Evans turned to the *Autobiography* when she was unable to finish her fifth novel for Basil Blackwell.[12] What she was publishing, and what she was writing, were two different matters. The shape and impetus of her imaginative engagement was not necessarily congruent with the texture of her published work.

This is particularly true in terms of her output in the 1950s. Despite her deteriorating health and the domestic instability under which she laboured, she nevertheless managed to complete and publish her account of the illness which was overtaking her, *A Ray of Darkness* (1952), as well as her prizewinning collection of poems *A Candle Ahead* (1956). She was also writing for radio, including an autobiographical play, *December Day*, which was broadcast on Monday, 31 December 1956. These visible outputs from her creative imagination account, however, for only a small fraction of her work.

Margiad Evans's papers and notebooks are littered with scraps and fragments, with starts that lead nowhere, with experiments in writing that may show occasional flashes of what she is capable of, but fail to attract to themselves the necessary spark of creative life. These trialled and abandoned pieces suggest a writer who is attempting, and failing, to broaden the scope of her imaginative engagement. They also show a writer who is constantly drawn back to old themes and usages, to what Sue Asbee has characterised as 'the intensity of a highly charged emotional family life' where 'married couples practise untold cruelty upon one another, while rivalries and bitterness are rife in all kinds of relationships.'[13] In other words, Evans was still embroiled in the emotional storm and domestic disarrangement that had characterised her earlier writing and her life.[14]

An attempt to broaden her approach to a theme that was dear to her is evident in a dialogue called 'Balance'[15] which appears to have been written around 1952. In this fragment, 'The Atom' berates 'Man' for upsetting the delicate balance of the universe. 'First you divided God from Eden, split the Unity of him who saw yourself and God as one. Now you would kill the universe.' Despite Man's protestations that he is 'only exploring' in the cause of 'scientific perfection', he is roundly condemned in terms which anticipate the fervour of twenty-first century ecological debate: 'Oh race suicidal, think of the balance you had in me, the equity of a body still young and most beautiful!' Here, Evans has moved from her former intense contemplation of the minute patch of nature that is the south Wales border land, to a more cosmic or even metaphysical approach. Unfortunately,

the piece peters out, condemned perhaps by its own formal restrictions, or by an as yet insufficiently developed imaginative engagement with the larger issues of the contemporary post-war world.

Evans was also attempting during this period to engage with the burgeoning possibilities of technology, in particular with the new medium of television. However, she seems to have had little understanding of the demands of this new medium. 'A Borrower: A Tragic Comedy for Television' occupies a few abandoned pages of manuscript that languish in her archive among notebooks, poems, scraps of fiction, sketches, and numerous photographs of her dogs. Her quite long cast list (eleven characters 'plus extras') which includes a chapel deacon, a rector, an atheist, a farm girl, a landlady 'from Vowr arms' and 'an old-age pensioner' seems fundamentally unsuited to the contemporary exigencies of the televisual mode. The opening camera direction, slow and static and 'show[ing] us long distance the rectory garden of Vowr-Vaughan in Summer with a Church tower topping some trees'[16] bears out this impression. The leisurely particularity of the world Evans is addressing, and the characters who seem, indeed, to have sprung from the same impulse out of which the characters of *The Old and the Young* emerged, point to a stasis that dooms the attempt at experimentation.

The piece is subtitled 'a tragic comedy', and the darkly comedic possibilities that hover in *The Old and the Young* do lurk in its conflicting moral imperatives of belief, atheism, and the old-world wisdom of 'neither a borrower nor a lender be', upon which the piece seems predicated. The opening dialogue gives a hint of these possibilities:

'We had an atheist in this parish once', [Deacon Davies says] 'Yes, mind.'
He rubs his hands and continues about the mulberries – 'they nasty squashy things – dirty they are. But you will eat 'em, sir. Meant for birds.'[17]

Evans seems unsure, though, how to construct and direct her material. The visuality is merely an add-on, and the heart of the writing focuses on the aural and the descriptive – strengths which had distinguished her short fiction. However, the distinct focus on individual circumstance that characterised *The Old and the Young* or *Country Dance* is here dissipated or absent. The generalisation of character that was directed and framed to advantage by nature – what has been referred to as Evans's engagement with the 'representative rather than [the] individual'[18] – is, in the creative context of visuality and

dialogue, exposed and weakened. 'Nature' in the televisual medium can no longer function as protagonist but becomes a backcloth. The comedy flounders and there seems a distinct lack of Evans's previous mainstays: emotional conflict or the hoped-for potential for tragedy.

If the territory of earlier work is revisited in 'A Borrower', albeit in dissipated and soon abandoned form, a more successful revisiting occurs in Evans's broadcast radio piece, *December Day*. It seems at first that she is here regurgitating earlier, autobiographical material, but in fact there are important shifts and differences in this successful production, which provide some clues as to where the fount of her creative imagination may have been tending. On the surface the piece is a calm and meditative reflection on a fruitful and happy period spent at Llangarron in the 1940s. However, a closer examination reveals the strains and conflicts that are at work.

There are two 'Margiad Evanses' in *December Day*. One is the controlling narrator, the other is the Evans character-as-narratee. The play consists of a poetic recollection or enactment of a Christmas Day, which begins with the voice of Margiad Evans (narrator):

> Christmas time in Llangarron. Under the snow the fields are a dark, purplish red. They look like a roan horse's back as they lift to the horizon with snow on them [. . .] the memory is life-lasting.[19]

The familiar, romantic territory of unity with nature is revisited ('a complete fusing of Seeing and Being').[20] In this idyllic realm and time, inner and outer landscapes are as one, the inner landscape, oddly, 'humanised' by its conflation with the outer. Scenes of seasonal domestic harmony on a snowbound landscape are interspersed with darker connotations:

> Only the sky told the truth. The sun shot up and into one lowering cloud. A wind which seemed to have circled some icy northern star, spun slowly round our cottage. Oh it was cold![21]

'Only the sky told the truth': the metaphorical use of the weather opens the way for psychological and emotional fissures to be revealed in apparently mundane conversation. Husband and wife have dressed up for the Christmas party – a tie is required for the husband, and for 'Margiad Evans' 'some lipstick and an angora jersey'. During the festivities, a neighbour asks Margiad Evans whether she ever thinks of herself, to which the Evans-character replies:

No, I don't believe I do. Oh – one thinks of cooking, and so on, but I wouldn't if I weren't obliged to . . . I don't call cooking and housekeeping 'thoughts'.[22]

Evans-as-narrator has written herself as a post-war housewife, dressed up in middle-class garb (the angora jersey is a telling detail) and obliged to fulfil a domestic role which is uncongenial. Just how frustrating this uncongenial role is becomes apparent when she exclaims: 'Oh Edna, if I were a poet I wouldn't mind anything! Not illness, not weariness, not grief. Poetry would be everything.'[23] The frustration is borne out in her 1950s Notebook,[24] where it is evident that the darker elements of life on the border were taking their toll. 'My life is spent in heaven, in hell, at the sink, the washtub and the Pictures', she exclaims. It is no accident that her unpublished 1950s novel 'The Churstons' has in its character list 'Mrs Luchardi, a nobody' where the 'nobody' is crossed out and the word 'WIFE' is inserted in definite blue biro.[25]

If the differential placing of the two Margiad Evans personae (narrator and character) have perhaps encouraged a critical/analytical distance which enables the fault lines of the borderland existence to be revealed, this placing also allows the distance between Evans and her country milieu to become clearly visible. Jack Waters, characterised as '(Very countrified with a slight tilt [*sic*] to the words)', is intent on nothing but getting his sheep 'into the parlour'; while Gwenyth [*sic*] Petty, an equally stock character, '(also with a Welsh tilt [*sic*] but more educated)',[26] assists him, portrayed in a ponderous attempt at comedy about her bad back. Old Morgan 'trudging and grumbling as he banged the snow off "morning wood"'[27] criticises Margiad Evans (as character) for her writing, which he regards as having 'Too many words', which is 'improper [. . .] Bad for a man, but wholehearted improper for a woman'.[28] The yawning cultural divide between Evans and her neighbours is evident,[29] while once again the gender divide looms.

In many respects the frustrations that Margiad Evans is depicting epitomise difficulties faced by many women in the aftermath of the war. Margiad Evans spent much of her married life separated from Michael Williams. During the war he was on active service in Motor Torpedo Boats, and she led a harsh but largely self-sufficient existence, attending to manual tasks that might usually have been considered the province of the male. The nature of this existence is clear from her *Autobiography*:

Each day is spent in hard labour. I carry, I bear, I lift, I fight, not with angles but with spadefuls of muck. My adversaries are wet, cold and hunger, my tempter is the fire. My sleep is a dog's. It's my life to dig and saw, cook and wash and gather sticks to warm my sleepy evenings.[30]

No wonder the 'cooking and housekeeping' of *December Day* are so readily dismissible. The difficulties for women in adjusting to the return of the male and the taking up of the more traditional domestic role has been the subject of much comment, and finds its most prominent image in the 'Rosie the Riveter' trope, that of the woman brought into the labour market and offered greater freedom and possibility than hitherto, only for this to be removed quite summarily when the men come back from the war and wish to resume their place in the economic structures. This point is taken up by Deborah Philips in her contention that the writing of romance during the 1950s was influenced by this shift in roles, which inevitably challenged the previously accepted balances between masculine and feminine,[31] and by Katie Gramich in her argument that women in Wales 'were subject to contradictory pressures, pushed back towards traditional domestic roles and femininity on the one hand [. . .] impelled forward to a greater liberation by economic and technological advances, as well as by their own ambitions.'[32]

Class, cultural and gender divides are, then, feeding in to Margiad Evans's dissatisfactions and frustrations in the early 1950s period. While there are hints of the emotional conflict that might appertain in the creative frustrations of the life depicted, these frustrations become more fully evident in the unpublished notebook entries and fictions of the time.

An exclamation from Evans's Notebook demonstrates the degree of emotional turbulence to which she was subject in that unstable, early 1950s period:

> My God you vile thing!
> You demon viper vampire
>
>   you
>
> who have the power to
>
>   blacken out the
>   world
>
> to dull joy's eyes –
> Bugger bugger bugger
> three times bugger
> and buggered![33]

Wavering between the beginnings of a poem and an outright *cri de coeur*, this exclamation attests to a woman existing on a tight-drawn emotional and artistic edge. Immediately abutting it in the notebook is a draft of something similarly tight-strung:

> While they were out together I lay alone enduring all I knew [. . .] Does all happiness cost somebody as much as their two hours together cost me? Some women cry, some tear off their clothes. I *suffer* the pain of the body. My hand goes to it. *I want to groan and beat myself. Oh for someone to cool me with healing!* The door is opening on madness when I would do anything *to myself* – fall, run . . .[34]

This extract depicts quite clearly the anguished cry of a triangulated relationship, in terms reminiscent, in the amalgamation of physical and emotional pain, of Arabella's sufferings in *The Wooden Doctor*.[35]

The nature of the triangular relationship, and the price it extracts in emotional and creative terms, are further explored in the draft of a short story titled 'The Letter'. The story's chief protagonist is Geraldine, a writer who is having a love affair with someone who sends her letters which make her laugh and cause her to be joyous. Geraldine is writing her goodbye to her lover – but only because her lover is no longer writing to her: 'it was the kind [of letter] that a woman writes only a few times possibly only once in her life'.[36] The absence of communication from the lover has caused Geraldine anguish: 'When no letter had come that day she had wanted to die [. . .] Once she had been in love with his very handwriting – that vivid scrawl which told so much more about him than he ever did'.[37]

The biographical parallels in this story are striking. The family are in financial trouble, as were Evans and her husband, Michael Williams. The fictional husband, Humphrey, gets dunning letters which make him 'yellower and yellower and more and more spiteful'.[38] They are to be evicted from their home, just as Evans and Williams had been in the late forties. When Geraldine asks her husband whether things are bad, he says, 'Yes. Worse than I'd thought. We'll have to clear out. There, now you know.'[39] The physical description of Humphrey, although he is described as ugly, bears a striking resemblance to Michael Williams: 'He had magnificent dark eyes and melancholy musical brows, inherited from Spanish Jewish ancestry, the sort of [?] brows one sees in a sad Velazquez face.'[40] Elsewhere Evans had described how 'Looking at [Michael Williams] [. . .] I think of those fierce Spaniards hurled on the coast of Pembroke hundreds

of years ago, one of whose *black* names he has'.[41] Geraldine, at forty-five (precisely Evans's age at the time of writing the story) is getting nowhere with her writing and finding that 'the rejection slips for the short stories were getting more plentiful and without friendly editorial comment'.[42] The artistic challenges that Geraldine faces are redolent of Evans's situation: 'There was the new novel . . . and the one they asked for that she wanted to write; but she had never focused the beginning.'[43] At the heart of her creative difficulty is a dilemma which reflects directly on, but turns on its head, the Margiad Evans (narrator) recollection of unity expressed so cogently in *December Day*. Rather than enjoying a 'complete fusing of Seeing and Being', Geraldine finds that 'now nothing is *seeable*. I don't mean visible, but nothing passes through my eyes beyond them to my mind.'[44]

One final correspondence between Geraldine and Margiad Evans is illness. 'The Letter' manuscript is marked as written at 'The Bungalow, Hartwell, Hartfield, Sussex, March 1954'. By this time, Evans would have been more than aware of the potential seriousness of her own illness, and she portrays Geraldine's condition movingly and unflinchingly from the perspective of 'Nannie', the last remaining servant in the household. Having been 'seized by an emotional anguish so intense that the pain was physical', Geraldine calls Nannie and asks for 'two codeines'. When Nannie brings them, 'Geraldine's face was white. It hadn't altered otherwise but somehow it looked as if all the features beneath the pretty skin had been sucked in. "She'll look like this when she loses her teeth", Nannie thought'.[45]

Deirdre Beddoe has characterised this period in which Evans was struggling to find appropriate modes of expression as 'the frustrating fifties'.[46] Certainly the theme of frustration permeates Margiad Evans's work at that time. To the frustrations of the uncongenial domestic role depicted in *December Day* have been added, in 'The Letter', artistic, financial and emotional disappointments, as well as the challenges of indifferent health.

Two unpublished works from the 1950s probe deeper the question of frustration and its impact. The unbroadcast radio play 'Dear Desdemona',[47] featuring Byron and Lady Frances Webster, focuses on the theme of frustrated sexuality. Lord Webster, having extolled the virtues of his wife lady Frances, confesses to Byron that although his wife 'dotes on' him, they do not have a sexual relationship. '[T]hat woman,' he confesses, 'she – she insists on – well, she *is* like a nun! There! She will not live with me.'[48]

An attraction inevitably develops between Byron and Lady Frances, but this too is similarly unproductive in terms of intimacy. Byron asks her whether she loves her husband. Having prevaricated, she admits that 'I can't . . . He is so strange.' Byron asks: 'Then it is true? That you don't live together?' And Lady Frances responds: 'It is true (faintly). In the beginning I tried. But lately I cannot – I cannot'.[49]

It is not a reluctance, however, confined to her relation with the unfortunate husband. Having taken her in his arms, Byron proposes that as they are 'totally alone, utterly in love – and in my house' a consummation of their passion would be in order. Lady Frances, however, although she shares Byron's feelings, finds herself unable to acquiesce, for complex reasons:

> Lady F: (pitifully) I cannot. I cannot! I am entirely at your mercy. I own it. I give myself up to you. I am not *cold* whatever I may seem to others . . . Oh what nervousness this is I cannot tell you but *it is as though I were watching myself.*[50]

A single occurrence of self-denied passion might be attributed, particularly given the rather clichéd style Evans is employing, to an exploration of the tried and tested methods of the romance genre – a latter-day depiction of the pure heroine holding out against the allurements of a rapacious world. It is clear, however, that Evans's preoccupation with sexual frustration is more deep-seated.

The Wooden Doctor focuses on the obsession of the young Arabella, tormented by an indefinable illness that may be psychosexual, for her physician, Dr O'Flaherty, a man thirty years her senior. Evans's own obsession with the physician of her youth, one Dr Leeper Dunlop, has been well documented. Ceridwen Lloyd-Morgan recounts how Evans 'telephoned and wrote constantly, despite [his] attempts to discourage her'[51] and, as Sue Asbee puts it:

> In an early draft of *The Wooden Doctor* there are times when the author forgets she is writing fiction and refers to her character Arabella by her own name of Peggy. Notions of identity, then, are complex in Evans's work, shifting between the usual boundaries critical readers are taught to observe between life and fiction.[52]

The theme recurs in 'The Churstons', an unpublished novel which Evans was working on in the early 1950s. Tyrannical Guy, a physician and brother of Adelaide Churston, has extracted, in their youth, a promise from Adela and his other siblings never to marry, because their sister Priscilla had died of an 'hereditary [. . .] mania'.[53] The

figure of the powerful practitioner, so dominant in *The Wooden Doctor*, resurfaces in 'The Churstons' in multiplied form. For here there are not one but two doctors – Professor Luchardi is the beloved physician whom Adela, because of her promise to her brother, has rejected and sent away. This cataclysmic parting from the doctor, enacted despite his assurances that the mania will not touch any other member of the family, is retrospectively recounted in the manuscript draft as follows:

> What had so wrinkled her face? Was it an indication of the long while she had resisted her love for the now extremely famous neurologist, Professor Luchardi, who had attended Priscilla? The Churstons never knew Adelaide's feelings, they only knew that she had sent him away, first to unhappiness, then to a successful second attempt at devotion.[54]

Karen Caesar positions the sexual and emotional trajectories within *The Wooden Doctor* as pertaining to the trope of the abused woman, and as situating themselves on the fault line between fact and fiction, between autobiography and art. Evaluating the novel as 'fictionalised autobiography',[55] Caesar explores the possibility that Evans may have suffered sexual abuse during her girlhood, such abuse leading to, among other things, a reluctance to make the transition from girl to woman, thereby entering into 'reproductive reality'.[56] According to Caesar, 'It has been found that the experience of abuse often results in gender precariousness and a high degree of splitting and projection.'[57] From Lady Webster's split personality, 'watching herself' and denying the possibilities of surrender, to Dr Luchardi's assertion in 'The Churstons' that 'promise is so much better than fulfilment, don't you agree?'[58] an unwillingness to assume fully the mantle of sexualised being is indicated.

Evans herself acknowledges, albeit tongue-in-cheek, the extent to which 'The Churstons' may not be a fictional work. Whereas in relation to *The Wooden Doctor* she somewhat disingenuously insisted that her characters were 'purely imaginary',[59] of this text she says quite the opposite: 'Not quite every character is a living person in this story. And not quite the reverse.'[60] An autobiographical reading of Evans's output is further justified by her own assertion, expressed in relation to Emily Brontë, that a writer at her best and most expressive, 'writes herself'. Catharine Earnshaw's 'brief soliloquy at the window [in *Wuthering Heights*] is out of character as the wilful and shallow Catharine's but is in character as Emily Brontë's [. . .] Read her, understand, what is the love of death in a strong soul.'[61] It could

similarly be argued that the theme of sexual frustration, so tellingly cast as celibacy in 'The Churstons' and 'Dear Desdemona' is based in a comparable autobiographical reality.

The trope of the unreceived letter, standing for lack of communication from a loved and desired other, lies at the heart, as we have seen, of Evans's unpublished story of that name. Such letters also feature powerfully in her poetry of that period. In a poem titled 'No Capital Punishment Here' and annotated 'Margiad Evans Cheltenham 1952', the non-arrival of an agitatedly awaited letter from a lover is delineated:

> Do not say 'I' to any body
> but whisper it to your own breast
> 'I, I, I' privately. For it is sacred.
> And do not believe your heart is broken;
> a broken heart doesn't hurt like this,
> doesn't kill [?], comes round, does work, a model prisoner.[62]

The reason that the 'heart is hard' lies in the fact that 'the message [. . .] that would have saved it' has not arrived, has, rather, 'never been posted through the letterbox'. The subject of the missing or unreceived or unsent letter is not confined to Evans's poetry. It recurs in the Notebook, in the plaintive utterance: 'This morning I thought I shall hear from you. But there was no letter [. . .] The light mocked my wretched meditation.'[63]

It is perhaps, at one level, unsurprising that letters should loom so large in Evans's life at this period, given her uprooted and destabilised domestic and familial experience. In a letter to Gwyn Jones on 9 June 1948 she had laid out the coming upheaval, or at least its first stages, as follows: 'It looks as though we may have to shuffle into another cabin again soon. Farm to be sold.'[64] The sale of the farm, as Moira Dearnley recounts, was the beginning of a sustained period of domestic upheaval. Evans spent a year following the departure from the farm staying with relatives. After a trip to Ireland with her husband, they moved to the Black House at Elkstone, on the border, in March 1950, and during the ensuing period Michael Williams, who was training to be a teacher, spent week nights staying away from home and near his training college. In May, Evans suffered her first epileptic fit, becoming pregnant shortly afterwards and giving birth on 22 March 1951. And then, after only a year at the Black House at Elkstone, the real exile began.

The removal from Elkstone and away from Evans's beloved border country heralded a time of separations and letters, of visible trials and subterranean inconsistencies. Whether in relation to motherhood, illness or personal relationships, Evans seems to have been constantly in a state of flux. In a letter dated 7 August 1954, written from Surrey, Evans sketches the continuing trials of motherhood in the following, rather weary, manner:

> Cassie has gone to sleep after the usual bottle over her dinner. She was very good at my sister's but is much worse than ever now. Still not long to go before school only a year and a half.[65]

Continuing tensions of a somewhat different complexion are evident in a letter of 15 July 1956, again from Surrey:

> Cassie [. . .] has had a mouldy holiday with me ill and her Pa in Paris. But I begin to mend instead of dying – which I'll see stops Paris. The doctor says the improvement is extraordinary. Pity to die suddenly and spoil it. I think I will write a short story on that ironical theme.[66]

Estrangement and marital tension, of one kind or another, are clearly evident, along with a rather bitter and defiant tone. Other letters, received rather than sent, and from a correspondence begun rather earlier in the decade, exhibit a different tone altogether.

The warm regard felt for Margiad Evans by her surgeon, Frederick Golla, is present in the subject matter and emphasis of the letters he sent to her. The correspondence from April to December 1952 reveals the development of his feelings. In the beginning he addresses his patient as 'Dear Mrs Williams' and writes of the illness and what she may expect with it. He then progresses to exhortations of courage and so on in later letters. By October there are discussions of beauty and unity and Plotinus. 'Burdens Neurological Institute' is crossed out, and the more personal address of 'Newlands Frenchay' is substituted. By 22 October, written on 'Union Club' paper and headed 'As from Newlands', there is a discussion of love, pity and Radakrishnan.[67] Golla is by now phrasing his communications in a quite intimate way: 'I am writing from a bedroom in a club as I had to come up for a futile meeting this afternoon and get back to the West tomorrow.' By December 1952, he is writing of an impending visit that 'I shall come up on your account only'.[68]

On 5 August 1953, Golla sends a note suggesting alternative times for what he refers to in quotation marks as their 'consultation'.[69] The note is unmistakably written much more as a very close friend than as

a doctor. By 13 October 1953, a line seems to have been crossed, and Golla is linking love, possession and pity in his feelings for Margiad Evans: 'I have been reading your letter for the nth time with infinite pain' he writes, and goes on to elaborate:

> Pity hurts [. . .] like unrequited love for after all what is pity but the intense longing for the good of those we pity and is this other than love? [. . .] Love without the immediacy of possession is not love. I don't know but to feel that certain beings that I reverence are suffering [. . .] gives me an intense longing to be everything to them that others seem to mean by love.[70]

Whether that 'everything [. . .] that others seem to mean by love' was ever enacted is irrelevant here. Frederick Golla and John Leeper Dunlop, the model for *The Wooden Doctor*, are paralleled. Dunlop was about twenty-eight years older than Margiad Evans, and Golla, in his early seventies when Evans was in her early forties, is almost the same number of years older. Even the initials of the two men are closely mappable. Dunlop's were F.L.D., while Golla's were F.L.G. If the progress of Arabella's love for the doctor in *The Wooden Doctor* is intertwined with that of her hysterical illness,[71] and that relation is based on Evans's obsession with Doctor Dunlop, it seems clear that the relation with Golla some thirty years later is tragically entwined not only with Evans's illness in her real life, but also with her faltering creativity. The emergence of the two doctors in 'The Churstons', and their relation to the theme of celibacy, takes on new resonance in the light of Golla's letters.

That Margiad Evans was emotionally engaged with a love that may or may not have been 'unrequited' is illuminated by a poem dated 1955 and written at 'The Bungalow Hartwell', which addresses directly the theme of passion lost or unrequited: 'The world is woven round me, but/I remember only that you went', the lament goes. 'The world is woven round me tightly, and/the world is spent'.[72] The object of these feelings of loss and abandonment is clear. The poem is titled 'To F.L.G', and the titling is underlined three times.

In the radio play *December Day*, Margiad Evans (the narrator) points up the price Evans (the narratee) pays for her double role of writer and outsider. Having been criticised by 'Old Morgan' for her unwomanly, writerly propensities, the recollecting Evans muses: 'Sometimes I wish I could be more of a person and less of a reflection of what is here. After all, I may lose it, and what happens then?'[73]

The question is, in hindsight at least, prophetic. In 'The Nightingale Silenced', Evans states her belief that 'It is true that somewhere centrally a calm and solemn detachment persists and has always persisted amid my extravagance [. . .] From this central theme of the spirit has sprung all my work including the tragic and the comic.'[74] The 'detachment' is directly related to the idea of being 'a reflection of what is here'. A mirror, after all, is eternally detached from that which it is reflecting. Evans's character in 'The Letter', Geraldine, so closely related to her creator in many ways, similarly characterises herself as 'born to observe'.[75] The inference here is that detachment and observational space are essential to the processes of creativity for the writer. 'I may lose it, and what happens then?' is at once a prediction and a question born of fear.

I have argued elsewhere that although the border Evans inhabits is on one level that of Wales and England, it is, more importantly, that of Peggy Whistler and Margiad Evans, a psychological, emotional and spiritual border whose aspect mirrors the prevailing cultural anxiety of a Britain seeking, in its marginal spaces, rootedness.[76] It would seem that this psychological, emotional and spiritual borderland was vital to Margiad Evans in providing a liminal territory where the necessary detachment could be practised that would enable her to carry forward her craft.[77]

Evans's character Geraldine, lamenting the fact that she cannot create because 'nothing is seeable', observes that she is 'clogged with recollection'.[78] The recollection with which Margiad Evans was 'clogged' resulted in the publication of *A Ray of Darkness* (1952) and two unpublished autobiographical pieces – 'The Nightingale Silenced'[79] and 'The Immortal Hospital',[80] but did not offer any fresh direction for Evans's more purely imaginative creativity. A passionate exclamation in her Notebook speaks, in its violent image of self-immolation on the exigencies of literary production, of the degree of desperation Margiad Evans suffered through this failure: 'I have taken out my heart and stuffed it with paper', she writes. 'I have wiped my bloody fingers in books.'[81]

If *The Wooden Doctor* came directly out of the mental and emotional turmoil she experienced in her relationship with John Leeper Dunlop, she came to the conclusion that the pain of the experience was justified by the artistic output:

> I was unhappy – what of that? I have conveyed my misery – what of that? Ah a great deal. I have wrought bones, muscles, a beating heart. My book's alive and it was worth it.[82]

By the 1950s, however, Evans seemed unable to utilise the storms and tribulations, including those of her relation with the second doctor, Frederick Golla, to creative advantage. Writing of Arabella in *The Wooden Doctor*, Sue Asbee asserts that 'there is also a sense in which his [the doctor's] care provides not so much a solution as part of the continuing problem'.[83] The same could be said of the care provided by Golla, at least in the emotional storms to which it apparently contributed, and which Evans seems unable, this time, to translate into the 'live' material of art.

Despite the tendencies exhibited in *A Candle Ahead*, Evans's work in the 1950s was not mystical, neither was it looking outward from the self towards nature. She was listening, as ever, to the 'human tune' which, she acknowledges, had always obsessed her and which 'has a great many limitations and has narrowed my work'.[84] That tune though was now heard without mediation. In her earlier work, Margiad Evans had taken the 'human tune' to herself, had capitalised on unease and disturbance, using them to generate creative impetus and energise her fiction with a quality that Tim Longville has characterised as 'dark, edgy, odd [and] wild'.[85] Now, however, exiled from the place she regarded as home, ill and alone, she writes in a 1956 poem 'Christmases' of her own alienated and despairing humanity:

> To-night is Christmas again and I sitting alone
> weave sleep for my child in my arms,
> my arms which are forced
> into the old cradle shape, a bitter woman, ill to the bone.[86]

Here she is writing the self without the mediating force of a detached, constructed and observing alternative identity. Not only has she physically left behind the country that allowed her the precarious detachment of otherness and provided a platform for refraction; she also acknowledges that the liminality on which it was based was illusory.

Katie Gramich remarks on there being only one poem in *A Candle Ahead* that mentions Wales, and that poem to do with an idyllic (not to say romanticised) version of childhood unity with nature.[87] At the beginning of a sonnet titled 'On the Burning of my Letters Unread', Margiad Evans seems, finally, to have come full circle and confronted her own necessary self deception. 'For forty years and more, Earth's *English* ways/I have admired'[88] (my emphasis). Gone is the half-understood allure of the border country, swept away by this casual utterance. The 'one drop of Welsh blood' that she claimed to

have in her veins has been dissipated. Her 'psychological, emotional and spiritual identification with the Border'[89] has been fractured. Margiad Evans has unwritten herself. Peggy Whistler has returned to take her place.

Notes

[1] Margiad Evans 'The Nightingale Silenced', National Library of Wales (hereafter NLW) MS 23368B, p. 34.

[2] Idris Parry, 'Margiad Evans', *Speak Silence* (Manchester: Carcanet, 1988), pp. 306–23.

[3] D. S. Savage, *The Withered Branch: Six studies in the Modern Novel* (London: Eyre and Spottiswoode, 1950). Cited in P. J. Kavanagh, 'Margiad Evans', *The Listener*, 11 November 1972, 640.

[4] NLW MS 23370D, p. 12.

[5] NLW Margiad Evans MSS 42, 'Notebook'; unpaginated. Emphasis in the original.

[6] Margiad Evans, *A Ray of Darkness* (London: Arthur Barker, 1952), p. 16.

[7] For further discussion of Margiad Evans's lack of direction in the 1950s, see Cerdiwen Lloyd-Morgan, *Margiad Evans* (Bridgend: Seren, 1998), p. 130.

[8] Lloyd-Morgan, *Margiad Evans*, p. 85. Sue Asbee however believes *Autobiography* to be a 'contemplative account of her inner life'. Cited in Sue Asbee, 'Introduction', in Margiad Evans, *The Wooden Doctor* (Dinas Powys: Honno, 2005), p. xviii.

[9] Katie Gramich, *Twentieth-Century Women's Writing in Wales: Land, Gender, Belonging* (Cardiff: University of Wales Press, 2007), p. 88.

[10] Lloyd-Morgan, *Margiad Evans*, p. 85.

[11] Gramich, *Twentieth-Century Women's Writing in Wales*, p. 113.

[12] Asbee, 'Introduction', p. xviii.

[13] Ibid., p. xvi.

[14] For further discussion of Evans's family life see Asbee, pp. vii–viii; and Karen Caesar, 'Patient, doctor and disease in Margiad Evans's *The Wooden Doctor*', in Aleksandra Bartoszko and Maria Vaccarella (eds), *The Patient: Probing Interdisciplinary Boundaries* (Witney: Inter-Disciplinary Press, 2011), *www.inter-disciplinary.net/ptb/persons/patient/pat1/caesar%20paper.pdf*, p. 6. Consulted 25 June 2011.

[15] NLW Margiad Evans MS 4/1–144, No. 10.

[16] NLW Margiad Evans MS 23365D, p. 1.

[17] Ibid.

[18] Diana Wallace, 'Mixed marriages: three Welsh historical novels in English by women writers', in ed. Christopher Meredith, *Moment of Earth* (Aberystwyth: Celtic Studies Publications, 2007), pp. 171–84, p. 175.

[19] NLW MS 23373E Radio Scripts, p. 10.

[20] Ibid.

[21] Ibid., p. 13.

[22] Ibid., p. 22.

[23] Ibid.

[24] NLW Margiad Evans MSS 42, 'Notebook'; unpaginated.

[25] NLW MS 23363C, 'The Churstons', p. 2.

[26] NLW MS 23373E Radio Scripts, p. 13.

[27] Ibid., p. 15.

[28] Ibid., pp. 15–16.

[29] As Sue Asbee points out, in relation to *The Wooden Doctor*, Evans's 'need to research background, self-referentially inscribed within the novel itself, functions as a signpost to her position as an "outsider"'. Asbee, 'Introduction', p. xxi.

[30] Margiad Evans, *Autobiography* (London: Calder & Boyars, 1974), pp. 10–11.

[31] Deborah Philips, *Women's Fiction 1945–2005* (London: Continuum, 2006), p. 36.

[32] Gramich, *Twentieth-Century Women's Writing in Wales*, p. 106, citing Deirdre Beddoe, *Out of the Shadows: A History of Women in Twentieth-Century Wales* (Cardiff: University of Wales Press, 2000), p. 134.

[33] NLW Margiad Evans MSS 42, 'Notebook'; unpaginated.

[34] Ibid. Emphasis in the original.

[35] For a discussion of Arabella's suffering in *The Wooden Doctor* see Asbee, 'Introduction', pp. viii–x, or Caesar, 'Patient, doctor and disease', p. 7.

[36] NLW Margiad Evans MSS 17, 'The Letter', p. 2.

[37] Ibid., p. 3.

[38] Ibid.

[39] Ibid.

[40] Ibid.

[41] Evans, *Autobiography*, cited in Moira Dearnley, *Margiad Evans* (Cardiff: University of Wales Press, 1982), p. 28.

[42] NLW Margiad Evans MSS 17, 'The Letter', p. 3.

[43] Ibid., p. 4.

[44] Ibid.

[45] Ibid., p. 2.

[46] Deirdre Beddoe (ed.), *Changing Times: Welsh Women Writing on the 1950s and 1960s* (Dinas Powys: Honno, 2003), p. 5.

[47] NLW MS 23373E 'Radio Scripts'. Annotated by Margiad Evans: 'The scenes are indicated in the course of conversation but I have a copy with the television sets described.'

[48] Ibid., p. 38.

[49] Ibid., p. 44.

50 Ibid., p. 69. My emphasis, except for original emphasis on 'cold'.
51 Lloyd-Morgan, *Margiad Evans*, p. 36.
52 Asbee, 'Introduction', pp. xiv–xv.
53 NLW MS 23363C, 'The Churstons', p. 53.
54 Ibid., p. 14.
55 Caesar, 'Patient, doctor and disease', p. 1. This view is supported by Sue Asbee in her 'Introduction', p. vi.
56 Caesar, 'Patient, doctor and disease', p. 3.
57 Ibid., p. 4, citing Rosalind Minsky, *Psychoanalysis and Culture: Contemporary States of Mind* (Cambridge: Polity Press, 1998), p. 91.
58 NLW MS 23363C, 'The Churstons', p. 87.
59 Cited in Caesar, 'Patient, doctor and disease', p. 1.
60 NLW MS 23363C, 'The Churstons', p. 2.
61 NLW MS 23371B, p. 16.
62 NLW Margiad Evans MSS 4/1–144, No. 14.
63 NLW Margiad Evans MSS 42, 'Notebook'; unpaginated.
64 Cited in Moira Dearnley, *Margiad Evans* (Cardiff: University of Wales Press, 1982), pp. 48–9.
65 NLW MS 22432D, Margiad Evans's Letters; to Dorothy from The Bungalow, Sarwell, Hartfield, Surrey, 7 August 1954.
66 NLW MS 22432D, Margiad Evans's Letters, 15 July 1956.
67 NLW Margiad Evans MSS 900.
68 NLW Margiad Evans MSS 900. Dated 'Paddington 12.45pm 3 Dec 1952' and addressed to Evans at 69 Leckhampton Rd.
69 NLW Margiad Evans MSS 901–21 (1953–4); letter dated 5 August 1953; letter 905.
70 NLW Margiad Evans MSS 901–21 (1953–4), letter 908.
71 See Asbee, 'Introduction', pp. vii–viii.
72 NLW Margiad Evans MSS 4/1–144, No. 136.
73 NLW MS 23373E, p. 16.
74 Margiad Evans, 'The Nightingale Silenced', NLW MS 23368B, pp. 33–4, cited in Asbee, 'Introduction', p. xix.
75 NLW Margiad Evans MSS 17, 'The Letter', p. 3.
76 Clare Morgan, 'Exile and the kingdom: Margiad Evans and the mythic landscape of Wales', *Welsh Writing in English: A Yearbook of Critical Essays*, vol. 6 (2000), 89–118, 98.
77 Rhodri Hayward's belief that 'the imagined landscape of Ross on Wye could be seen as a practical mnemonic' that fed into Evans's sense of identity, supports this contention. See 'Between flesh and friendship: Margiad Evans, F. L. Golla and the struggle for self'. Cited in Asbee, 'Introduction', p. xx.
78 NLW Margiad Evans MSS 17, 'The Letter', p. 4.
79 NLW MS 23368B, 'The Nightingale Silenced'.
80 NLW MS 23369C, 'The Immortal Hospital'.

81 NLW Margiad Evans MSS 42, 'Notebook'; unpaginated.
82 NLW MS 23366D, p. 141. Cited in Caesar, 'Patient, doctor and disease', p. 7.
83 Asbee, 'Introduction', p. viii.
84 NLW MS 23368B, 'The Nightingale Silenced', pp. 33–4.
85 Tim Longville, 'It was my religion to look', *Country Quest* (October 2003), 32.
86 NLW Margiad Evans MSS 4/1–144, No. 142.
87 Gramich, *Twentieth-Century Women's Writing in Wales*, p. 113.
88 NLW Margiad Evans MSS 4/1–144, No. 83.
89 Asbee, 'Introduction', p. xxi.

12

Margiad Evans: Memory, Fiction and Autobiography

SUE ASBEE

'Not quite every character is a living person in this story. And not quite the reverse'[1]

In 1957 when Margiad Evans was forty-eight and aware that she would not live for very much longer, she dedicated two pieces of writing to her daughter, Cassandra. The first was a novella called 'The Churstons',[2] the second a memoir called 'The Immortal Hospital or Recollections of Our Childhood';[3] each is headed *To my daughter Cassandra*. Evans's intention was to publish them together with a third minor work, 'The Green Shade' ('These two short pieces are intended to go with the first one, The Churstons'),[4] but the proposal was turned down by Pearn, Pollinger & Higham and it seems unlikely that she made further attempts to publish. This essay focuses on the two more significant autobiographical pieces, 'The Churstons' and 'The Immortal Hospital'. The two texts could not be more different from each other and although it is not hard to understand why they were not perceived as a commercial proposition by the publishers, they are of great interest for the different ways in which Evans represents her memories.

'The Churstons' concerns six eccentric adults, four sisters and two brothers, from a 'very old and very distinguished family' who have taken vows of celibacy because of the family's 'ancient hereditary suicidal mania'.[5] They divide their time between their home in London and their farm in the country. This odd fictional text is fractured in several places by the appearance of, or reference to 'Margiad Evans', and therein lies its main interest for this study: the way in which she appears first as a character, and later as 'herself' in the text. 'The Immortal Hospital' is, as far as genre is concerned, more

conventional. It is a memoir of the period in Evans's childhood when she and her sister stayed with an uncle and aunt on their farm just outside Ross-on-Wye. Although it remains unpublished, this is the text that any biography or introduction to Evans's work quotes from, as it describes – and in doing so mythologises – a formative moment in her life. Her first view of the river Wye provoked 'some powerful emotion' within her and she could only sob 'Oh don't, don't take me away from this place'[6] when her father indicates that it is time to leave. At the end of her life, then, she identifies a key moment in childhood, locating this place and that moment, as a foundation for her lifelong mystical and spiritual relationship with nature.

By calling the childhood memories 'The Immortal Hospital', Evans locates her present *writing* moment as she faces death, in her youthful, pastoral self: 'Immortal hospital for every kind of misery, physical and mental that a human being can suffer is the remembrance, whole and in parts, of my Uncle Donavan's farm in Herefordshire.'[7] Her use of the words 'immortal' and the reference to suffering suggest a strong spiritual dimension, potent imagery which Mary Warnock also draws on in her study of memory: 'Memory then comes like a saviour. Like a Messiah, it is to save us from the otherwise inevitable destruction brought by death and time.'[8] Thinking of and writing against a future in which she would have no part, Evans returns to the past. The account, then, of the eccentric household of her own childhood, with stories of moonlight gallops on runaway hunters, of a servant girl's pale blue satin blouse and a land girl's unplanned pregnancy, of playing in the churchyard and studying birds' eggs, is a way of asserting identity in the face of destruction. Dedicated to Cassandra, it is also intended to supplement absence, a present to her daughter of her past, standing in for the anecdotes about her childhood that she will never be able to tell. In spite of the dedication, which may suggest private writing, Evans always intended 'The Immortal Hospital' for publication. In the first paragraph, she asks, reasonably enough, 'why should not recollections of my childhood reveal themselves in time to be very inviting reading indeed? For I show every symptom of becoming a rare cult after I am dead: I may indeed sell, for I never have living'.[9]

What exactly is the relationship between these two apparently diverse texts? Her idea that they be published together suggests that in Evans's mind they supplement each other, and that raises interesting major questions about genre, for she finds two very different ways of

talking about and recording her childhood and youth. If 'The Immortal Hospital' is straightforward memoir or autobiography, 'The Churstons' is not. Evans's nephew suggests that her father's nine older brothers and sisters, the Whistler siblings, may be a possible source for the Churstons,[10] but it was her mother's side of the family that had the Buckinghamshire connection where the Churston family live. Thus, if there is a biographical basis for the Churstons, maternal and paternal families merge, and are fictionalised. But the movement between fiction and memory functions as a sharp dislocation at a number of points in the text where the conventions of fiction are ignored. Evans's hybrid narrative is predominantly but not consistently written in the third person. It is neither straightforward fiction, nor first-person autobiographical account, but a rather disconcerting combination of the two. Charting the history of auto/biographical criticism, Laura Marcus says that 'the perceived hybridity which troubled earlier critics is now celebrated, at least by some critics, as a powerfully transgressive property of autobiographical fiction'.[11] Evans's hybrid narrative predates this observation by about forty years.

In an early version of 'The Churstons'[12] which runs to just fifteen pages in a red exercise book, Margiad Evans refers to herself in the third person right at the beginning of the narrative:

> Some said that the name originally was cherry stone, not Churston. However, for over two hundred years it had borne its present form in their native country. There were six of them, Margiad remembered to count although she had only been well-acquainted with a few. Now, as she walked drawing block in hand, through the gardens where a red rose still shone among the box hedging, she recalled them with affection which latterly had been useless. The Churstons were dead it was her youth she was worshipping as she looked at the beautiful little farm-house they had kept so dirtily and so queerly.[13]

In this early draft, 'Margiad' is the perceiving consciousness, aware of the importance of the farmhouse in recollections of her own youth which she 'is worshipping'. But paradoxically the use of her pen name does not work to suggest the kind of straightforward autobiographical pact that a first-person account would do. On the contrary, it deliberately sets out to complicate any such relationship: is 'Margiad' one and the same as the writer of this text, or is she a persona at one more remove from Peggy Whistler, her given name, and the name she would have been known by at the time, as a child? This instability is

complicated two pages later, for 'Margiad' suddenly elides into 'Peggy': 'Peggy looked up at the little farm house which as a child had captured her imagination, as a young woman her delight, as a middle-aged one, her taste.'[14] The movement from pen- to actual name is probably a simple slip, but nevertheless an interesting one. At this stage of composition, the six Churstons' names are not fixed either; this is after all an unfinished exploratory draft, but a writer writing herself into her text always poses interesting questions about the nature of identity and fictionality, and this particular elision from Margiad to Peggy is symptomatic of Evans/Whistler's use of personas evident in her writing elsewhere. In an early diary she refers to herself as 'Arabella', the name she gave her counterpart in the autobiographical fiction, *The Wooden Doctor*.[15] She wrote that novel under the name 'Margiad Evans', but adopted her own initials to sign the frontispiece illustration, which has 'P.W.' in a corner: 'nobody knows I did that too', she wrote in her journal when the book was published.[16] In this early version of 'The Churstons', it may be Margiad who sets off through the gardens with a drawing block in her hand, but it is Peggy the illustrator who 'propped up the drawing block' so that her mother, the Churstons' 'life-long friend', should have something to remember Elm Flowers by.[17] Evans's multiple use of proper names complicates notions of identity, preventing the construction of one single notion of self.

In this early version the Churstons are introduced through Peggy – 'Peggy herself had known of six brothers and sisters & was aware that one had died in infancy, and one had poisoned himself' – juxtaposed against the present moment of the text as Peggy 'the incompetent artist'[18] sketches and takes rose cuttings from the garden after the last of them is gone.

> The pen and wash drawing when it was done, was *irrecoverably* not a likeness. The little house looked too tall and thin, its perfect proportions, of a type to be found nowhere but in England, had slipped *away*, though garden and trees were as exact as an epitaph should be. Elm Flowers! What was its spell? Beauty? Early childhood, or something subtler that meant Escape from Londonism in the very centre of it. Defiance? Peggy had hated the suburban world which she had lived in as a child: though she loved the young sycamore tree in the front garden and even spent hours standing by it and clasping it in her arms. This childish communion was the foundation and the substance of her feeling for Elm Flowers and the Churstons.[19]

If the importance of the River Wye for Evans's emotional and spiritual relationship with nature is fixed for ever by her depiction of the
moment her father says it is time to leave in 'The Immortal Hospital',[20]
'The Churstons', which pre-dates that work, establishes the importance of communion with nature even earlier in her life.

The writing is elegiac, not only for an extant family, but for Peggy's
own past, as well as for a disappearing England: Elm Flowers stood
'so firmly against the rows of mud-cast villas scarcely a mile away. Its
land, cornfields and orchards was the country before it had been
marked.'[21]

Given this tone, it is perhaps hardly surprising that before long the
writer forgets herself – or alternatively and more significantly –
remembers herself so that eventually (if briefly) the narrative shifts
into the first person. We move from a description of 'the beautiful,
pale Guy', whose room in the Churstons' London house was
floor-to-ceiling with books and who 'passed forever out of Peggy's
world' to 'I see myself, when staying there escorted by Ada, walking
candle ahead through the passage to his bed [. . .] turning the right
angles between dark brown calf stain until I reached my pillow.'[22] The
fictional contract is broken and while one effect is of layers peeled
away until the 'real' Margiad/Peggy stands revealed before us, another
effect is inevitably reviewing what has gone before to see where, if
anywhere, truth lies in that narrative. If the writer herself feels the
sketch of the house is unsatisfactory as a likeness, language and
narrative too 'slip away', leaving open the question of where, if
anywhere, truth might lie.

This same movement from third- to first-person occurs in the
version of 'The Churstons' that Evans sent to the publishers, suggesting that here it is not a slip, but a deliberate strategy. The effect is even
more acute, and more sustained as literary conventions suggest that
fiction cedes to recollection. It is evident that genre was much in her
mind when she revised, for an epigraph quixotically declares that 'Not
quite every character is a living person in this story. And not quite the
reverse',[23] in other words, some of the characters are 'living persons'
while others are inventions. Again, at the beginning of the narrative
she says that her story is 'not a crime story, not a love story, not a
novel, but a remembrance'.[24] The decision to adopt a hybrid style
between fiction and autobiography is, then, quite deliberate. Of
exactly whom or what it is a remembrance is less immediately apparent. In keeping with her published novels, she begins with a cast list of

(almost certainly) fictional characters; but Margiad Evans herself, her sister, and her mother, all of whom appear at various points in the narrative, are neither listed nor fictional. They were, at the time of writing, all 'living'. On another level – given the complexities of all representations – in this text they occupy a different level of fictionality from the cast list.

'The Churstons' begins as fiction. The opening sentence of this final draft is brisk and ambivalent about potential readers: 'The first and most important part is to provide a key to the family in case anybody should want to read their extraordinarily uproariously tragic history.'[25] The individual family members, typified by motifs, would seem more at home in a fairytale than a realist novel. Their characteristics are designed to parallel or double each other, rather than suggest any notion of complex characterisation:

> Though there were only six alive and two dead they were a cross word of a family because, as in square dance, they had selected partners. From these they never swerved all their lives.
>
> It is true that Guy Churston and his brother Basil were not at all attached to each other, and seldom looked in each other's faces without dislike, yet their random appearances in both family residences, provided the check or tartan thread, as it were, in this family pattern.
>
> Miss Adelaide and Miss Edith Churston had chosen to be a pair [. . .] Adelaide was the oldest and ugliest, Edith the youngest and loveliest. Miss Thomasina and Miss Elsie were the corresponding couple and the distinction was the same: Thomasina, elderly, plain [. . .] Elsie, younger, handsomer, but not so handsome or so firm as Edith.[26]

With homes in Albermarle Street, London, and Elm Farm, Buckinghamshire, thirty-three miles from London and 'set in deep cherry orchards', the pairs of sisters 'travelled unremittingly to and fro every fortnight, carrying all their clothes, pets, china and saucepans with them on every journey'.[27] The symmetry of pairs of siblings, the town house and the country house, together with the patterned movements between them, all declare that realism was not the main aim of this narrative; it is quite different from the earlier version in this respect, in spite of being designated a 'remembrance', which would have been an apt word for the early draft, but which seems misplaced here. Any possible basis on the Whistler family is concealed, and yet these Churstons interact with the author, her mother and her sister.

Margiad first appears here as:

that queer girl Margiad Evans who writes – you know! – so badly – you may remember her. We invited her to come and stay and write her blasted book. Well she wanted to know when. Of course Thomasina wrote back at once and told her we hadn't really *meant* it.

'She must be crazy,' they all gloomily agreed.[28]

This is one way in which Evans breaks the fictional frame that has been established, by writing her *writing* self into the text while paradoxically remaining absent – invited, but uninvited. She represents herself in several ways in that brief exchange: as someone who writes badly, as a poor judge of social situations, as 'queer' and as 'crazy'. The fictional frame is broken more fundamentally and more interestingly towards the end of the narrative when the third-person point of view quite deliberately shifts into the first-person:

> Every Churston is alive. It is at this period that I begin to know them, for their toleration of me as my mother's crazy daughter has become something warmer and they sometimes invite me and my sister Sian to Albermarle Street when we are routing out publishers. But we don't often leave our Herefordshire home for it is far, unprofitable, and the publishers are obdurate.[29]

The declaration 'Every Churston is alive' sits oddly with the initial statement that 'Not quite every character is a living person in this story. And not quite the reverse',[30] for the Churstons, as we have seen, undoubtedly conform to fictional conventions. Their dialogue and the patterning and structuring devices of the narrative declare that this is a novel, whereas the first-person 'remembrances' that follow the extraordinary claim that 'Every Churston is alive' convey a conviction of personal recollection:

> Memories of our very early childhood begin to mingle with the Churstons at this stage. One moment, as I write, I seem to be sleeping with Sian [identified as her sister Nancy] in a spied-round terrifying bedroom with green baize curtains and Maria's white alabaster hands folded on the mantelpiece under glass, a grown-up young woman; the next I am a baby girl in a pinafore at one of the famous 'cherry-parties'. I will try to take these disorderly memories in sequence.[31]

The first memory is a very early one – she is 'a baby girl' in a push-chair. Her description of 'that eternal feeling of being' is very similar to Virginia Woolf's 'moments of being' in her essay 'A sketch of the past',[32] and indeed the memory itself, like Woolf's early recollection of sitting on her mother's lap on a train or omnibus, and of the 'red

and purple flowers on a black ground'[33] – the material of her mother's
dress – is not of a particular event as such, but crystallises a moment
which, retrospectively, becomes a formative moment, a feeling or
sensation, significant in forging the beginnings of individuality and
identity. Like Woolf's memory, Evans's too includes vivid colour
imagery:

> I am with my mother and sisters at Elm Flowers in Home Orchard. The
> trees are pink or purplish black with fruit and their leaves droop. Great
> wicker baskets full of cherries as shiny as beads stand against the
> tree-trunks . . . it is the day, the famous Day when Edith, Adelaide and
> Basil have asked us to a cherry party. I am too young to pick and I sit in
> the shade in a pushchair – then called a push-cart – looking at meringues,
> sugar cakes, bread and butter plates, of white and black hearts that glis-
> ten and almost flash where they crowd the tables [. . .] But far and
> beyond all these details which are yet one, the essentially ecstatic nature
> of the afternoon, its specialness, its beauty, its preciousness. And above
> all, that eternal feeling of being which the brightest memories of child-
> hood never lose in a lifetime, however long or sad. The almost visionary
> quality is still with me, and the cherry party is part of it; although I do
> not even know whether it is one cherry party or if there were several.[34]

Here, like Woolf, Evans writes uncertainty into her account, acknow-
ledging that memory can be unreliable. Phrases like 'I think', 'I
suppose', 'Perhaps' and 'more probably' qualify Woolf's recollection
of her childhood journey to St Ives,[35] settling eventually on the solution which is 'more convenient artistically'. The facts – one cherry
party or more, a journey going to or from – are far less significant
than the sensations which are recalled with confidence and clarity,
and which are assembled into a story: 'I will try to take these
disorderly memories in sequence.'[36] Like Woolf, Evans reflects on her
writing practice as the narrative unfolds. Her account continues:

> From that moment of peaceful contemplation Elm Flowers became
> myself, a self so dear that now when all the Churstons are dead and the
> farm sold I sneak round with a pen and block and make a drawing of it
> as it was, before any alterations can spoil it.[37]

The sudden time-shift into the present tense at the end of that passage
produces a dislocating jolt. The sentence which begins by declaring
that 'Elm Flowers became myself', and reiterates that that self is 'so
dear', shifts into the notion of loss – ostensibly the death of the
Churstons, but effectively, and perhaps too painfully to be stated
directly even to herself, the imminent loss of that same 'dear self', as

the writer confronts her own death, only months in the future. In the timescale of her life, the recollection of sketching the place functions as an earlier attempt to fix the memory. The scene of the artist drawing Elm Flowers which opened that early draft of 'The Churstons' reappears here then, but the emphasis is quite different; instead of making the sketch as a remembrance for her mother, here the link with the past, the memory of the self as a young child, becomes the very foundation of identity: 'Elm Flowers *became myself*' (my emphasis). The same memory is recounted, but the two very different ways of expressing it change the significance profoundly. Stephen Crites's discussion of his own memories is relevant here:

> . . . some things only slowly [clarify] themselves as I become aware of their significance for my story. From this point of view 'experience' is a single, vast story-like construct, containing many sub-plots, richly illustrated by visual images and accompanied by sounds and rhythms . . . This narrative construct, furthermore, is constantly changing, shifting its accents; some episodes that had seemed important becoming trivial and others emerging from obscurity into central importance.[38]

Evans's revisions of the sketching episode provide evidence of similar shifts of accents, and demonstrate that, inevitably, the self recorded in this narrative is a consequence of the narrative itself. As Laura Marcus says, 'the self does not pre-exist the text but is constructed by it',[39] and multiple narratives will produce multiple selves.

The cherry orchard memory is one of those moments that Mary Warnock identifies as 'the discovery of the individual "me" . . . the subject of all future events and memories of events'.[40] It is pre-verbal; like Woolf as a child in St Ives, waking and hearing waves break on the beach, at the time of the cherry-orchard moment Evans did not have the facility with language to describe what it meant to her; it was, quite simply, a feeling. Similarly, in the River Wye episode in 'The Immortal Hospital', Evans recalls the way that 'the fields and river lay dormant in [her] consciousness' and she would repeat to herself '"They are There", not in language but in mind'.[41] Pre-verbal or not, as Warnock goes on to say,

> Without the recognition of this 'I' to be the subject of all future experiences, there can be nothing on which to latch the kind of memory which is self-conscious recognition. As I value myself, so I value my life, the past that I have.[42]

The moment of recognition of the self as an independent perceiving consciousness is as important as the initial sensation that triggers this recognition – an awareness that both Woolf and Evans demonstrate in the ways in which they present these earliest memories. It is only in the very last months of Evans's life that these moments are written down and identified as formative memories; committing them to paper represents the effort to assert the value of her life when identity and consciousness are under threat of imminent disintegration. Recording them in this way is as much an effort to assert the value of her life as it is to preserve it.

This last period of production is highly significant: in the previous eight years she confronted her illness directly in two narratives. *A Ray of Darkness* (1952) gives an account of the diagnosis of her epilepsy, of her pregnancy and the birth of her daughter. This may make some sense of the Churstons' hereditary 'suicidal mania' and decision to remain celibate, as Evans herself had to make decisions about whether to continue with her pregnancy, needing medical advice about the genetic nature (or not) of her seizures.[43] It is perhaps projecting into the future when she imagines Cassandra reading her text, a veiled way of conveying to her daughter the awful dilemma that she faced. Later, in Tunbridge Wells Hospital in 1954, Evans wrote the unpublished 'The Nightingale Silenced',[44] a pathography which continues to chart the progress of her illness in its more acute stages. Those two texts are first-person accounts, directly confronting terminal illness; each defines, reassesses, and works to assert a sense of identity within her new constrained circumstances. In contrast, writing 'The Churstons' in the third person as her condition deteriorates could be seen as a writer's holiday, freeing her imagination, while the self that she represents within the narrative never reaches an age when illness has to be confronted. Hereditary problems are displaced onto fictional characters. 'The Immortal Hospital', on the other hand, is a reminiscence designed to alleviate 'every kind of misery, physical and mental that a human can suffer'[45] by returning to memories of childhood at Benhall Farm (referred to as Hill Hall in her narrative) near Ross-on-Wye:

> When lying awake, half teased by sleep or by my disorder or the horrible associations this disorder has brought. When burnt by sorrow and hollowed by pain, when all the misery and narrowness of that nature which is often a writer's makes me writhe like a snake over my own length of Self which I have collected behind me, at moments I can still be little Margiad at Hill Hall, if I try. Memory does not repose there

ordinarily – a brooding mind seldom broods on happiness – but memory can be *sent back* by deliberate will. And once there, an ethereal happiness permeates me and penetrates my restless mind. Some unhurried, incorrupted [*sic*] peace the scenes bring to me which seem to soothe my young troubled self to sleep in my old body.[46]

Mary Warnock suggests that 'childhood experiences . . . are not to be understood, as Freud might seem to understand them, as *causing* us to be as we are. It is rather that we cannot understand or explain what we are without reference to our childhood.'[47] This is very much Evans's position, for her narrative begins by drawing attention to the past in relation to the moment of writing: 'I was nearly eleven years old when I went with my sister Sian to live with my Uncle and Aunt.' She follows this very soon after with 'I am now forty-eight'.[48]

The imagery she draws on to describe her memories in this text recalls Woolf's description of how she 'digs out beautiful caves behind [her] characters'[49] in the work that was to become *Mrs Dalloway* (1925). Evans's initial image is a less active, but equally potent one: 'Writing about childhood one channel leads into another, as in one of those huge prehistoric caves and each chamber, decorated with its fanciful drawings more absorbing than the last.'[50] The way each writer used the idea of caves says a great deal about how they thought of memory as foundation for the self. Caves, after all, are of indeterminate space, dark, possibly dangerous, perhaps beautiful. Woolf, constructing fictional lives, digs her caves behind her characters. Evans's cave walls are painted, one leading to the next, reminiscent of Woolf's interior monologues where association of ideas are the bedrock of individual consciousnesses.

Neither Woolf nor Evans thought of the self as a single and autonomous entity, but a complex composite. The subtitle of 'The Immortal Hospital' is 'Recollections of Our Childhood', recognising that any sense of self or identity is not formed in isolation, but also built upon relationships. 'Our' refers not to Evans's cousins, but to her younger sister, Nancy, referred to throughout this narrative, as she was in 'The Churstons', as 'Sian'. Evans distinguishes herself from her sister, 'she the younger, bolder spirit, who had in her already the spirit to dislike, to rebel' but equally emphasises their closeness: 'Sian and myself so different, yet so closely bound in our harmony with natural time and natural laws'.[51] While the cherry party memory and the moment by the River Wye recall essentially solitary foundations for the construction of identity, Evans also insists (as she did in 'The Churstons' by

showing how those fictional lives intersected with hers) on social aspects of development:

> If I write the words 'the old playroom' there comes to me a sense of so many things, past even then, that I forget my own past, and am once more part of my cousins' who had grown up and left it as fledglings fly from the nest. Objects I thought forgotten materialise in my mind; smells, books, and the empty grate in which Sian and Katherine, my youngest cousin who was sixteen, sometimes lit a blaze of fir cones [. . .] Oh enough memories in that one room alone to make up a whole person. And none of them solitary or isolated [. . .] but rubbed and worn together, inseparable as the beads of a Rosary.[52]

In Hermione Lee's terms, identity here becomes 'an undifferentiated part of a greater whole',[53] as Evans's own individuality is subsumed in the past of cousins who had already grown up and gone before she inhabited their playroom. This preoccupation is developed as she dwells again on the connectedness of memory and lives: 'I am only trying to gather the impressions and recollections of one year, but now that I have begun one leads into another, and so on, until it seems not only my own childhood entire, but Sian's and our cousins' too'.[54] Later in the narrative she returns to her original image: 'So chamber leads into chamber, passage into passage of remembrance, as in the garden the smell of lilac leads us on to the violets and the first pansies.'[55] These apparently artless recollections are not without structure and organising devices.

In this example from 'The Immortal Hospital' there is a clear similarity to ways in which memory and identity are shaped by place in 'The Churstons'. The words 'memory' and 'remember' are repeated throughout that text, while the house is a repository for them:

> Basil took the parrot and disappeared with her somewhere in the shadows and murmurs of the great house. What shadows they were! What murmurs! They were like recollections that had escaped from the Churstons and materialised themselves into this form of memory – the memory of a house that has a sort of being. 'It was Here. It was Here' every Churston would murmur from time to time, for they had lived there since childhood.[56]

Sense of place in each text is important not only for individual, but also collective identity, and in addition stresses the interdependence of the two.

Both texts end abruptly with deaths, but whereas 'The Immortal Hospital' has a final elegiac note, 'The Churstons' has a final 'nobody

cares' flourish. The family buy a Baby Austin, and Edith (the 'young-est and loveliest')[57] learns to drive. This leads to the last first-person memory. On their journey to tour Wales, the Churstons visit Margiad and her mother who give them tea, load their car with vegetables, and push their car down the hill, for it has run out of petrol: 'What happened at the bottom of the hill we never heard; we never saw the Churstons on earth again.'[58] All later die in a car crash, except Adelaide who ends her days in a nursing home 'seeming to try to untangle the look of memory on her face'.[59] Far from being valued, the letter she wrote expressing her lifetime's thoughts about love, existence and the meaning of life is found after her death and dismissed with a scribbled word at the bottom which 'might have been "courage" or "all rubbish". Nobody knew or cared which. THE END.'[60]

'The Immortal Hospital' concludes almost equally abruptly after the chapter heading 'VI An Animal Tragedy. The End'. Uncle Donavan's 'beautiful strong colt, superb in bone and promise of growth' and only five years old, has to be destroyed.[61] It hardly needs saying that this appears to function as a displacement for her own death, which by definition she will never write. Within this same penultimate paragraph she moves from Uncle Donavan's reaction to the horse's death – 'he minded very much' and was 'silent for days' – to general comments about her narrative and all the 'various versions of our childhood' which she has not included. Completeness, she says, was not her intention, for the writing is 'not a record but a refuge for joy'.[62] Effectively, she says that her gaps and silences are eloquent and she draws on a painterly image to explain: 'in the tender pictures painted by the English watercolourists where suddenly, it may be at the very heart of the scene, the artist's hand has deliberately halted, and left space to speak of luminousness'.[63] The abruptness of both these endings suggests the understandable pain of concluding these narratives for a woman who has spent her life expressing herself, whichever genre she wrote in, and who recognises that she lacks the strength to undertake another major writing project.

Notes

[1] National Library of Wales (hereafter NLW) MS 23363C, p. 2.
[2] NLW MS 23363C, 'The Churstons'.

3 NLW MS 23369C, 'The Immortal Hospital'.
4 NLW MS 23363C, 'The Churstons', p. v. 'A Green Shade' (Margiad Evans MSS 22) is a short fictional account of an eleven-year-old girl's conversations with an older woman. It is of little interest and is not discussed in this essay.
5 NLW MS 23363C, 'The Churstons', p. 5.
6 NLW MS 23369C, 'The Immortal Hospital', p. 17.
7 Ibid., p. 1.
8 Mary Warnock, *Memory* (London: Faber and Faber, 1987), p. 141.
9 NLW MS 23369C, 'The Immortal Hospital', p. 1.
10 Email from Jim Pratt, 18 March 2010.
11 Laura Marcus, *Auto/biographical Discourses: Theory, Criticism, Practice* (Manchester and New York: Manchester University Press, 1994), p. 9.
12 NLW Margiad Evans MSS 19. (There are two other, incomplete, versions of 'The Churstons': 'The Churstons' vol. I (second copy), NLW MS 23361A; and 'The Churstons' vol. II, NLW MS 23362A. These are incomplete drafts, discussion of which would over-complicate this essay.)
13 NLW Margiad Evans MSS 19, 'The Churstons', p. 1.
14 Ibid., pp. 2–3.
15 Margiad Evans, *The Wooden Doctor* (Oxford: Basil Blackwell, 1933).
16 NLW MS 23366D, journal entry for 17 March 1933.
17 Margiad Evans MSS 19, 'The Churstons', p. 4.
18 Ibid., p. 7.
19 Ibid., pp. 5–6. Emphasis in the original.
20 NLW MS 23369C, 'The Immortal Hospital', p. 17.
21 Margiad Evans MSS 19, 'The Churstons', p. 6.
22 Ibid., p.10.
23 Ibid., p. 2.
24 Ibid.
25 Ibid., p. 1.
26 Ibid.
27 Ibid., p. 2.
28 Ibid., p.12.
29 Ibid., p. 99.
30 Ibid., p. v.
31 Ibid., p. 99.
32 Virginia Woolf, 'A sketch of the past', in Jeanne Schulkind and Hermione Lee (eds), *Moments of Being: Autobiographical Writing* (London: Pimlico, 2002), p. 82.
33 Schulkind and Lee (eds), *Moments of Being*, p. 78.
34 NLW MS 23363C, 'The Churstons', pp. 99–100.
35 Schulkind and Lee (eds), *Moments of Being*, p. 78.
36 NLW MS 23363C, 'The Churstons', p. 99.
37 Ibid., p. 100.

[38] Stephen Crites, 'Storytime', in Theodore R. Sarbin (ed.), *Narrative Psychology: The Storied Nature of Human Conduct* (New York and London: Praeger, 1986), pp. 152–73, p. 161.

[39] Marcus, *Auto/biographical Discourses*, p. 180.

[40] Warnock, *Memory*, p. 133.

[41] NLW MS 23369C, 'The *Immortal* Hospital', p. 17.

[42] Warnock, *Memory*, p. 133.

[43] Margiad Evans, *A Ray of Darkness* (London: John Calder, 1978), pp. 128–9.

[44] NLW MS 23367B and NLW MS 23368B, 'The Nightingale Silenced'.

[45] NLW MS 23369C, 'The Immortal Hospital', p. 1.

[46] Ibid., p. 37.

[47] Warnock, *Memory*, p. 115.

[48] NLW MS 23369C, 'The Immortal Hospital', p. 1.

[49] Anne Olivier Bell (ed.), *The Diary of Virginia Woolf*, Vol. II, 1920–4 (Harmondsworth: Penguin, 1981), p. 262 [June 1923].

[50] NLW MS 23369C, 'The Immortal Hospital', pp. 4–5.

[51] Ibid., p. 22.

[52] Ibid., p. 5.

[53] Hermione Lee, introduction to Schulkind and Lee (eds), *Moments of Being*, p. 18.

[54] NLW MS 23369C, 'The Immortal Hospital', pp. 15–16.

[55] Ibid.

[56] NLW MS 23363C, 'The Churstons', p. 7.

[57] Ibid., p. 1.

[58] Ibid., p. 115.

[59] Ibid., p. 119.

[60] Ibid., p. 123.

[61] NLW MS 23369C, 'The Immortal Hospital', p. 54.

[62] Ibid., p. 55.

[63] Ibid.

13

'Eternity is Now my Mood': A View of the Later Writings of Margiad Evans

MOIRA DEARNLEY

Writing about her sister, Margiad Evans, Mrs Nancy Nightingale once observed that 'Looking back I sense that maybe all her life she was influenced by her comparatively early death and that much of her writing was written so to speak from her death bed.'[1] D. S. Savage, an early critic of Evans's work, considered that she was obsessively concerned with the idea of death but failed to take into account in his comments on *Autobiography* (1943) that as a deeply religious writer she was essentially preoccupied with the apprehension of 'eternity'. Even if one puts aside what this might have meant to her in terms of mystical experiences in the course of her everyday life, it is not a straightforward matter to summarise what she understood by the afterlife. Her conviction that death was to be welcomed as a means of final union with God and that in some form or other she would live on joyfully as part of the natural world – ideas most cogently expressed in the verse included in *A Ray of Darkness* (1952) – was probably eroded, though never totally destroyed, during the long illness that followed her first major attack of epilepsy in May 1950. At the same time, Christian doctrines that she claimed to wholly reject clearly influenced her thinking about the subject. Tracing her thought processes on these matters, particularly in the last few years of her life, is complicated by the fact that many of the poems that were almost certainly written during this period are undated and survive only in manuscript. Even so, a tentative attempt in this essay to 'make sense' of Margiad Evans's perennial concern with 'the last things' is offered in the belief that to do so is essential to a full understanding of her work.

In an autobiographical essay, 'The Immortal Hospital', written shortly before she died, Evans makes it clear that while she believed in

God, she rejected orthodox Christian belief. Writing of the year of family crisis when she and her younger sister stayed with an aunt and uncle at Benhall, a farm near Ross-on-Wye, she recalled attending matins at Bridstow parish church:

> I loved the words. But I wasn't a Christian. Neither at eleven years old did I intend to be. Perhaps it has brought me much misery: I can only say that it wasn't by my choice. The thing seemed fixed and settled. At the naming of Jesus Christ both Sian and myself resolutely refused to bob our heads, though scolded for this lack of grace. Neither influenced the other; we never discussed it. I am not even aware of her state of heart then, but I am of my own. With all the other voices I would state confidently:
>
> 'I believe in God the Father Almighty, Maker of Heaven and Earth . . .' and than [*sic*] close my lips *intentionally*, determined not to utter untruth in that place, even to please Aunt Fran. I was quite conscious *why* the continuation was unatterable [*sic*] and the opening of the Creed of the Church of England has been my only 'religious' belief in all my life that I could with truth expose in words.[2] (Emphasis in the original)

Margiad Evans believed in God the creator, though she could not declare 'with truth' even as a child that she believed in 'The Resurrection of the body, And the life everlasting'. By the time she published *Autobiography*, her idea of eternity was inseparable from her reverence and love for the natural world and in particular for 'my own country' on the Herefordshire border.[3] For Savage, *Autobiography* was a work that 'smells of mortality', one to be castigated as the 'final repudiation of personal values and [a] calmly despairing desire for the merging of the soul into the life of the natural universe'.[4] Evans certainly felt an ecstatic sense of oneness with the created universe but in 'The Winter Journal', for instance, she clearly experiences anything but despair as she joyously tramps the countryside with M[ichael], her future husband, while the newly budding trees in the woods afford her a glimpse of eternity:

> Take my soul to Paradise
> in February harmonies.
> And some old and dove-worn tree,
> bud-tinted, be eternity.[5]

Evans's conviction that 'the soul pours outward from us to join all in the world that is grown from light to merge with the universal atmosphere within and about the body of the earth and the sky' (*A*, p. 80) persuaded her that she might become an inseparable entity of the

natural world she loved so intensely. In a passage in 'Journals at Dawn', she describes a day spent alone on a hillside, her 'ghost' potentially brought into being by her love of place: 'Yet there were pangs in me – a ghost. I don't know what it means, my love, nor what tongueless uttering I overhear, but it is true, my love, for these lands will make a ghost of me.' Later in the same passage, however, it seems doubtful whether her 'ghost' will haunt the hills she loves: 'The thought of this spot is eternity, itself in all disguises. My country, my *body*, why must I die and leave you, why was I born away from you, why am I not your native spirit? To me the sun rises over Chase and sets over Garway' (*A*, p. 93). Evans used a quotation from this passage in *Autobiography* to preface 'To the Mountains', first published in *Poems from Obscurity* (1947). Here, the Herefordshire hills have been transformed into a mountainous landscape imbued with spiritual significance, 'of a purity high ranged/Above all disbelief'. Describing the mountains as 'a psalm of the ages, and earth's word/For "evermore"', she can feel her soul linked to their creation and their 'abiding', though she does not fully understand how this can come about ('Only my ghost guesses, or I guess the ghost love makes'). She welcomes the remoteness and distance of the mountains from herself, and is happy to 'have them guessed' even when they are invisible: 'For then it is enlightened with the certainty of forecast,/ I feel my spirit's path within my living feet'.[6]

Other items in *Poems from Obscurity* suggest, however, a more troubled view of her 'spirit's path'. In 'Resurrection', first published in 1945, the poet looks into her mirror by candlelight as a gale creates a whirlwind of dead leaves outside her window. As the leaves are metamorphosed into 'risen trees again', the image of the poet's 'resurgent hands' holding the mirror suggests that she too is 'risen . . . again'. But as she stares at her image in the glass, 'weedy with brown hair', she does not recognise her resurrected self: 'Oh, who is there?' (*PO*, p. 15).[7] Even more perplexing is 'The Inner One', which appears to form a pair with 'Resurrection' ('LAST night I looked into the glass/Under the candle flame . . .'), though the poems are not placed side by side in the published volume. Here the speaker discovers that she has lost 'that inner one/ Who loved the climate of my soul'. She had expected that this inmost self would survive after death as her 'ghost':

> I thought that it would never leave,
> That it would be the ghost
> Which when its eye-lit world was done
> Would find recession in my dust.

But she is wrong. As she lifts her hands tentatively to the mirror, she sees a change in her reflection ('Blank eyes, blank hair'). The tilted flame pouring through the glass lights 'on that empty place/I must call me, since that has gone/ Which hidden was my face' (*PO*, p. 34). Her horror at the idea of this loss of identity is evident in an unpublished poem, 'Halt here or there', which survives in a manuscript dated September 1947. Tearfully protesting 'I *cannot* die' and that to leave 'myself in me' is too bitter, too frightful to bear, she longs to survive as part of the created universe, but with her identity intact:

> But I would die whole
> like the sun
>
> in a passion of ending,
> to re-arise as myself
> in the fields which are my joy.[8]

There can be little doubt that Evans was referring to the 'inner one' (and possibly to 'myself in me') when, in an essay on Byron and Emily Brontë published the following year, she defined mysticism as 'A singling out of *the* self among the Selves'. It is also evident that she was already frightened of death even though she could write confidently that for one 'who consciously holds sustained relations with the absolute', the ultimate state of mysticism is 'pacifism towards death', reached when he or she cannot live without God.[9]

Shortly after the essay was published, Evans was forced to leave her 'own country' when the farm on which Michael Williams, her husband, worked was sold and they lost their cottage. Temporarily homeless, she went to stay with her younger sister in Buckinghamshire. 'So terrified and bewildered were my husband and I at our separation from each other and our lovely county (Herefordshire) that he lost his head one day and had a dog we both adored put down.'[10] She found herself 'dissolving into desolation' in the aftermath of these traumatic events and even when she began to recover from her 'terrible grief' her writing was dark indeed:

> grief is never unlearned. My entranced youth was over, prolonged as it had been by feeling through the imperishable earth. I wrote until early mornings in my bedroom, listening to the sound of the pine trees above my room whose shadow it seemed I could hear in the dark. And my poems were all on death, were all requiems. Derek Savage, in his survey of the modern novel *The Withered Branch*, said he had discovered 'the death wish' in my work written years before. I had never felt it until then, in fact I do not think it was in truth present before. (*RD*, pp. 17–18)

A number of the poems written at this time were included in *A Ray of Darkness*. In the first of three requiems which reflect the exalted state of being at one with nature celebrated in *Autobiography*, she bids fare-well to the 'green life' but asks rhetorically:

> What statelier fate
> could Immortality create
> or Prayer provide
>
> than to be buried in your native star
> with all of pompous space as sepulchre?

In 'Requiem II' the soul goes silently 'with stars to burial' and in 'Requiem III' the last look the poet releases on earth travels with the sun towards night, 'Until winds close and skies begin/their lofty lantern climb' (*RD*, pp. 25–6). In 'Traveller's Joy', written during the same period, the speaker imagines herself 'travelling in the grave' as old man's beard (*clematis vitalba*): 'a thoughtful eye on Nature's constancy/is bound to meet me often coming home'. Here again, as she explains in a note on the poem, she was expressing her conviction that 'my being and all natural life were in substance and spirit, one, and that in one form or another, life lives on' (*RD*, p. 22).

On a first reading of 'The Will', also written during this period, it appears that Evans is once again averring that in life and death she is at one with nature. The poet bequeaths her possessions to the universe: to the stars, for instance, she leaves 'the praying habit of my eyes,/For there God took them' and to the sun – even more enigmatically – 'my Hopes/to breed, a golden spread of sight'. She will take with her 'gold untellable' to wall, to floor and to roof her coming night:

> for with the gold I leave and take
> much I may build of visions to entomb
> Egyptian me, with seeds and weapons left
> intact beneath an empty throne.

The author's comment on this poem suggests, however, that although she had rejected the Christian faith while she was still a child, she was not unaffected by its promise of eternal life:

I remember how pleased I was at finding the word 'Egyptian' in my mind, with its associations with the long quiet dead. Yet there is in 'seeds' and 'weapons' an idea of a resurrection. I had, and perhaps still have, no faith which will contain my worship of the earth; and I do not think I believe in an Eternal separate identity of the soul. Yet the sight

of loveliness, the sound of Bach's music would, each time, make even this for a little while possible. And the greatness and goodness of some men. Who, meeting a good man of whatever faith in God, has not felt the Resurrection? And who of us has not, though he can turn to no church, a priest in his heart? (*RD*, pp. 23–4)

It is perhaps not overstating the case to suggest that despite her 'worship of the earth', Evans may have longed to 'believe in an Eternal separate identity of the soul'. Indeed, the terror of realising that this might not be so almost certainly generated 'Resurrection', 'The Inner One' and 'Halt Here or There'. In an untitled poem, probably written a few months after 'The Will', while she was still homeless and staying with her sister-in-law in Gloucester,[11] Evans appears to be contemplating a lifetime of spiritual loneliness spent in the shadows before she is gathered into God's eternal embrace:

> Never send thy thoughts for me,
> I will stay in loneliness
> living till all shadowless
> droops on me Eternity.
>
> When so patient, thou in bliss
> and peace and sight shall gather me
> to mingle in thy breast with thee
> forgiving the abyss.
>
> Never send thy voice from thee
> nor let the seldom trumpet call
> only when my hour befall,
> only send thy heart for me.

Although Evans wrote this poem before she experienced her first major epileptic attack, it is used in *A Ray of Darkness* to help sustain her argument that an epileptic is spiritually needy:

. . . I think his disease is not a quality but a lack of quality. Either psychically, or spiritually or even religiously, he is hungry and he is not fed. He can speak to us at least of appetite; and his glimpses of the whole, the Oneness of God, may be as the thought of bread, pure and simple, to the hungry, who do not have visions in their extremity, of a diversity of deliciousness, but of one plain pure satisfaction and peace. (*RD*, p. 159)

Evans was, of course, ascribing to her fellow sufferers her own longing for 'satisfaction and peace'. She insisted that 'THIS spiritual lack does not take the form of a hunger for any formal religion. It is the

personality, not the presentation of God, that I long for' (*RD*, p. 181). Yet the notion of 'the personality' of God is a Christian one, as indeed is the representation in 'Never send thy thoughts for me' of a loving and eternal relationship with a personal and merciful God 'forgiving the abyss'. (At some point she scribbled what was perhaps an anguished 'oh God!' on one of the manuscript copies of the poem.)[12]

In March 1950, six months after Michael Williams began a teacher training course at St Paul's College, Cheltenham, she and her husband moved into the Black House in Elkstone. On 11 May, while she was alone in the cottage writing a sonnet addressed to the pantheon of 'great men' to whom she frequently paid homage, she experienced her first major epileptic fit, falling 'through Time, Continuity and Being' (*RD*, p. 78). From this time onwards, her health deteriorated inexorably, though the brain tumour that would eventually kill her was not diagnosed until 1956. Writing in her journal on 23 May 1950, less than a fortnight after the attack, she reiterated her view that there is 'no *modern* religious belief which at once contains and worships the earth' (*RD*, p. 91). But referring to the separation that had come about between herself and the earth in recent years, she confessed that she did not expect to be so happy again. A part of her spirit had broken away from life and seemed to be calling her to go after it:

> I know that that is so. That something in me is demanding *its share of death*: and through all my natural and normal fears when death does indeed seem possible, that distant demand, this cry for the experience, sounds profoundly and insistently. It is as though the spirit knows it can't become acquainted with God here. (*RD*, p. 92; emphasis in original)

In the same entry, she claimed that what had happened 'the other night' (which at that stage had not been confirmed as an epileptic fit) had given her 'a glimpse': 'Death is the soul's delight, Death is God, Death grows to be our daily appetite. Give us our necessity' (*RD*, p. 92). The echo of 'Give us our daily bread' in the Lord's Prayer would reverberate in her comment on 'Never send thy thoughts for me'.

Within days of her first epileptic attack, Evans returned to the book she was currently writing on Emily Brontë. Pursuing her thesis that alone of all the women she had read, Emily Brontë 'seemed to have grasped the importance of dying', she refers to Albert Schweitzer's biography of Bach, one of Evans's revered 'great men':

The love of death, as Schweitzer sees it [,] as the truly religious, [*sic*] regard it, is not a morbidity. It is not the love of the grave, of the dark, of the end, but the love of resurrection, the love of freedom, renewal, and the hope of transfiguration. And it arises not from misery and melancholia and disappointment in life, but from a sense of completion.[13]

But she soon abandoned the book. Emily Brontë's mysterious and isolated figure 'was expanding over all the creative figures of literary or thoughtful or poetic greatness' and absorbing the universe as she conceived it (*RD*, p. 14). She could not control the ideas that streamed in upon her:

I felt that I understood the experience she had undergone, which too was a circle having at its centre, death. But in trying to put this understanding into words I merely reproduced more circles of my own. And the few dominant, dead personalities who had been in my life such profound influences and interests protruded also into her life – or rather her work, as I saw it. (*RD*, pp. 95–6)

Evans recognised that 'The book as contemplated was nearer to madness than I could face' (*RD*, p. 14).

Soon after the epileptic attacks began, she discovered that she was pregnant but was advised that a termination was unnecessary. On 22 March 1951, a few days after her forty-second birthday, she gave birth to her only child, Cassandra, and in the years that followed she continued as far as she was able to live a busy life as a wife, mother and writer, first in Cheltenham and then in Sussex after her husband took up a teaching post in Hartfield in 1953. In May 1954, following a sharp deterioration in her condition, she was admitted to the Burden Neurological Institute in Bristol where Professor Frederick Golla had treated her as an out-patient for the previous four years. She was discharged in July. After a number of further spells in hospital, she entered the National Hospital for Nervous Diseases in London in January 1956 where an operation, performed by Dr William G. Lennox on 8 February, revealed a gliomatous brain tumour.[14] *A Candle Ahead*, Evans's final collection of verse, was published in the same year.[15]

'Poem' ('I feel it in my being/fast waiting me!'), one of forty-two items included in the volume, had been written while Evans was staying with her sister in Chalfont St Giles. What cryptically 'thickens every window . . . dapples every door!' was made clear to readers when a longer version of the poem was published the following year

as 'Cure' with its deliberately shocking opening line, 'It might do me good to die' (*CA*, p. 18).[16] Yet despite the deteriorating state of the author's health, few of the poems in *A Candle Ahead* refer directly to her illness. One notable exception is 'A Lark Sonnet', addressed to her lover as though from the grave itself ('our name is enrolled/with other dead names in the mason's fold/of wrinkled stone') which provides a metaphor for the coldness that exists between the pair: she points out that she should not feel the weather where she lies 'within the heart's cooled climate'. She claims that 'Eternity/is now my mood', though one suspects that she writes this with bitterness, if not with uncharacteristic irony. Certainly, there is little consolation to be found in the poem: she reminds her lover of the misfortunes that have 'killed' her ('All, all was taken while complete in strength/the hopeful life, its love, its living dream/of joyousness') and ends with the sombre reflection that 'all passion is short voiced, all love lark-length' (*CA*, p. 20).

In the sonnet sequence inspired by Thomas Hardy's 'The Well-Beloved' – in which the poet berates her lover for his indifference, arrogance and contempt (and for burning her letters unread) – sonnet XI is addressed to him in the full knowledge that she will shortly die. Having accused him of striping her universe with shadows, she tells him that 'the evening brings the sound of aerial hearse/ among the topmost leaves, and I have seen/the funeral go by'. Yet she assures him that she is 'reconciled to chill and coming dark, and I/though younger am as sure as you to die' (*CA*, p. 37). In Sonnet III (not obviously a love poem), the speaker's heart stirs 'in its box of darkness' on a still evening of 'complete/quiet, such as I never heard' to repeat again and again '"Lost, loss, lost, loss, lost, loss, loss"/soon to be underlined with death' (*CA*, p. 33). There seems a clear connection with 'Sonnet Number 7' (not part of 'The Well-Beloved' sequence) which laments the double blow the speaker has sustained ('the vision and the place where it could show'), which almost certainly refers to the loss of Evans's visionary sense of 'the earth' and the move from the border country: 'I only know – my heart is lost in loss' (*CA*, p. 23).

'The Forest' had appeared in *The London Magazine* before the publication of *A Candle Ahead* and in Evans's view was one of only two 'significant pieces of writing' she had ever done.[17] She began writing the poem on 6 April 1954 in an over-excited state of mind following a slight epileptic fit and admitted in her journal that it puzzled as well as satisfied her: 'What is the meaning exactly I don't

know – it is not the soul, it is not suffering, but it is some deep experience without a substance of reality *as such* in my life'.[18] The speaker
walks alone in the darkness of the forest, her happiness conveyed in
an extraordinary simile:

> happy in the way no human being should be happy
> in silence, alone, and in shadow.
> I was like the heart of a dead man
> singing in the grave, to be buried forever.

When she encounters 'a stone man with fresh white honeysuckle/
crowning its blindness' – clearly the god Apollo[19] – she recognises the
figure as an effigy of her joy ('holy stone and white scent/linked to me,
sightless') – a reminder of the 'visionary piercing scent' of 'Oh Only
One!' and the 'scent and silence' of 'Cherry Orchard in Bloom'. But
when the bald eyes of the stone figure have 'glared into tears', she
experiences inconsolable grief: 'And I wept deeply, nor sang for the
leaves sang so loudly./And I wept deeply. And I weep always' (*CA*, p.
27).[20] For the present reader, the poem appears to record symbolically
the poet's realisation that at that moment she no longer wished for
death as a rapturous merging of the solitary self with nature: gravely
ill, she now had a desperate need for pity and consolation. Like the
effigy of the poet in 'On Milton's Bust At His Cottage in Chalfont St.
Giles', written while she was temporarily homeless, the stone god is
overcome with grief:[21] both sculpted figures are surely weeping for *her*.
However, Evans's own interpretation of 'The Forest' has a different
emphasis. As she recorded in her journal, she gradually came to realise that the (male) poet walks through his grievous life without
understanding that he is one of the most miserable beings ever born.
Singing with joy in the silence and ecstasy of being alone, he sees the
image of Apollo as a symbol of his happiness until the stone eyes flow
with tears and the silence is broken by music. The poet weeps always
because he has discovered that 'he cannot separate himself from the
misery, pain and loneliness of humanity' (NS, pp. 116–17). Evans's
interpretation is without overt self-pity, but only a few weeks after
writing the poem she found that the most beautiful thing in the Burden
Institute was compassion (NS, p. 7). Here, too, she found comfort in
praying to St Teresa of Avila, whose 'ecstasy in Christ . . . meant nothing to me', but 'who had spread over my body one fold of her habit
and given me respite' (NS, pp. 43, 50). As she observed in her account
of her stay in the hospital: 'In *Autobiography* there was hinted the

belief in God the Creator; *A Ray of Darkness* was to some extent the affirmation of God the Inspirer; in this the latest and saddest M.S. there is a feeling towards God the Compassionate' (NS, p. 9).

Despite the speaker's assertion in 'A Lark Sonnet' that 'Eternity/ is now my mood', there is relatively little reference in *A Candle Ahead* to the afterlife. In 'Poem' ('Sleeping too long the other day'), her dream of the dead who walk into the sun when she awakes ('I could not look where they had gone/into white light') and her sense of being left alone in a single downward ray clearly echo Henry Vaughan's 'They are all gone into the world of light!/And I alone sit lingering here', though Vaughan's apostrophe to 'Dear, beauteous death!' celebrates the 'true liberty' of eternal life that lies beyond the grave, while in Evans's poem the brilliance of the sunlight falling on her bed brings little consolation:

> I slept, then woke, to see
> only the coffin shape of me;
> and other shapes condemned to die
> like me below.[22]

In 'Oh Only One! (Walter de la Mare)', however, the speaker is afforded – or so it appears – a glimpse of that 'world of light'. The poem was probably inspired by de la Mare's 'Alone', his lament for the absence of the nightingale chiming with Evans's own sense of desolation (she describes in 'The Nightingale Silenced' how she was haunted by the memory of the nightingale that had been frightened away from her Cheltenham garden by her home help – 'the absolute symbol of all the joy in existence, the seizures and their treatment never done to me' (NS, p. 187)):

> The abode of the nightingale is bare,
> Flowered frost congeals the gelid air,
> The fox howls from his frozen lair:
>   Alas, my loved one is gone,
>   I am alone;
>   It is winter.[23]

De la Mare laments the absence of a loved one, just as Evans mourns that 'no lover binds my limbs/with his limbs, no kiss/embosses my mouth with lips'. But in de la Mare's lyric, the candle that sheds 'a silent fire' as 'Starry Orion hunts o'erhead' becomes in Evans's more complex poem a metaphor for eternity:

> Owner of miracles I
> when I fade to my bed with a candle ahead

of eternity:
with a candle ahead I die,

when I fade into spinneys of sleep
when I faint into furrows of night.
Oh bright and deep
watcher of miracles I!

Despite the bleakness of waking life for 'the only one', she experiences in 'bright and deep' dreams a vision of eternity: 'seer of miracles I/and lonely for them to be done' (*CA*, pp. 16–17). As for the miraculous vision hinted at as 'a visionary piercing scent' ('the essence/ without its habiliment'), this is possibly made explicit in the poem that follows in *A Candle Ahead*, in which the cherry orchard in bloom is brought into being by an unspoken word in the darkness:

So the stillness and the dark
told to me the orchard:
all its scent and silence in
a mute, white word. (*CA*, p. 17)

As the final poem in *A Candle Ahead* attests, Evans had not abandoned the idea that she would survive as an element in the natural world. This is also evident elsewhere in her work, as in 'The Mistletoe Sonnet', an unpublished poem written in 1954, where she asks to be grafted like mistletoe seed onto a new stem and promises that she will not pine

for the great winds, the bursting appenine
of cloud-edged sun, for life, for breath, so
I shall not be a buried love, forgotten down below
but still green and glorious shall blow.

She imagines being pulled along by boys: 'I shall not die:/oh I would like to be with other joys,/the mistletoe of love: you, that I live by'.[24] In Sonnet XVI, the last poem in 'The Well-Beloved' sequence (once again not obviously a love poem), the speaker demands of the future 'which ghost I can command/best?' While sleeping the previous night she had planned all but the form of her spirit, 'Which blew about like sand/changing from dream to dream without outline', but she now decides that her ghost will not inhabit a place, a stone or a plant – no mountains or mistletoe here. As a spirit even more amorphous than sand blowing about without outline, the voice announces that 'love and memory/I'll be. Thus I my life, when dead, shall exceed' – the enigmatic final words in *A Candle Ahead* (p. 50).

It is undeniable that Evans's poetry is occasionally morbid, even though in her essay on Emily Brontë, she had pinpointed 'the one disfiguring flaw in her poetry . . . her imperfect symbolization of the death emblem – tombs, graves, in every poem that is at all inferior'.[25] Thus, in an undated poem, 'The Day of Ressurrection' [*sic*], the reluctant dead respond to the Last Trump by apostrophising the 'dear black grave' they are leaving behind and complaining that they 'wither in the trumpet-light'.[26] In 'Endor', also undated, the poet has been summoned 'to the séance of my ghost' but is slow to attend the resurrection of her soul as she is still 'loyal to Death who mothered me in earth and snow and sighing'.[27] Both poems include macabre details which have no part to play in 'The Wish', also undated, in which Evans describes the place where she would like to be laid to rest:

> I wish I were in some old place
> where [nearest?] noise the water is,
> straightening its back for the mill race.
>
> There, unwinding like a ball
> silvery, the lark sings over all;
> and the quiet insects crawl.
>
> Let the sight of hills be there,
> blue, old-fashioned, as they were,
> crumpling up the distant air –
>
> Folding space into tall heaps,
> (heap upon heap) and no one speaks
> except the wind, when it shrieks.
>
> I myself folded away, to be
> forgotten, and yet presently
> the stream, hills and all will see
>
> There is pity, there is peace
> and rest where no remem[b]ered face
> clings to the grass in sad embrace.[28]

It is beyond question that she wished to be 'mothered . . . in earth' in her beloved border country – as is evident from the reference to the blue hills 'crumpling up the distant air'. ('Sussex is just horrible', she once told Gwyn Jones. 'Never a blue hill. Dull coloured earth.')[29] But it is not entirely clear whether, forgotten as an individual and unmourned by a lover, she still expects to survive after death by merging her identity with the streams and hills of the landscape. Her longing for pity – divine pity perhaps – as she rests in peace may be a

faint echo of Blake's 'The Divine Image' ('To Mercy, Pity, Peace, and Love') and his conviction that where these dwell 'There God is dwelling too'.[30] Yet a poem Evans sent Gwyn Jones shortly before she died, 'In spring 1957', is a stark reminder that 'God the compassionate' had ultimately shown no mercy in her suffering:

> How could I match such love
> with an unkempt human one?
> Turning, I whispered, 'mercy Lord'
> and God replied, 'I've none'
>
> Love I have to share, and Truth
> Vengeance they say is mine
> But what you ask for my sick child
> transcends the divine.

The speaker strolls away, observing that 'God was no longer there' and offering the only explanation 'that heaven has reverence/for anguish'.[31]

'The Wish' can be usefully read alongside 'Poem', one of Evans's finest poems and one of the last to be published in her lifetime:

> I MUST be dead as these dead vaults
> of skeletons the ark;
> when all can read by loud daylight
> my name, I shall be dark.
> No candlelight when in the Flood
> of earth these bones embark.
>
> The grass thrusts out its fragile sails,
> the wind comes, and the dews –
> not from *this* anchor shall we move,
> not from *this* harbour blow
> to Ararat this salvaged heart,
> this peace-bird from its yews.[32]

The sustained metaphor, in which the tomb becomes an ark anchored for ever 'in the Flood/of earth', conveys the impossibility of sailing to the safety of Mount Ararat. In death, the dove will never metaphorically return with an olive leaf in its beak to encourage Noah to remove the covering of the ark and thus to behold that 'the face of the ground was dry' (Genesis, 8.13). When in 'The Wish' people visit the poet's grave, 'all will see' that she is now at peace, but in this poem 'when all can read' the poet's name, she will be in darkness. There will be 'no candlelight' in the grave – not a vestige here of the 'candle ahead' that

provides the metaphor for eternity in 'Oh Only One!' Yet by means of a curious contrapuntal movement in the poem, the darkness is offset by the fact that in the grassy churchyard the wind blows and the dews fall. The speaker may not be blown along to Ararat, but she is nevertheless safely at anchor in harbour, while the poignant phrase, 'this salvaged heart', suggests that like a ship's cargo salvaged from the sea she has been metaphorically 'saved'. The dove may not carry a leaf from Ararat but remaining near at hand among the churchyard yews, its presence signifies perhaps that, as in 'The Wish', 'There is peace/ And rest' for the poet who suffered so much during her lifetime.

There is some evidence that as she approached the end of her life, Evans experienced consolation of a kind that her rejection of Christianity had generally denied her. 'Sonnet No. 8: On the Return of an Old Metre' (celebrating her rediscovery of the alexandrine metre), dated 15 November 1957, begins poignantly with a declaration: 'Dying, that ancient music returns to me/although my fading hand can scarcely hold the pen'. The comfort that the poetic form brought her at this time is conveyed in a remarkable simile, recalling perhaps the elevation of the host at Holy Communion:

> Too late to save its mission was
> to comfort. When the end comes like a priest
> still its old, proud, silent notes are heard not sounding wars
> but lifting the earthly skies and holding aloft the East.[33]

Another unpublished poem, 'Before and After', signed and dated on the last day of 1957, survives in several different versions and probably represents a polished version of an irregular sonnet composed at an earlier date.[34] It is possible that it may have been written originally in response to one of Professor Golla's letters. Writing to her at the Kent and Sussex Hospital on 12 July (probably in 1955), he had referred to the leitmotif running through all the letters he had received from her during the past few weeks, something often unconsciously disguised 'in a spirit of immature bravado – that is a fear of death'.[35] But in another letter, undated but probably written after the operation performed by Dr Lennox, he reassured her that she was in God's hands: 'We are all part of the universal spirit – we have nothing to fear and nothing of value can we lose – your work, your love for Cassie, your realization of beauty your feeling for others are all part of Reality, they can never perish for they belong to the world of eternal value.'[36] In 'Before and After', the speaker approaches her ordeal with courage (not 'bravado'):

When we are come to death we need have no fears,
nor spread our hands to catch at our shadows' weft.
We are nobly the dead! we are not the bereft.

The consolation that dries the tears of those about to die is that at the end, nothing appears to be altered, discarded or changed. The good and the evil alike leave behind all arrears: 'We are content, we are debtors forgiven the debt', as though she and all mankind have received a merciful response to the petition in the Lord's Prayer, 'And forgive us our debts, as we forgive our debtors' (St Matthew 6.12). The five lines that end the poem look to the possibility of life after death, but the dream of eternity here is a dark one, not illuminated even by 'a candle ahead':

A dark dream lies before us unwinding its length;
we will forget what in life most brightly was shown,
we will forget what was so gaudily grown,
we will forget ourselves in the glass where we saw
ourselves we had sworn – but before – but before.[37]

The final couplet, which appears in another version as 'And you will forget yourself in the glass where you saw/yourself as you thought you were shown – but before',[38] recalls the speaker's changed face in the mirror in 'The Inner One' and 'Resurrection' in *Poems from Obscurity*, though in 'Before and After' she appears to accept that the knowledge of the self before death is illusory: implicitly, she will at last know herself after death (perhaps alluding to but reversing the image of the dark mirror in I Corinthians 13.12, 'For now we see through a glass darkly; but then face to face: now I know in part; but then shall I know even as also I am known').

But in 'For My Friends/New Year 1958', probably written the day after Evans made the fair copy of 'Before and After', there is no mistaking the bitterness she felt as death approached: 'What does one care relentlessly forced into dying/Whether the faces are laughing or lying?'[39] She was admitted to the Kent and Sussex Hospital for the last time on 19 January[40] and died there on 17 March 1958, her forty-ninth birthday. We cannot know whether the end came 'like a priest . . . lifting the earthly skies and holding aloft the East' or whether she was vouchsafed 'a candle ahead/of eternity' in the darkness – but hope that it was so. She was buried on 20 March, in the parish churchyard in Hartfield. Her longing for a final resting-place 'in some old place' in the border country remained unfulfilled but its image – blown by the shrieking wind and filled with silvery lark song

– survives (like the cherry orchard brought into being in the darkness by the power of the word) in a bundle of manuscripts in the National Library of Wales, here transcribed where 'all can read'.

Notes

1. Letter from Mrs Nancy Nightingale to the author, postmarked 2 July 1981.
2. National Library of Wales (hereafter NLW) MS 23369C, pp. 42–3. In 'The Immortal Hospital', Evans refers to her younger sister, Nancy, as Sian, and to her aunt, Mrs Annie Lane, as Aunt Fran.
3. Margiad Evans, *Autobiography* ([1943] London: Calder and Boyars, 1974), p. 18.
4. D. S. Savage, *The Withered Branch: Six Studies in the Modern Novel* (London: Eyre and Spottiswoode, 1950), pp. 122–3. The essay was originally published as 'Margiad Evans and the cult of nature', *South Atlantic Quarterly*, xlv, 2 (April 1946), 222–41.
5. Evans, *Autobiography*, p. 41. Hereafter *A*.
6. Margiad Evans, *Poems from Obscurity* (London: Andrew Dakers, 1947), pp. 40–1. Hereafter *PO*.
7. First published in *The Welsh Review*, IV (March, 1945), 21.
8. NLW, Margiad Evans MSS 1.
9. Margiad Evans, 'Byron and Emily Brontë', *Life and Letters Today*, 57 (June 1948), 193–216, 193, 194, 202, 203.
10. Margiad Evans, *A Ray of Darkness* ([1952] London: John Calder, 1978), p. 17. Hereafter *RD*.
11. One manuscript of the poem, 'The Only Meeting', is endorsed 'Present address 15 St Aldate Street Gloucester'; another is entitled 'Send for Me' (NLW, Margiad Evans MSS 4/3, 4/8).
12. NLW, Margiad Evans MSS 4/8.
13. NLW MS 23371B, p. 15.
14. In September 1954 Margiad Evans was admitted to the Kent and Sussex Hospital, Tunbridge Wells, and spent 'a few hours' at Hurstwood Park Hospital, Haywards Heath, from which she discharged herself (information gathered by W. Arnold Thorpe, NLW, Margiad Evans MSS 20, June 1982 Deposit). She probably returned to the Kent and Sussex Hospital in the summer of 1955 (letter dated 12 July [1955] to Evans from Frederick Golla, NLW, Margiad Evans MSS 925).
15. Margiad Evans, *A Candle Ahead* (London: Chatto & Windus, 1956). Hereafter *CA*.
16. 'It might do me good to die' was written in Evans's journal on 26 October 1948 (NLW, Margiad Evans MSS 40). 'Cure' was published in *New Poems 1957*, ed. Kathleen Nott, C. Day Lewis and Thomas Blackburn (London: Michael Joseph, 1957), pp. 44–5.

17 NLW MS 23368B, 'A Nightingale Silenced', p. 116. Hereafter NS.

18 NLW, Margiad Evans MSS 27.

19 Evans's association of Apollo with honeysuckle is explained in *A Ray of Darkness*, p. 15n.

20 'The Forest' was first published in *The London Magazine* (September, 1954), 11.

21 Evans, *A Candle Ahead*, p. 18. A version of 'On Milton's Bust' was written in Evans's journal a few days after she visited the poet's cottage at Chalfont St Giles on 16 October, 1948 (NLW, Margiad Evans MSS 40).

22 Evans, *A Candle Ahead*, p. 24; Louis L. Martz (ed.), *Henry Vaughan* (Oxford: Oxford University Press, 1995), pp. 107–9.

23 De la Mare, *The Collected Poems of Walter de la Mare* (London: Faber & Faber, 1979), p. 100.

24 NLW, Margiad Evans MSS 4/30. Other versions of the poem survive in manuscript (Margiad Evans MSS 4/28 and 4/29).

25 Evans, 'Byron and Emily Brontë', 206.

26 NLW, Margiad Evans MSS 4/98.

27 NLW, Margiad Evans MSS 4/104, untitled. Another version of the poem has the title 'Endor' (Margiad Evans MSS 4/105).

28 NLW, Margiad Evans MSS 4/71. Another version, 'A Wish', which ends 'To be/forgotten, and yet presently/(beside the stream) memory', echoes perhaps sonnet XVI in *A Candle Ahead* where the poet's 'ghost' will take the form of 'love and memory' (Margiad Evans MSS 4/72).

29 Letter from Margiad Evans to Gwyn Jones, 21 January, 1954 (NLW, Gwyn Jones Papers 74/165).

30 Alfred Kazin (ed.), 'The Divine Image', *The Portable Blake* (Harmondsworth: Penguin Books, 1976), p. 91.

31 NLW, Gwyn Jones Papers 74/167/6.

32 See *New Poems 1957*, ed. K. Nott, C. D. Lewis and T. Blackburn (London: Michael Joseph, 1957), p. 45.

33 NLW, Margiad Evans MSS 4/75. Another version with the same date has the title 'Sonnet No. 8: On the Return of the Alexandrine Metre' (Margiad Evans MSS 4/76).

34 Among various versions of the poem that survive in manuscript (NLW, Margiad Evans MSS 4/65, 6/67, 4/135), one is endorsed with a note from the author ('I am sending you the first muddled version. Can you return it to me for correction & typing?') (Margiad Evans MSS 4/67).

35 NLW, Margiad Evans MSS 925.

36 NLW, Margiad Evans MSS 933.

37 NLW, Margiad Evans MSS 4/65.

38 NLW, Margiad Evans MSS 4/67.

39 NLW, Margiad Evans MSS 4/70.

40 Information gathered by W. Arnold Thorpe, loc. cit.

Bibliography

Primary

Unpublished sources

For a summary of the contents of these collections, please see the appendix to Ceridwen Lloyd-Morgan's essay on pp. 19–21. All items are at the National Library of Wales unless otherwise stated.

Bryher Papers. General Collection, Beinecke Rare Book and Manuscript Library, Yale University. MSS 97.

Margiad Evans Manuscripts (Margiad Evans MSS, nos 1–987).

Margiad Evans Papers (1–38).

NLW MS 23361A: The Churstons vol. I.

NLW MS 23362A: Churstons vol. II.

NLW MS 23363C: The Churstons.

NLW MS 23365D: 'And Every Day of their Lives'; 'The Haunted Widow'; 'The Equerry's House'.

NLW MS 23366D: Journal 1933–4.

NLW MS 23367B: The Nightingale Silenced.

NLW MS 23368B: The Nightingale Silenced.

NLW MS 23369C: The Immortal Hospital.

NLW MS 23370D: Autobiographical Notes *c.*1934–*c.*1955.

NLW MS 23371B: Essays, Poems, &c. *c.*1953, unpublished writing by Margiad Evans (donated 1995).

NLW MS 23372 C: 'How do the children?'; 'Famous unknown children, with a digression upon Wordsworth's psychological intuitions of childhood'.

NLW MS 23577C: Journal September 1935–9.

Margiad Evans in other collections at the National Library of Wales

NLW MS 22744D, ff. 145–6 (Letters from Margiad Evans to Keidrych Rhys).

Gwyn Jones Papers 4/117–18.

Gwyn Jones Papers 74/18–74 (1978 reprint of *A Ray of Darkness*).

Gwyn Jones Papers 74/207, 218–221 (5 February–26 March 1958, letters from Michael Williams and Mrs Katherine Whistler).

Gwyn Jones Papers: 74/115–73 (letters from Margiad Evans to Gwyn Jones).

NLW MS 20062B, item 1 (letter from Margiad Evans to Kate Roberts).

Published works (in chronological order of publication)

Evans, Margiad, *Country Dance* (London: John Calder, 1978; Cardigan: Parthian, 2006 [original edn: London: Arthur Baker, 1932]).

Evans, Margiad, *The Wooden Doctor* (Dinas Powys: Honno, 2005 [original edn Oxford: Basil Blackwell, 1933]).

Evans, Margiad, *Turf or Stone* (Oxford: Basil Blackwell, 1934; Cardigan: Parthian, 2010).

Evans, Margiad, *Creed* (Oxford: Basil Blackwell, 1936).

Evans, Margiad, 'The Black House', *The Welsh Review* 1 (1939), 242–6.

Margiad Evans, 'Book reviews: *Welsh Border Country* and *Old English Household Life*', *Wales*, 10 (October 1939), 285–6.

Evans, Margiad, *Autobiography* (Oxford: Basil Blackwell, 1943; London: Calder and Boyars, 1974).

Evans, Margiad, *Poems from Obscurity* (London: Andrew Dakers, 1947).

Evans, Margiad, 'Byron and Emily Brontë, *Life and Letters Today*, 57/130 (June 1948), 193–216.

Evans, Margiad, *The Old and the Young*, ed. Ceridwen Lloyd-Morgan ([1948] Bridgend: Seren, 1998).

Evans, Margiad, *A Ray of Darkness* (London: Arthur Barker, 1952; London: John Calder, 1978).

Evans, Margiad, *A Candle Ahead* (London: Chatto & Windus, 1956).

Evans, Margiad, 'Cure' and 'Poem' ('I must be dead as these dead vaults'), *New Poems 1957*, ed. Kathleen Nott, C. Day Lewis and Thomas Blackburn (London: Michael Joseph, 1957), pp. 44–5.

Secondary

Unpublished sources

Cambridge, King's College Library, Rosamund Lehmann Papers, MISC 42A/17.

National Library of Wales, NLW MSS 23005–14: Ceri Richards correspondence.

Published sources

Aaron, Jane, 'A national seduction: Wales in nineteenth-century women's writing,' *New Welsh Review*, 7/3, 27 (1994), 31–8.

—— 'Introduction', *A View Across the Valley: Short Stories by Women from Wales c.1850–1950* (Dinas Powys: Honno, 1999), pp. ix–xx.

—— *Nineteenth-Century Women's Writing in Wales: Nation, Gender and Identity* (Cardiff: University of Wales Press, 2007).

—— 'Taking sides: power-play on the Welsh border in early twentieth-century women's writing', in ed. Jane Aaron, Henrice Altnik and Chris Weedon,

Gendering Border Studies (Cardiff: University of Wales Press, 2010), pp. 127–41.

Anderson, L. A., *Autobiography* (London and New York: Routledge, 2001).

Alvarez ,Walter C., *Minds That Came Back* (Philadelphia & New York: J. B. Lippincott, 1961).

Asbee, Sue, 'Margiad Evans's *The Wooden Doctor*: illness and sexuality', *Welsh Writing in English: A Yearbook of Critical Essays*, vol. 9 (2004), 33–49.

—— '"To Write a Great Story": Margiad Evans's illness narratives', in *The Patient: Probing Interdisciplinary Boundaries*, ed. Aleksandra Bartoszko and Maria Vaccarella (Witney: Inter-Disciplinary Press, 2011). E-book, available at *www.inter-disciplinary.net/publishing/id-press/ebooks/the-patient/* (28 November 2011).

Atwood, Margaret, *The Penelopiad* (Toronto: Knopf, 2005).

Austen, Jane, *Northanger Abbey*, ed. Anne Ehrenpreis ([1818] London: Penguin, 1985).

Avrahami, E., *The Invading Body: Reading Illness Autobiographies* (University of Virginia Press, 2007).

Bachelard, Gaston, *The Poetics of Space*, tr. Maria Jolas (Boston: Beacon Press, 1994).

Bates, H. E., 'Review: *A Summer's Day*', *The Welsh Review*, 5 (1946), 217–20.

Barker, Juliet, *The Brontës* (London: Weidenfeld and Nicolson, 1994).

Baumann, C. R., V. P. Novikov, M. Regard and A. M. Siegel, 'Did Fyodor Mikhailovich Dostoevsky suffer from mesial temporal lobe epilepsy?', *Seizure*, 14 (2005), 324–30.

Baxendale, S., 'Epilepsy at the movies: possession to presidential assassination', *Lancet Neurology*, 2 (2003), 764–70.

Beard, Mary R., *Woman as Force in History* (New York: Macmillan, 1946).

Beddoe, Deirdre, 'Images of Welsh women', in ed. Tony Curtis, *Wales: The Imagined Nation* (Bridgend: Poetry Wales Press, 1986).

—— (ed.), *Changing Times: Welsh Women Writing on the 1950s and 1960s* (Dinas Powys: Honno, 2003).

Bell, Anne Oliver (ed.), *The Diary of Virginia Woolf, Vol. II 1920–1924* (Harmondsworth: Penguin, 1981).

—— (ed.), *The Diary of Virginia Woolf, Vol. III: 1925–30* (Harmondsworth: Penguin, 1982).

Bell, G. H. (ed.), *The Hamwood Papers of the Ladies of Llangollen and Caroline Hamilton* (London: Macmillan, 1930).

Benson, D. F., 'The Geschwind syndrome', *Advanced Neurology*, 55 (1991).

Benstock, Shari (ed.), *The Private Self: Theory and Practice of Women's Autobiographical Writings* (Chapel Hill and London: University of North Carolina Press, 1988).

'Bibliographies of modern Welsh authors: no. 4 Margiad Evans', *Wales*, 5 (Summer 1938), 181–2.

Bhabha, Homi K., *The Location of Culture* (London: Routledge, 1994).

Blake, R., S. Wroe, E. Breen and R. McCarthy, 'Accelerated forgetting in patients with epilepsy: evidence for impairment in memory consolidation', *Brain*, 123 (2000), 472–83.

Bland, Lucy, *Banishing the Beast: English Feminism and Sexual Morality 1885–1914* (London: Penguin 1995).

Bogousslavsky, J. and F. Boller (eds), *Neurological Disorders in Famous Artists* part 1 (Frontiers of Neurology and Neuroscience, vol. 19) (Basel: Karger, 2005).

—— and M. Hennerici (eds), *Neurological Disorders in Famous Artists*, part 2 (Frontiers of Neurology and Neuroscience, vol. 22) (Basel: Karger, 2007).

——, M. Hennerici, H. Bazner and C. Bassetti (eds), *Neurological Disorders in Famous Artists*, part 3 (Frontiers of Neurology and Neuroscience, vol. 27) (Basel: Karger, 2010).

Bohata, Kirsti, 'Apes and cannibals in Cambria: images of the racial and gendered Other in Welsh Gothic writing', in *Welsh Writing in English: A Yearbook of Critical Essays*, vol. 6 (2000), 119–43.

—— 'Excessive appetites: cannibalism and lesbianism', in Wojciech H. Kalaga and Tadeusz Rachwal (eds), *Spoiling the Cannibals' Fun?: Cannibalism and Cannibalisation in Culture and Elsewhere* (Frankfurt am Main: Peter Lang, 2005), pp. 81–91.

Bowen, Elizabeth, *The Collected Stories* (London: Jonathan Cape, 1980), pp. 468–70.

Brittain, Vera, *Honourable Estate* (London: Victor Gollancz, 1936).

—— *Lady into Woman: A History of Women from Victoria to Elizabeth II* (London: Andrew Daker, 1953).

Brontë, Emily, *Wuthering Heights*, ed. and introduction by Ian Jack (Oxford: Oxford World's Classics, 1981).

Brown, Tony, '"Stories from foreign countries": the short stories of Kate Roberts and Margiad Evans', in Alyce von Rothkirch and Daniel Williams (eds), *Beyond the Difference: Welsh Literature in Comparative Contexts* (Cardiff: University of Wales Press, 2004), pp. 21–37.

Caesar, Karen, 'Patient, doctor and disease in Margiad Evans's *The Wooden Doctor*', in Aleksandra Bartoszko and Maria Vaccarella (eds), *The Patient: Probing Interdisciplinary Boundaries* (Witney: Inter-Disciplinary Press, 2011). E-book, available at *www.inter-disciplinary.net/publishing/id-press/ebooks/the-patient/* (28 November 2011).

Castle, Terry, *The Apparitional Lesbian: Female Homosexuality and Modern Culture* (New York: Columbia University Press, 1993).

Clare, Horatio, 'The borders of reason: a reflection on boundaries', *Planet: The Welsh Internationalist*, 201 (February 2011), 50–61.

Connolly, Claire, 'Introduction', Sydney Owenson, Lady Morgan, *The Wild Irish Girl: A National Tale*, ed. Claire Connolly and Stephen Copley, foreword by Kevin Whelan ([1806] London: Pickering and Chatto, 2000).

Crites, S., 'Storytime', in T. R. Sarbin (ed.), *Narrative Psychology: The Stories Nature of Human Conduct* (New York and London: Praeger, 1986).

Davies, John, *A History of Wales* ([*Hanes Cymru* (1990)] London: Penguin, 1994).

De la Mare, Walter, *The Collected Poems of Walter de la Mare* (London: Faber & Faber, 1979).

Dearnley, Moira, *Margiad Evans* (Cardiff: University of Wales Press, 1982).

Derrida, Jacques, *Specters of Marx*, tr. Peggy Kamuf (New York: Routledge, 1994).

Doan, Laura, *Fashioning Sapphism: The Origins of a Modern English Lesbian Culture* (New York: Columbia University Press, 2000).

—— and Jane Garrity, *Sapphic Modernities: Sexuality, Women, and National Culture* (Basingstoke: Palgrave, 2006).

Dolan, Frances E., *Marriage and Violence: The Early Modern Legacy* (Philadelphia: University of Philadelphia Press, 2008).

Donoghue, Emma, *Inseparable: Desire Between Women in Literature* (Berkeley: Cleis Press, 2010).

Eagleton, Terry, *Literary Theory: An Introduction*, 2nd edn (Oxford: Blackwell, 1996).

Edwards, O. M., introduction to *Cymru'r Plant*, vol. XVI (1907).

Eliot, George, *Silas Marner: The Weaver of Ravelow*, ed. Terence Cave (Oxford: Oxford World's Classics, 2008; reissue edn).

Farr, Ruth, *Will You Go Back?* (Tunbridge Wells: The Dorothy Kerin Trust, 1970, new edn 1977).

—— 'Healing and making whole', reprinted in *Burrswood Herald* (Spring 1984), 50–3.

Fisher, R. S., B. W. van Emde, W. Blume et al., 'Epileptic seizures and epilepsy: definitions proposed by the International League Against Epilepsy (ILAE) and the International Bureau for Epilepsy (IBE)', *Epilepsia*, 46 (2005), 470–2.

Ford, S. F. and A. J. Larner, 'Neurology at the movies', *Advances in Clinical Neuroscience & Rehabilitation*, 9/4 (2009).

Frank, Arthur, *The Wounded Storyteller: Body, Illness and Ethics* (Chicago: Chicago University Press, 1995).

Freud, Sigmund, 'Beyond the pleasure principle', *Complete Psychological Works*, vol. XVIII (London: Hogarth, 1961), pp. 171–84.

Geschwind, N. 'Interictal behavioural changes in epilepsy', *Epilepsia*, vol. 24: S4 (1983).

Goetland, Jan Nordby, *Eudora Welty's Aesthetics of Place* (London and Toronto: Associated University Presses, 1994).

Golla, Frederick, 'This is a work of great importance', *John Bull Magazine*, 18 October 1952.

Gramich, Katie, *Twentieth-Century Women's Writing in Wales: Land, Gender, Belonging* (Cardiff: University of Wales Press, 2007).

Gray, Richard, *The Literature of Memory: Modern Writers of the American South* (London: Edward Arnold, 1977).

—— *Writing the South* (Cambridge: Cambridge University Press, 1986).

Griffiths, T. D., 'Capturing creativity', *Brain*, 131 (2008).

Gunn, Daniel, *Psychoanalysis and Fiction: An Exploration of Literary and Psychoanalytic Borders* (Cambridge: Cambridge University Press, 1988).

Hackett, Robin, *Sapphic Primitivism: Productions of Race, Class, and Sexuality in Key Works of Modern Fiction* (Piscataway, NJ: Rutgers University Press, 2004).

Hammill, Faye, *Women, Celebrity, and Literary Culture Between the Wars* (Austin: University of Texas Press, 2007).

Harris, John, 'Not a Trysorfa fach', *New Welsh Review*, 3/3 (1990–1), 28–33.

Hawkins, Anne Hunsaker, *Reconstructing Illness: Studies in Pathography* (West Lafayette: Purdue University Press, 1993).

Heaton, K. W., 'Faints, fits and fatalities from emotion in Shakespeare's characters: survey of the canon', *BMJ*, 333 (2006), 1335–8.

Henderson, James, 'The Gothic novel in Wales', *The National Library of Wales Journal*, 11 (1956–60), 244–54.

Humble, Nicola, *The Feminine Middlebrow Novel 1920s to 1950s: Class, Domesticity, and Bohemianism* (Oxford: Oxford University Press, 2001).

Iniesta, I., 'Epilepsy and literature', *Medical Historian*, 20 (2008–9), 31–53.

—— 'On the good use of epilepsy by Fyodor Dostoevsky', *Clinical Medicine*, 8 (2008), 338–9.

James, William, *Varieties of Religious Experience: A Study in Human Nature*, centenary edn ([1902] London and New York: Routledge, 2002).

Kavanagh, P. J., 'Margiad Evans', *The Listener*, 11 November 1972.

Kazin, Alfred (ed.), *The Portable Blake* (Harmondsworth: Penguin Books, 1976).

Knight, Stephen, *A Hundred Years of Fiction* (Cardiff: University of Wales Press, 2004).

Kristeva, Julia, *Powers of Horror: An Essay on Abjection*, tr. Leon S. Roudiez (New York: Columbia University Press, 1982).

Lacan, Jacques, *Écrits* (Paris: Seuil, 1966).

Larner, A. J., 'Dostoevsky and epilepsy', *Advances in Clinical Neuroscience & Rehabilitation*, 6/1 (2006).

—— '"Neurological literature": epilepsy', *Advances in Clinical Neuroscience & Rehabilitation*, 7/3 (2007).

—— 'Has Shakespeare's Iago deceived again?', *www.bmj.com/cgi/eletters/333/7582/1335* (2 January 2007).

—— *Neuropsychological Neurology: The Neurocognitive Impairments of Neurological Disorders* (Cambridge: Cambridge University Press, 2008), pp. 115–24.

—— '"Neurological literature": headache (part 4)', *Advances in Clinical Neuroscience & Rehabilitation*, 7/6 (2008).

—— 'Demise of botany in the medical curriculum', *Journal of Medical Biography*, 16 (2008).

—— 'Illusory visual spread or visuospatial perseveration', *Advances in Clinical Neuroscience & Rehabilitation*, 9/5 (2009).

—— '"A ray of darkness": Margiad Evans's account of her epilepsy (1952)', *Clinical Medicine*, 9 (2009).

—— 'Margiad Evans (1909–1958): a history of epilepsy in a creative writer', *Epilepsy & Behavior*, 16 (2009).

—— 'Syncope', in T. M. Cox et al. (eds), *Oxford Textbook of Medicine* (5ᵗʰ edn) (Oxford: Oxford University Press, 2010), pp. 4838–41.

—— *A Dictionary of Neurological Signs* (3ʳᵈ edn) (New York: Springer, 2011).

——, S. J. M. Smith, J. S. Duncan and R. S. Howard, 'Late-onset Rasmussen's syndrome with first seizure during pregnancy', *European Neurology*, 35 (1995).

Lawson, R., 'The epilepsy of Othello', *Journal of Mental Science*, 26 (1880), 1–11.

Lee, H., *Biography* (Oxford: Oxford University Press, 2009).

Lennox, W. G. and M. A. Lennox, *Epilepsy and Related Disorders* (London: J. A. Churchill, 1960).

Lewis, Gwyneth, 'The poet I might have been', *New Welsh Review*, 91 (Spring 2011), 9–13.

Lloyd, G. E. R. (ed.), *Hippocratic Writings* (London: Penguin, 1978).

Lloyd-Morgan, Ceridwen, 'Diwrnod o haf: llythyrau Kate Roberts a Margiad Evans', *Cylchgrawn Llyfrgell Genedlaethol Cymru/National Library of Wales Journal*, 33 (2003), 201–16.

—— *Margiad Evans* (Bridgend: Seren, 1998).

—— (ed.), *Gwen John: Letters and Notebooks* (London: Tate Publishing, 2004).

Location Register of 20th Century English Literary Manuscripts (*www.locationregister.com*).

Löffler, Marion, 'A romantic nationalist', *Planet: The Welsh Internationalist*, 121 (1997), 58–66 (60).

Longville, Tim, 'It was my religion to look', *Country Quest*, 32 (October 2003).

Loring, D. W., S. Marino and K. J. Meador, 'Neuropsychological and behavioural effects of antiepilepsy drugs', *Neuropsychology Review*, 17 (2007), 413–25.

Marcus, L., *Auto/biographical Discourses: Theory, Criticism, Practice* (Manchester and New York: Manchester University Press, 1994).

Martz, Louis L. (ed.), *Henry Vaughan* (Oxford: Oxford University Press, 1995).

Miller, Julia Anne, 'Acts of union: family violence and national courtship, in Maria Edgworth's *The Absentee* and Sydney Owenson's *The Wild Irish*

Girl', in Kathryn Kirkpatrick (ed.), *Border Crossings: Irish Women Writers and National Identities* (Tuscaloosa and London: University of Alabama Press, 2000), pp. 13–37.

Moers, Ellen, 'Female Gothic', *Literary Women* (London: The Women's Press, 1986).

Morgan, Clare, 'Exile and the kingdom: Margiad Evans and the mythic landscape of Wales', *Welsh Writing in English: A Yearbook of Critical Essays*, vol. 6 (2000), 89–118.

—— 'Margiad Evans: a writer in her time', Margiad Evans Centenery Conference, National Library of Wales, Aberystwyth, 15 May 2009.

Owenson, Sydney, Lady Morgan, *The Wild Irish Girl: A National Tale*, ed. Kathryn Kirkpatrick ([1806] Oxford: Oxford World's Classics, 1999).

Panayiotopoulos, C. P., *The Epilepsies: Seizures, Syndromes and Management* (Chipping Norton: Bladon Medical Publishing, 2005).

Parry, Idris, 'Margiad Evans and tendencies in European literature', *Transactions of the Honourable Society of Cymmrodorion* (1971), 224–36.

—— 'Margiad Evans', *Speak Silence* (Manchester: Carcanet, 1988).

—— 'Margiad Evans', *PN Review*, 15.3 (1989), 29–32.

Philips, Deborah, *Women's Fiction 1945–2005* (London: Continuum, 2006).

Pratt, Jim, 'Margiad Evans: centenary of an artist with epilepsy', paper delivered to the 28th International Epilepsy Congress, Budapest, 28 June–2 July 2009.

Prys-Williams, Barbara, 'Variations in the nature of the perceived self in some twentieth-century Welsh autobiographical writing in English' (unpublished PhD thesis, University of Wales Swansea, 2002).

—— *Twentieth-Century Autobiography: Writing Wales in English* (Cardiff: University of Wales Press, 2004), pp. 32–57.

Punter, David, *The Literature of Terror: A History of Gothic Fictions from 1765 to the Present Day* (London: Longman, 1980).

Report of the Commissioners of Inquiry into the State of Education in Wales (London: William Clowes, 1847).

Rosa, V. P., G. M. A. Filho, M. A. Rahal, L. O. S. F. Caboclo, A. C. Sakamoto and E. M. T. Yacubian, 'Ictal fear: semiologic characteristics and differential diagnosis with interictal anxiety disorders', *Journal of Epilepsy and Clinical Neurophysiology*, 12 (2006), 89–94.

Savage, D. S., *The Withered Branch: Six Studies in the Modern Novel* (London: Eyre and Spottiswoode, 1950).

Scarry, Elaine, *The Body in Pain: The Making and Unmaking of the World* (Oxford: Oxford University Press, 1985).

Scott, Walter, *Ivanhoe*, ed. Graham Tulloch ([1819] London: Penguin, 1998).

—— *Waverley: Or, 'Tis Sixty Years Since*, ed. Claire Lamont ([1814] Oxford: Oxford World's Classics, 1986).

Sedgwick, Eve Kosofsky, *Tendencies* (London: Routledge, 1994).

Sontag, Susan, *Illness as Metaphor and Aids and its Metaphors* ([1978 and 1989] London: Penguin, 1991).

Stacey, Jackie, *Teratologies: A Cultural Study of Cancer* (London and New York: Routledge, 1997).

Stirling, Jeannette, *Representing Epilepsy: Myth and Matter* (Liverpool: Liverpool University Press, 2010).

Stopes, Marie, *Mother England: A Contemporary History* (1929), reproduced in Lesley A. Hall (ed.), *Marie Stopes: Birth Control and Other Writings*, vol. I (Bristol: Thoemmes Press, 2000).

Thomas, R. H., J. M. Mullins, T. Waddington, K. Nugent and P. E. M. Smith, 'Epilepsy: creative sparks', *Practical Neurology*, 10 (2010), 219–26.

Thomas, R. S., *Song at the Year's Turning* (London: Rupert Hart-Davies, 1955).

Torgerson, Beth, *Reading the Brontë Body: Disease, Desire and the Constraints of Culture* (New York and Basingstoke: Palgrave MacMillan, 2005).

Trumpener, Katie, *Bardic Nationalism: The Romantic Novel and the British Empire* (Princeton, NJ: Princeton University Press, 1997).

Vaughan, Hilda, *Here Are Lovers* (New York and London: Harper & Brothers, 1926).

Vicinus, Martha, *Intimate Friends: Women who Loved Women 1778–1928* (Chicago and London: University of Chicago Press, 2004).

Wallace, Diana, 'Mixed marriages: three Welsh historical novels in English by women writers', in ed. Christopher Meredith, *Moment of Earth* (Aberystwyth: Celtic Studies Publications, 2007), pp. 171–84.

Warnock, M., *Memory* (London: Faber and Faber, 1987).

Watkins, Vernon, *Collected Poems* (Ipswich: Golgonooza Press, 1986).

Webb, Mary, *Gone to Earth* ([1917] London: Jonathan Cape, 1974).

Welty, Eudora, *One Writer's Beginnings* (Cambridge, Mass.: Harvard University Press, 1983).

—— *A Writer's Eye* (Jackson: University of Mississippi, 1994).

—— *The Golden Apples* (New York: Harcourt, Brace and World, Inc., 1949).

Wieshmann, U. C., L. Niehaus and H. Meierkord, 'Ictal speech arrest and parasagittal lesions', *European Neurology*, 38 (1997), 123–7.

Williams, Daniel G., 'Welsh modernism', *The Oxford Handbook of Modernisms*, ed. Peter Brooker, Andrzej Gasiorek, Deborah Longworth and Andrew Thacker (Oxford: Oxford University Press, 2010), pp. 797–816.

Williams, Daniel G., *Black Skin, Blue Books: African Americans and Wales 1845–1945* (Cardiff: University of Wales Press, 2012).

Woolf, Virginia, *Collected Essays*, vol. 1 (London: The Hogarth Press, 1966).

—— 'Women and fiction', in *Virginia Woolf on Women and Writing*, selected and introduced by Michèle Barrett (London: The Women's Press, 1979).

—— *Three Guineas* ([1938] London: Hogarth, 1986).

—— *A Room of One's Own* ([1929] Orlando VA: Harcourt, 1989).

—— *The Waves* (Oxford: Oxford University Press, 1998).
—— 'A sketch of the past', in Jeanne Schulkinel and Hermione Lee (eds), *Moments of Being: Autobiographical Writing* (London: Pimlico, 2002).
Zamyatin, Yevgeny, *We* ([1924] London: Penguin, 1993).

Index